I've done nothing to deserve gratitude;
I saw some fine work, said it was fine,
and thereby only did my simple duty by
the republic of letters (which is the
only kind of republic I believe in,
a kind of republic that can't exist
in a political republic).

Allen Tate to John Peale Bishop, 1933

THE
REPUBLIC
OF LETTERS
IN AMERICA

The Correspondence of

John Peale Bishop
& Allen Tate

Edited by
Thomas Daniel Young
& John J. Hindle

THE UNIVERSITY PRESS OF KENTUCKY

Library of Congress Cataloging in Publication Data

Bishop, John Peale, 1892–1944.
  The republic of letters in America.

  Includes index.
  1. Bishop, John Peale, 1892–1944—Correspondence.
2. Tate, Allen, 1899–1979—Correspondence.   3. Authors,
American—20th century—Correspondence.   I. Tate, Allen,
1899–1979.   II. Young, Thomas Daniel, 1919–
III. Hindle, John J., 1946–   IV. Title.
PS3503.I79Z483   1981   811'.52'09   [B]   80-5186
ISBN 0-8131-1443-8   AACR2

Publication of this book has been assisted by a grant
from the National Endowment for the Humanities.

Scholarly publisher for the Commonwealth,
serving Berea College, Centre College of Kentucky,
Eastern Kentucky University, The Filson Club,
Georgetown College, Kentucky Historical Society,
Kentucky State University, Morehead State University,
Murray State University, Northern Kentucky University,
Transylvania University, University of Kentucky,
University of Louisville, and Western Kentucky University.

Editorial and Sales Offices: Lexington, Kentucky 40506

For Arlease & Joan

CONTENTS

*Manuscript poems appear on
pages 176–177*

ACKNOWLEDGMENTS

The editors wish to express their gratitude to all those who have contributed to the publication of this correspondence, especially the following: the staff of the Firestone Library of Princeton University for their courtesy and helpfulness in locating and retrieving manuscripts; Professors Emerson Brown and Jean Leblon of Vanderbilt University for their assistance in identifying troublesome references; Donna Stinson and Louise Durham for their patience, timeliness, and attention to detail in the preparation of the manuscript; the Graduate School of Vanderbilt University for research grants that materially enhanced the quality of the edition. To Jonathan Bishop and the late Allen Tate go our deepest thanks for their permission to publish the correspondence.

INTRODUCTION

Few writers of the twentieth century have been so profoundly dedicated to the vocation of letters as was Allen Tate. A young English poet publishing his first poem in an obscure little magazine received from Tate a few days after the poem appeared a letter of commendation and detailed comment on the strengths and weaknesses of the poem. Moved that an established man of letters would devote so much attention to the work of a novice, this young poet (Geoffrey Hill) pursued his craft with increased diligence and confidence. It is clear, as Lewis P. Simpson has pointed out, that Tate felt that one of the responsibilities of the man of letters was the restoration of an age of faith at a time when science was becoming a dominant force in every area of human thought and activity. Quite early in his career he realized that the artist in the materialistic economic pattern of the American system was working against society, not with it, so he endeavored to set up a literary community, what Simpson calls "an idealized community of alienation." To accomplish this purpose Tate deliberately set about a campaign to establish a "Republic of Letters in the Modern World" by unifying writers and would-be writers around the concept that they composed a community set against an alien world. The unceasing and ever-important task of the artist, he reiterated, following the leadership of T. S. Eliot, one of his acknowledged "masters"—the other was John Crowe Ransom—was that of confronting the "dissociation of sensibility" as the dominant cultural phenomenon of his age. The poetic community had the dual function, he argued, of making the world aware of the cultural crisis it faces and of preserving the health and vitality of the language.

In an attempt to establish and maintain a vocation of letters, Tate undertook a voluminous correspondence with a broad range of writers—some virtually unknown, some well established—in England, America, and France. Among the persons with whom he corresponded regularly over long periods were T. S. Eliot, John Crowe Ransom, Donald Davidson, Robert Penn Warren, Cleanth Brooks, Herbert Read, Andrew Lytle, and Robert Lowell. Less frequently he exchanged letters with Peter Taylor, Geoffrey Hill, Kenneth Burke, Howard Nemerov, Randall Jarrell, Ernest Hemingway, Archibald MacLeish, Malcolm Cowley, Edmund Wilson, and many others. As Radcliffe Squires has observed, however, the tone of Tate's correspondence with John Peale Bishop is different from that of all the others. Although there are exceptions—particularly in letters to Andrew Lytle—Tate's letters to his other correspondents tend to form a definite pattern: those to Donald Davidson, on the plight of the artist in the modern world and on their shared interest in Agrarianism; those to John Crowe Ransom (though few of these survive), on the details of operating a literary quarterly and on the development of a theory of literature as a means of cognition; those to Edmund Wilson, on interpretations of individual works of art and on the functions of literature in a democratic society. The letters to Bishop were more personal, and, as Squires has noted, to both men they were a source of strength:

> To look through their correspondence is to discover how fully each trusted the other, and how fresh their friendship stayed. Their criticism of each other's work was never the usual harmless compliments which old friends seem to deliver almost as a reflex action. It was careful criticism; they often suggested specific emendations of words or lines to each other. Upon occasion they wrote "companion pieces," poems which were variations on one of the other's poems and themes.

Tate was introduced to Bishop in a New York speakeasy by Kenneth Burke in September 1925. Three years later, while Tate was in Paris on a Guggenheim fellowship, Robert Penn Warren came over from Oxford, where he was a Rhodes Scholar, and Bishop joined the two for a night on the town, coming in from his home in Orgeval, about twenty kilometers outside the French capital. The three had a memorable evening together, sampling the wine in some of Bishop's favorite cafes and concluding the celebration over a bottle of Scotch in Tate's apartment. Sometime around midnight, Bishop responded to a request that he read some of his poetry. Although Bishop had been writing verse for many years—he published one volume, *Green Fruit*, shortly after his graduation from Princeton, and collaborated with Edmund Wilson on another, *The Undertaker's Garland*—and although he was a close friend of Ernest Hemingway, F. Scott Fitzgerald, Archibald MacLeish, and Edmund Wilson, his literary career had come to a standstill. His literary friends often asked him to read and comment on their work, but they apparently regarded him as a man with an assured income (his wife's family apparently was fairly wealthy) who merely dabbled in the arts. The incisive and complimentary commentary on Bishop's poems by Tate and Warren had a stimulating effect. About five years later he wrote Tate that "it was from that evening" that he decided he was talented enough to pursue a career in the arts.

Not only was there a noticeable increase in Bishop's output in poetry but in fiction as well. Almost immediately he published a poem in the *New Republic,* a short story in *Vanity Fair,* and won the 1930 Scribner's short story prize of $5,000 for "Many Thousands Gone." In 1931 a collection of his short stories appeared. His letters to Tate, after they began corresponding regularly in 1929, reflect Bishop's increased confidence in his abilities as an artist, almost in direct ratio to the serious, careful, and helpful commentary that were always accorded the poems or stories he had sent to Tate.

What proved tonic for Bishop, however, proved even more salutary for Tate. Although Tate was deeply engrossed in the Agrarian movement, and his letters to his friends in Nashville were filled with details of this movement—projects proposed and rejected, comments of various critics weighed and analyzed—his letters to Bishop barely mention Agrarianism and never in any detail. The verses he sent Bishop were always perceptively and wisely scrutinized. Bishop gave detailed criticism of meter, rhyme, diction, and structure. Comparison of the versions of the poems Tate sent Bishop with those published demonstrates quite clearly how much Tate profited from Bishop's suggestions. Bishop never achieved Tate's literary stature or reputation because his work was too uneven and his productivity too sporadic. Although there is no indication that the friendship was adversely affected by this fact, the correspondence shows that both men considered Tate the superior artist. But in many respects Bishop supplemented Donald Davidson's criticism, and the two of them gave Tate the most useful commentary his poetry ever received. When Bishop died on April 4, 1944, most of Tate's best poetry had been written.

Time after time in these letters Tate refers to the helpfulness of Bishop's honest, practical criticism. In 1931 Tate wrote: "I rewrote the *Ode to Fear,* adopting most of your suggestions. I hope you are getting as much out of our correspondence as I am." In dedicating one of his finest and most evenly sustained poems, "Seasons of the Soul," to Bishop, Tate insisted that he had "reason apart from sentiment" because some of Bishop's suggestions were incorporated verbatim into the poem. A letter Bishop wrote Tate very early in the correspondence illustrates the kind of detailed and technical criticism, as well as the helpful encouragement, Tate always received from Bishop:

> Your own two poems are very fine, particularly the Anabasis, which is noble and grave and pure. At first, I was inclined to think that the rhythm halted in one or two places.

Now, I am not so sure. But I will put down my comments for what they are worth. Line 2—Dash instead of comma. 1. 3—Substitute 0 for A or qualify "woman" with an adjective of direct address. l. 5—for, l. 8, "unstudiously" for "unstudiedly"; l. 12 ⊙ for , l. 13; avoid accent on "that" (it shall—. that shall, possibly) l. 19: is "The" right? l. 22, 23, 24 Obscure.

Although a careful study of Tate's poetry written in the thirties and early forties demonstrates quite clearly the seriousness with which he always received Bishop's perceptive criticism (many of the suggested changes affected the final form of the poem), Bishop's most profound assistance, perhaps, came in connection with "Picnic at Cassis," later retitled, at Bishop's suggestion, "The Mediterranean." On October 31, 1932, Tate wrote to Bishop: "I enclose one which is not one of my best, but it has a few nice phrases. I've tried to keep it direct and classical, suppressing the dramatic irony that usually I try to put in." Bishop's response was immediate and enthusiastic: "You're wrong. 'Picnic at Cassis' is not one of your best poems. It is the best. . . . It is—I hesitate, but it is—a great poem. Never I think, has the feeling of the Mediterranean from one of Northern blood (which you are) been so well expressed. Maybe The Mediterranean or something vague like that would be [a] better [title]." Bishop then listed a series of specific changes, many of which, after careful consideration, Tate rejected. But he did adopt Bishop's title, and Bishop's unqualified praise of the poem changed Tate's attitude toward it. For the remainder of his life it remained one of the three or four of his poems that he valued most highly. ("Ode to the Confederate Dead" was not among these.)

Tate replied, thanking Bishop for his praise, and although he was deeply engrossed in a biography of Robert E. Lee, which he was finding difficult to conclude, he put that manuscript aside and attempted to alter the poem in the manner Bishop had suggested. Again Bishop responded promptly, asserting that the revised version of the poem was not as good as the first. As always he expressed his objection in specific terms:

I may seem to be wrong in condemning your shift in time. But I can't think so. You describe in your poem a place—the shore of the Mediterranean. The time is continuous with the progress of the verse. But behind this time is the arrival of Aeneas on these same or similar shores and this carries you to another arrival on other shores. You make the reader aware of Trojan time. I don't think you need devote a stanza to it.

The information contained in it . . . had better be put in your motto. What that should be is the Latin for your first motto, or perhaps better, your translation of the Virgil.

Bishop concluded by indicating rightly that "Aeneas at Washington," which Tate had written as a companion piece to "The Mediterranean" was "vastly inferior to the earlier poem."

Bishop was the author of a prize-winning book of short stories, and was working on his much-underrated novel, *Act of Darkness,* when Tate hesitantly and abashedly submitted for Bishop's reaction his first attempt at fiction. It was in late 1933, when Tate took another respite from the troublesome book on Lee, that he attempted his first short story—called "The Immortal Woman" (1933). He sent it to Bishop and asked him not to be "too severe with it." As usual Bishop's comments were detailed and helpful:

> I think the story has decided possibilities: As I see it your story takes place on three planes: The narrator's mind (his reminiscences and comment), his eyes (what he sees of the old lady), his ears (what he overhears Mrs. Dulany saying). There is, therefore, a great deal to be said for putting it all in one scene. That is, begin say with description of the old lady in the street (street or lady first as you choose), present her as seen: then as remembered, giving along with the recollection as much of the narrator's character and surrounding as necessary to understand, then place Mrs. Dulany.

Tate replies: "Your analysis of my so-called story is penetrating and exhaustive. . . . I'm not sure yet whether I will try to rewrite it or will go on with something else. If I do I will adopt your radical suggestion about making the whole action in two present scenes." Two days after Bishop received this letter, he wrote: "You really ought to finish it if only for the sake of discipline and technique." There is ample evidence to support the contention that Tate took Bishop's advice seriously and worked hard on the story trying to make its basic action less obscure. Realizing that most readers were not able to determine "what happened" in the story because of his inexpert handling of point of view, Tate worked hard on mastering this fundamental of fictional technique. As a consequence, although the story remains unnecessarily ambiguous and obscure (worse than even Henry James would allow, Donald Davidson wrote Tate), the labor accomplished much. One of the great strengths of Tate's only novel, *The Fathers* (1938) is his use of Lacy Buchan as the point of view, a retired doctor relating events fifty years in the past and reporting simultaneously his feelings about those events when they occurred and his feelings about them fifty years later.

After completing *Stonewall Jackson: The Good Soldier* (1928) and *Jefferson Davis: His Rise and Fall* (1929), Tate worked diligently for three or four years on a biography of Robert E. Lee. Finally in October 1932, he concluded he could not complete the biography. His reasons for reaching this decision are summarized in a letter to Bishop:

> The whole Southern incapacity for action since 1865 is rationalized in the popular conception of Lee.... Lee did not love power; my thesis about him, stated in these terms, is that he didn't love it because he was profoundly cynical of all action for the public good. He could not see beyond the needs of his own salvation, and he was not generous enough to risk soiling his military cloak for the doubtful salvation of others.... This is what I feel about Lee. Yet is it true? That is what keeps me awake at night. I can't "prove" a word of it. Of course, the facts do not in the least prove the current notion of him.

Bishop's response to Tate's determination to abandon a project that had consumed a major portion of his time for four or five years was most emphatic. "Proceed with your Lee," he wrote in mid-October, 1932; "if it is not true to the facts of Lee's life, it will be true to you. And that is more important.... So if you write the life of the Southerner (yourself, myself, all of us) in terms of Lee, so much more it will be than a life of Lee. I feel this now as a moral problem, and I urge you forward."

Tate had tired of Lee, however, and had his mind fixed on another project, a work more frankly autobiographical and fictional. He proposed to write of his own ancestry, bringing forward to the present the story of Robert Read who came to Virginia in 1638, and attempting to explain how two persons so much unlike as his brother Ben and he, each epitomizing a different kind of American, could belong to the same family. He designed the book to include one person representing each of the two contrasting types in each generation from the seventeenth to the twentieth century. In essence what he conceived was to trace the development of his father's bloodline and that of his mother, and thereby to demonstrate the development of two prominent American character types—that of the pioneer, with his restlessness and his chaotic energies and that of the Virginia Tidewater aristocrat with his cultural roots in tradition, stability, and order. Although he thought through this project sufficiently to outline it in detail, chapter by chapter, and to write a segment of it, he finally abandoned it too. He wrote Bishop on October 30, 1933: "I've been in a crisis. I have out of heroism or cowardice (take your choice) thrown over the ancestry book forever. The agony was great, but the peace of mind is greater. It was a simple problem that I could not solve. The discrepancy between the outward significance and the private was so enormous that I decided that I could not handle the material in that form at all, without either faking the significance or the material."

The effort that Tate had put into this autobiographical novel and into the biography of Lee was not wasted, however, for much of the thought and planning that had gone into these two projects were reflected in Tate's second short story, "The Migration" (1934), in the "Sonnets of the Blood" (1931), and most significantly in Tate's only novel, *The Fathers* (1938), which resembles in many ways Bishop's novel *Act of Darkness* (1935). Through this series of letters, too, one can follow clearly Tate's search for an authoritative source to give order, direction, and meaning to his personal life, from his early hope for the traditional society of the antebellum South to the dogma, doctrine, and the discipline of the Roman Catholic Church.

If this exchange of letters is important for the extent to which it reveals the intellectual and spiritual development of Allen Tate during a crucial period of his life, it is equally important for its effect on John Peale Bishop. By his own admission it resurrected his literary career and maybe saved his life. "You are a grand person, Allen," Bishop once wrote Tate, "and but for you I should probably have committed suicide more than three years ago. If not in the flesh, still in the spirit. I only hope I can keep to the level you are generous enough to accord me." Bishop dated the beginning of his career from the evening Tate and Warren first read his poems. *Green Fruit* (1917), which he wrote while a student at Princeton and published just before leaving for the Army in World War I, he classified as apprentice work, calling it "my attempt to swallow and digest . . . the French Symbolistes." Although since the end of the war he had been almost constantly in the circle of important English and American writers who had settled in France, literary aspirations were no longer a moving force in his life. In December 1933, several years after their meeting in Paris, he wrote Tate:

Do you remember the evening in the Rue Mignard which you and Warren spent with me over a bottle of Scotch? Well, it was pleasant enough and casual enough for you both. But it was from that evening, from the comment you two made on the verses I most shyly showed you that I conceived it might still be possible for me to make a place for myself as a poet. I do not think even you, who have been so much in my intimacy since, can know upon what despair and forlorness your words came. The confidence I had in youth was gone with youth. I saw myself with little done and that little had not only had no recognition that I was aware of, but I had almost convinced myself that it deserved none. . . . always I have known that but for that evening, . . . I should not now in any real sense exist.

Tate responded to this letter, with its extravagant praise and its almost embarrassingly frank relevation, in an uncharacteristically impersonal manner:

Yes, I remember the evening in the rue Mignard, but I could not understand all of its implications at the time, though I must confess that something in your response to what Warren and I said led me to reflect, a little later, on the kind of friendships with which you seemed to surround yourself. In fact, I became a little impatient though secretly with your suicidal disinterestedness. . . . I decided that your generosity and real love of craft had permitted you to surround yourself with the most unmerciful crew of bloodsuckers it had been my luck to observe. The really bad part of it was that they were nearly all highly gifted people, who in a sense deserved the attention you gave them; but because you clamored for little or no attention yourself you got none.

Tate ends his comment by saying that he deserves no praise for what he had done because he merely saw "some fine work, said it was fine, and thereby only did my simple duty by the republic of letters."

In the years following that "evening in the rue Mignard" Tate was unstinting, perhaps at times extravagant, in his praise of Bishop's work. "Your poem is splendid," he wrote on April 17, 1931. "I feel no need of being severe. I envy your power of setting the emotional tone so clearly that you don't have to keep telling us about it." Tate was also impressed by Bishop's fiction, commenting once about *Many Thousands Gone:* "There are few books in our day that are written out of a full and settled view of human nature. Yours is one of them." And even when he found serious technical flaws in Bishop's fiction, Tate nonetheless found room to praise it by seizing on its overriding virtues. While reading proofs of Bishop's novel *Act of Darkness* in the fall of 1934, for example, Tate wrote that he "became a little alarmed" at Bishop's shift of viewpoint for a crucial scene, adding that while he understood the reasons for the change, he wished "it could be done less violently where the scene is not so conspicuous." Later in the same letter, however, he adds that "the amount of social and human insight that you've put into this book vastly exceeds anything else I've seen from the South."

In spite of the high quality of Bishop's prose, however, Tate was convinced that his natural mode of expression was poetry. Tate wrote on November 5, 1931, "Perhaps your poetry is better than your prose for this reason: You have a *feeling for rhythm by phrases*, but not sentences, and your whole interest is in *emotion not action.*" So that Bishop would not think his praise of the poetry too effusive, Tate reminded him: "I never flatter anybody but women, so you must be aware that what I say about your poetry is the truth." Then he moved on to make specific technical comments about a poem Bishop had just sent him.

Perhaps posterity is justified in not finding as much artistic merit in Bishop's creations as Tate accorded them. One conclusion, however, is inevitable. Except for Tate's well intended and genuinely felt praise, the world of letters would not have two dozen or so highly original and structurally superior poems, a book of excellent short stories, an undeservedly neglected novel, and nearly a dozen perceptive and illuminating critical essays. Not a large quantity of work to be sure, but some of it is of a quality to merit more attention than it is currently receiving.

It is hard to believe that two men so obviously fond of each other, with so many perceptions, observations, and impressions they wished to share, were able to spend so little time together. For a while after their first meeting, they lived on two continents, but Tate spent almost two years in France on Guggenheim fellowships and the two friends had some time together. Later there was a memorable week in New Orleans, some of it shared with Andrew Lytle and the Robert Penn Warrens, and an occasional meeting at a writers' conference. A few times, while Bishop was living in South Chatham, Massachusetts, and Tate in Princeton, the two had a convivial weekend in New York, and Tate arranged for Bishop to give a lecture early in 1940 to the students in the Creative Arts Program at Princeton. During Bishop's visit he and Tate spent much time going over manuscripts of Bishop's poetry, editing and choosing for Bishop's 1941 *Selected Poems.* Time after time, however, these letters refer to missed connections, after weeks of careful planning for a brief reunion, or to misunderstood directions. For whatever reasons, Tate was not able to spend as much time with Bishop as he did with his other friends—Ransom or Warren, for example—or Bishop with Edmund Wilson or E. E. Cummings. Both men were always, it seems, trying to arrange a meeting—a speaking engagement at the same place at the same time, or one near enough the other's home for them to have some time together. When Tate was a member of the panel that presented the radio program "Invitation to Learning," he tried desperately to have Bishop join him on the panel, but instead Bishop became Tate's replacement. In November 1943, Tate, who had become consultant in poetry at the Library of Congress in September, persuaded Archibald MacLeish to create the position of resident fellow in comparative literature and to appoint Bishop to fill it. After two weeks in office, however, Bishop suffered a severe heart attack, from which he died a few months later. Tate's last communication informed Bishop that financial arrangements associated with their only cooperative literary venture, the anthology *American Harvest,* had been settled and that they could expect a royalty payment within a few weeks. Bishop did not live to receive his share.

This book has been edited with the informed reader in mind; therefore we have attempted to exclude unnecessary information from headnotes, endnotes, and chronologies. In the interest of conserving space, salutations and complimentary closes are placed on the lines with the text. For the same reason the place of origin is given only for the first letter written from any address; subsequent letters written by the same correspondent from that address are printed without it. Since both Tate and Bishop were traditionalists regarding style, spelling, grammar, and syntax, a few slips of the pen or typewriter have been silently corrected. All of the letters we are reproducing are printed in their entirety, and except for a few notes pertaining to travel plans, reporting on the health of one family or the other, and other such routine matters, all of the surviving correspondence between Tate and Bishop is included in this collection. Each letter is followed, at the right margin, by the abbreviation AL for autograph letter or TLS for typewritten letter, signed. In a few instances a hastily omitted signature has been supplied, in brackets. All of the letters are in good condition, and only a few words were not easily decipherable; these few were carefully studied by both editors and in each case our best guess is given in brackets. Any ellipses appearing in the printed text were in the original. We have generally avoided the use of *sic,* even for the titles of books, poems, and essays, casually and inexactly cited by both writers. We have reproduced these exactly as they were written. The British and French spellings resulting from Bishop's extended residence abroad have not been Americanized. Dates supplied by the editors have been enclosed in brackets. To avoid needless interruption, whenever practicable identifications of persons are placed in the index, following the entry for each name.

Our text, we hope, retains as much of the flavor of the original as possible.

1929-1934

After their introduction on September 23, 1925, an event over-shadowed in Tate's memory of that day by the birth of his daughter, Bishop and Tate did not meet again until 1928, in Paris, where their friendship truly began. Tate was working in France that year on a Guggenheim fellowship and was accompanied by his wife, Caroline Gordon. Bishop and his family had taken up permanent residence in a chateau near Paris in 1926, where they lived until 1933, six months after the Tates returned from a second sojourn in France. The correspondence begins in 1929, while Tate was still in Paris, and continues following Tate's return to the States at the end of 1929. It is in these first letters that we see the creative activity of both men increase with the stimulus of each other's careful and detailed criticism. Bishop produced a quality and quantity of verse and prose under Tate's prodding that he was not to achieve again until the last years of his life. Tate, on the other hand, was writing some of his best poetry and making his first attempts at fiction. We can also see the reaction of concerned, intelligent men like Tate and Bishop to the economic and social devastation of those years, which they saw as the inevitable result of capitalism. Yet we can also see their distrust of Utopian political remedies, a distrust born of a skepticism and sense of evil central to their southern heritage. This section of the correspondence ends in the fall of 1934 following Bishop's return to America and the completion of his novel, *Act of Darkness*. For Tate, too, the fall of 1934 was especially significant, for it marked the end of his efforts to support himself solely by his pen and the beginning of a long and distinguished academic career.

July 17, 1929

Tressancourt, par Orgeval
S[eine] et O[ise]

Dear Allen: Isn't it about time that you were delivered of Jefferson Davis?[1] As I remember the fifteenth was the date set for the cutting of the umbilical cord. If the event has taken place, let me know. I await anxiously the time when you'll again be available for discourse and drinking—My regards to your wife, JPB   AL

1. Tate completed *Jefferson Davis, His Rise and Fall: A biographical Narrative* (New York: Minton, Balch & Company, 1929) while in Europe on a Guggenheim fellowship.

[July 1929]

Dear Allen: I'm so sorry to hear about your mother's death.[1] It was two years earlier, almost to the day, that I learned in similar fashion of my own mother's death, and I know how grievous it is to be so far away. There is, as you say, no reason for returning once you know that she is dead, but it is impossible not to regret not having been there. I suffered for months afterward, and even now cannot quite forgive myself not having gone back, though at the time it was next to impossible, Margaret being with child and having a very bad time of it. To you, then, I can truly say that I sympathize with you.

I am, on the other hand, delighted that you have finished your book.[2] I hope now that you will devote yourself for a time at least to poetry.   Yours, John   AL

1. Tate's mother had died on July 17, 1929, at Monteagle, Tennessee.   2. *Jefferson Davis, His Rise and Fall.*

November 17, 1929   6 Place de l'Odeon / Paris, VIe,

Dear John: I read your story[1] the very night I brought it with me, and I have reread it since; but this is the first chance I have had to write to you about it; even now I am so rushed that I really ought to wait for the next conversation. It is a fine story beautifully written, and I hope you have enough of them like it to publish a book very soon.

If there is any criticism of it at all, it is, it seems to me, on two points only, which are really one point. The story tends to fall into two parts, and the style is two styles perhaps for that reason. It appears to me that what the professors call the "exposition" may be elaborated a little too much—the late war as the taking off place; and because this requires some manipulation to get you to the main character, the action is somewhat retarded; this same difficulty seems to place too much emphasis upon the hero's mother, who is obviously required as a further transition from the opening scene to the fine climax. All these difficulties are beautifully handled, but I believe that it would be a better story if they were eliminated altogether.

I have a suspicion: you are a very good short-story writer; and an extremely good novelist. It seems to me that, as a short-story, the piece should plunge right into the last incident with the minimum of preparation. As it is, it requires only the right amount of extension to make it a novel. There are two things that make me believe that you have primarily the instinct of a novelist. First, your tendency to elaborate a scene with reflections of, in this case, the "Marlow" of your method; and, secondly, your weakness (from the point of view of the short-story) for letting a character run away with you—which tends to clog the action. Old Mrs. Ambler is beautifully done, but her story blurs her son's because you get too much interested in her for her own sake. Shouldn't the treatment of minor characters in a short-story as a rule be more externalized? The old lady was obviously very rich material, and a great temptation. As the story stands, it would make a novel, or at least a fine long story, if it were twice as long: the various elements, for lack of even further elaboration, are suspended at present because the treatment is too intensive for a story, not intensive enough for a novel.

One difference between the story writer and the novelist is a difference between you and Hemingway. Hemingway has never surpassed the last episode of your story for pure narrative; but Hemingway, being only a story writer, would have got the character into that piece of action with a preparation of about two pages. On the other hand, he could never have given us Mrs. Ambler. He implies character through action; you arrive at action through character, and you are a novelist.

This is all very hasty and involved; I want very much to talk to you about it. In spite of all I say, if I were to find a book of stories like this one, I should say that here is a very good writer indeed, even if I should look forward to a novel by him.

Most of this I got from Caroline, who knows more about these things than I do.

We have been hoping you'd drop in some day, and if you all aren't doing anything in particular tomorrow afternoon, why not go to the bicycle races with us? The Walkers are going, and perhaps the Hemingways. If you can make it, meet us at Lipp's for lunch at 12:30, or at the Velodrome d'Hiver at 2, at the entrance on the street where the elevated tracks are. . . . Best regards to you both.   Yrs. Allen T.

TLS

1. "The Cellar."

March 24, 1930   4 Rue Mignard XVII/Passy 34-99

Dear Allen: *The child* turned out—to our amazement and Buffie's surprise—to be two children—in other words, twin boys, born Saturday night, easily and expeditiously.[1] They are a good size for twins, sturdy and disposed to feed, and as a consequence of her short labor, Margaret is sitting up looking as if nothing at all had happened.

I shall come over nonetheless, as soon as things are running with fair smoothness. Scribner's has taken *Many Thousands Gone* with enthusiasm and offered a—to me—more generous price.[2] I miss you both. John   AL

1. Bishop was married in 1922 to Margaret Grosvenor Hutchins. They had three sons—Jonathan, the eldest, and Robert and Christopher, twins—all born during their parents' prolonged European residence.   2. *Many Thousands Gone* was published by Scribner's in 1931.

August 9th, 1930

Dear Allen: I've been a devil of a time answering your letter. The water crisis undermined my morale so that I wrote no one; I wanted to say I was sailing, and not until I could say that, would I write. Well, we bathe now, all of us and the household is calmer than I can remember it. So I'm sailing on the Berengaria next Saturday, arriving in New York the twenty-second. I plan to be around there a few days only before going to Charles Town. My address is 311, S. George Street.

In New York, the only address I can think of at the moment is the Coffee House, 54 West 45th Street.

Your estate on the Cumberland River sounds on the grand scale.[1] I hope I can see it; it all depends on the money. The new well about broke us and just now I don't see how I am going to stay the two months I want in the land of tariff and Hoover. However, I'm coming and will stay as long as subterfuges and Scribner's check hold out.

I was delighted with Caroline's story.[2] Please congratulate her for me.

I haven't done a hell of a lot of work this summer, but think with a little revising at my sister's I can hand over the mss to Scribners before I return.[3] I've got everything in rough shape. Of course, give me time and I'll revise till the crack of doom.

I thought MacLeish's new book very good.[4] Well, even better than that. He has at last shaken off the sand of the Waste Land from his feet and written at least three poems that are about as good as one gets.

I had a good trip to London a month ago, to sojourn in the political atmosphere of the Stracheys. I heard nothing but the American Revolution—not that of '76 needless to say—so that at last I had to tell 'em just what the Revolution would come to in America. It would so obviously turn into a continental race riot that not a page of Marx would be left intact. Michael Gold and Dos Passos's provisional govt would last, on a liberal estimate, three days. Then the north Italians would begin killing south Italians, the Irish the Jews, everybody the niggers and at the end we'd all find ourselves safe and not so snug under a good hardboiled dictatorship, not of the proletariat. They were on the other hand amusing and maybe sound on the subject of the Social Rev. in England. Strachey gave us a good picture of Moscow receiving its first communication from His Majesty's Soviet Government.

I've heard nothing from Ernest except through the public prints. Scott F[itzgerald] has been in Switzerland with Zelda. She started with a nervous breakdown last winter and since has had to be confined, I can't say how strictly. He lies so I could only make out that her state is serious, or at least has been. But how near actual insanity she has been or is I've no idea.

But don't let me spread the impression that she is insane. I simply don't know. The rumor has gone about Paris, but is ultimately based only on Scott's drunken gossip and that depends upon whether he's trying to bolster himself up or make himself out a lowly Mid-Western worm. As you know.

My infants thrive. The new ones have been no trouble at all for all that they mean a lot of work. They eat, sleep and grow enormously. I don't think they had names when I wrote you. The elder was, inevitably, named for Margaret's father and is being called to his displeasure Robert—I'll have to say Grosvenor in his presence. The little one is Christopher, after Marlowe or Columbus, or anybody except A A Milne.

My best to Caroline and many apologies for not having written sooner. John   TLS

1. With a loan from Tate's brother Benjamin, the Tates had purchased "Benfolly," an estate near Clarksville, Tennessee.   2. "The Long Day," *Scribner's Magazine* 88 (August, 1930), 162–66. This was her first published short story.   3. Bishop is completing *Many Thousands Gone.*   4. *New Found Land* (1930).

December 12, 1930   Route 6 Clarksville, Tenn.

Dear John: Perhaps you are in town, but I'm sending this to the country, where, I hope, you are basking in the mild French winter, as we are shivering in the famous December of the sunny South. I can't tell you how sorry I was to get your farewell note back in October; I was sorry we had not gone to Virginia to live, for I am sure you would have visited us there. But perhaps we shall meet again within a twelve-month; Caroline has applied for a gift from the Guggenheims, and there's no reason to suppose she will be refused, since I got one. We should sail in September, and I should hope shortly after that to see you climbing those five flights of stairs at the Place de l'Odeon. I'll never have enough imagination to stay anywhere else.

I saw a very good poem of yours in a recent New Republic,[1] and I was pleased to see in the Contributor's Notes the news that you were the author of a volume.[2] Where is it and where may I get a copy? Much as I admire Many Thousands Gone I insist on putting your poetry far above your prose. I was saying that to some one here the other day, and was promptly accused of self-defense: I feel a mild nausea every time I see the biographies mentioned. I will probably come in the end to—"but you must read my verse"—humiliating enough in view of the fact that it will never set the house afire. However, I suspect that my preference, in your writing, will not be ungratefully received. I hope you are working like a demon, though I confess it is hard to see anything demoniacal in you. Visit Gertrude [Stein] often, and maybe you'll catch it. I pray for your continued immunity to the disease.

What is the gossip now? Hemingway evidently fell into an Arkansan swamp; I've had not a word from him since summer. Are the Fitzgeralds about? Remember me to them. Caroline liked Zelda extremely (not unreservedly, perhaps) and is sure she was victim to Scott's delusions of grandeur in a silk hat. Poor Scott! I fear he couldn't make up his mind whether I was a gentleman; I never announced that I was and I didn't think much of fashion. At this distance his best parts stand out, and I often think of him with real affection. [Ford Madox] Ford came down here for a week in October, and we had a very amusing time. He showed us pictures of his new and Jewish wife; I like her looks so far as virtue is concerned, but virtue in that case concerns Ford. Do you think they will have children? My feeling for decency is somewhat impaired by ten years of bad company in the metropolis, but it is not dead. . . . Please remember us both most warmly to Margaret. And the twins? I suppose Jonathan is looking out for himself.   Yrs. ever, Allen   AL

1. "To a Swallow," New Republic 65 (November 26, 1930), 37.   2. Green Fruit (Boston: Sherman, French & Company, 1917).

December 23, 1930

Dear Allen: Your news was most grateful. I have thought of you and Caroline much these last days, remembering that it is just a year since you left Paris. It does not seem so long; the years go with such appalling rapidity once you've come to the thirtieth. Longer it looks the nine months interval we must wait—at best—for your return.

I miss you. We touched at certain points where I have had no other contact. And then, like yourself, I am very well-disposed toward anyone who thinks I can write poetry. I'd rather do it than anything else in the world; prose must always be trivial beside it. But then one can get by with fairly good prose, and fairly good poetry is, like the well-known fairly good egg, impossible. I am not vain enough to think my poetry better than it is, which is the way, I suppose, that so many of our minor, our minuscule, contemporaries keep counting the iambs and scoring cacophonies. But I have decided, due somewhat to your and Edmund's persuasion, that there is no reason to be more modest than they. I might as well publish. It will do me good in many ways to do so, and now that I have got my mss to Scribners,[1] I am planning to go over all the verse I have with a volume in mind, adding to it, if possible, a long intellectual piece.

The stories are, I think, pretty good. At all events they are written and all arrangements concluded with Scribners to bring them out in the spring.

We plan to leave here for Switzerland—Hotel Regina at Caux around the 20th of January. The children will be dumped there with nurses, and Margaret and I, if money holds out, will gallivant onward, probably toward Vienna, do some two weeks sight-seeing and picture-seeing (I missed all the pictures in Vienna when I was there eight years ago) and then come back to Caux to pick up the nurseries. The boys are all as well and vigorous as could be desired, but M thinks Jonathan should have a change of air and doubtless considers even more the needs of his elders. I shall myself enjoy the snow for a week or ten days. Skiing is the only sport I have ever discovered which is fun when done badly.

Scott may be at Caux when we are there. He's been at Lausanne since early summer. Scotty is in Paris at school. Zelda is still under treatment at Glion. You know, I suppose, her serious state. It's hard to make out exactly how near she's been to insanity, but I gather near enough to make her cure a long and uncertain one. Scott is probably enough to drive her or any woman crazy, but I don't really blame him, unless sexually. I suspect that part of the trouble is there, but the need of a stronger man and male than FS could only produce trouble if combined with other and more (or perhaps less) profound disturbances. And one must always remember that the life of the Fitzgeralds was a common creation. They collaborated, even on S's drunkenness. And either, I think, might have emerged from their difficulties alone, but never together.

I see almost no one, for there is no one in Paris now that I care about. It's all right when working, but idle it's bad.

Your Jefferson Davis is having great success in England where Esther Strachey is passing it among the younger members of the Labour Party. They have been quick to draw from it conclusions unfavorable to Mr. MacDonald. It is not impossible that the example of Davis had something to do with the signing of the Mosley manifesto.[2] MacDonald is indeed rather like an older American statesman, though to my mind the resemblance to Buchanan is more true than that to Davis.

I like the sonnet[3] and even more the Ode to Fear. There are one or two places I think might be improved. I do not—and find it hard to say why—like the *strove, grove* rhyme. Somehow *strove* is a bad word to end a line on; and *drenched the grove* is not quite right. The word suggests trees, not the ground, which Laius would have spattered. And if you can get rid of the 'the' before sunlight in the last line—or perhaps it's 'by the' that is wrong. These are criticisms of the ear, which you can disregard if you like. Looking again at *strove* and *grove*, I think it's the nearness in sound of *stood* and *strove* that makes the trouble. *Pass* and *grass* at once suggest themselves as possible substitutions, for it was, as I recall, in a pass that Oedipus killed his pa.   Yours ever, John   TLS

1. *Many Thousands Gone.*   2. Bishop is referring to the "Mosley Memorandum," an economic plan drawn up by Oswald Mosley (1896–), and rejected by Ramsay Mac-Donald's cabinet on May 1, 1930. It was a plan for massive public works projects and pensions designed to handle Britain's soaring unemployment resulting from the depression.   3. Apparently this poem was never published, but it may have been an early version of one of the "Sonnets of the Blood."

March 2nd, 1931

My dear Allen: You will know by this time that I won the Scribner prize with *Many Thousands Gone,* a feat for which I am exceedingly grateful. Not only will it give the book a much better chance than it would otherwise have had, but it offers exactly that sort of recognition which is most telling with the family, mine and Margaret's. And you must know, as well as I and every other American, how much easy [sic] it makes things to have no explanations to give in that quarter. Moreover, the money end of it will at last see us out of debt.[1] And that, too, makes for freedom.

I shall, of course, have Scribner send you a copy, which I hope later to appropriately inscribe. For the stories certainly owe much to you, to your courage which was itself an encouragement, to your erudition, which was of the greatest practical assistance.

I think on the whole they are pretty good: the prose is dense as I could make it without retarding too much the speed; they seem to me not unsuccessful in rendering, succinctly and yet without a falsifying simplicity, the emotions which for me at least lie back of the Southern point of view. They are, as you know, conceived with the intent of providing a criticism, long in time, of the civilization from which we both derive.

Certain things are lacking. I could not deal directly with some of the elements, and those the best, which that civilization produced. I could not present heroism in terms of the gallant Pelham;[2] my hero who defends the earth from which he sprung is Charlie Ambler. My Southern belle is the faded and affected Celie Cary, my elaboration of the ancient courtesy is the tipsy and bewildered Dr. Burwell.[3] I know that these things were there but they cannot be recovered in their simplicity. The only thing we can do with them is to present them indirectly, with irony and with a touch of parody. The fault is not altogether personal; it's a failure of the time in which you and I live.

You yourself, I feel, were vastly more successful with Davis than with Jackson, and that not only because your biography of Davis was second; rather it was because Davis is a divided and harassed mind, which we are capable of understanding, whereas the luminous simplicity, the unity of character, of Jackson is something we can't get.[4]

But I am describing the stories to you myself, when what I really want is your own most difficult criticism. Already the book is behind me. But I want to know how much of the method I can retain in its successor. Exactly what that will be, I don't know. I think I ought now to do a novel, and I think it should be contemporary. Anything else would be for me a shirking of difficulties, and besides, there still seems to me a whole range of experience and emotion, belonging to our generation, which has scarcely been touched, much less exploited, in prose.

I realized after writing you the last time that I had not answered your query as to my book of poems.[5] Page Dr. Freud! I really forgot it.

Green Fruit I published just as I was going into the army. It's out of print, which is just as well. It contains a lot of unformed and experimental stuff, written at Princeton and in the summer of 1917. If I had a copy here, I should let you see it, but I haven't. Nor do I think there are any longer extra copies at home. It has, I should say, about the same value as some of Amy Lowell's stuff—that is to say it represents my attempt to swallow and digest (that process not complete) the French symbolistes.

Paris is not nearly as pleasant as it was last winter before you and Ernest left. Scott I heard from—over the telephone—on his return from America. He's having a dreadful time, but is coming through it on the whole well. His relations with Zelda had got so bad that any separation cannot but make for improvement. And he is actually in much better shape. I saw him over a week-end in Switzerland, just before his father's death took him suddenly to America. I saw Mac-Leish on his brief passage through last week. He is deep in his epic on the conquest of Mexico.[6] Except as providing stage properties, I can't see what the pre-Columbian and later aboriginal activities have to do with us. As far as I can find out the North American Indians were a lousy, dull lot of savages, about as uninteresting as any primitive people who ever lived. Ernest is probably the only American who ever acquired anything profitable from contact with them.

My family thrive, except for occasional runnings at the noise (misprint for nose, but let it stand; it's also true). Give my best to Caroline. How's her novel?[7]   As ever, John   TLS

1. Bishop won the Scribner Short Story Prize for 1930 with "Many Thousands Gone," first published in *Scribner's Magazine* 88 (September, 1930), 229-44, 334-44, and later in a volume of short stories bearing the same title published in 1931. The prize carried a cash award of $5,000, which enabled Bishop to repay debts of long standing, including one to Princeton owed since his graduation in 1917.   2. John Pelham (1838-1863) commanded the famed Stuart Horse Artillery at Antietam. Bishop's reference is apparently to a biography by Philip Mercer, *The Gallant Pelham* (1930).   3. Charlie Ambler is the protagonist of "The Cellar," Celie Cary appears in "Many Thousands Gone," and Dr. Burwell is a character in "Young Death and Desire," all stories from *Many Thousands Gone.*   4. Tate's *Stonewall Jackson, the Good Soldier: A Narrative* was published in New York by Minton, Balch and Company in 1928, and in London by Cassel and Company, Ltd., in 1930. A paperback edition was issued by Ann Arbor paperbacks in 1957. *Jefferson Davis, His Rise and Fall* has not been reprinted.   5. In a letter to Bishop on December 12, 1930, above, Tate had asked about Bishop's early volume of poetry, *Green Fruit.*   6. *Conquistador* (1932).   7. *Penhally* (New York: Charles Scribner's Sons, 1931)

March 12, 1931

Dear John: Yrs. of the 2nd makes me much ashamed: I had not answered your excellent letter of about Christmas time. Two weeks ago Edmund [Wilson] paid us a brief visit, and he first told me the splendid news of the Scribner prize. I read your competitors' work, and I had no doubt where the five thousand should go, but I feared it would not arrive; it seldom in such cases does. So far as the public is concerned, the prize should make the book circulate—which is of course highly desirable. And it *will* fix up these family matters: I know all about them. As you know, I persist in being a poet, but my family esteems me as a biographer, not only as a biographer who in spite of being modern has the right feeling about the lost cause, but as one who made a little money on his books. It is very amusing, and the effect is fortunately better than that; it brings relief. Here is an example: in 1924, when for about seven months I hardly knew if I should have a meal the next day, I *tried* to borrow sixty dollars from my brother; I really needed it. Last spring, when the problem of nutrition was not pressing, I asked for ten thousand, and got it without a murmur.[1] I feel that this story should be capped by some piece of high sentence, from the classics, on human nature. I can't think of one. Perhaps you can. Now, my dear John, that you have made five thousand dollars at a blow, more will come, more will come.

I am naturally much pleased that you feel that I offered some help with the stories. Really all I did, of course, was to tell you what was good, and any reader would have told you that. I'm looking forward to the book with great pleasure, and you will hear from me very shortly after it arrives. Until I can re-read it closely, I will not venture to answer any of the questions you put concerning the problem of the next book. In general, however, I should be sorry to see you leave the scene of the past so soon. It seems to me that there is too much made of the moral necessity to face the present: one can tell if an author has faced the present even though he write entirely about the past. It is simply a question of the imaginative focus. Mine is certainly on the past, and I believe yours is. And I believe the rich vein of the stories will yield a couple of more books. It is dangerous to interrupt a stream that is flowing. I suppose that we have to consult some oracle pretty deep down in order to find out if it indeed still flows; but obey the oracle by all means. Why not turn yourself loose again on those same characters, and write as a novel the background of the stories? Present Celie Cary when she was not faded and affected, Dr. Burwell when he was not bewildered. It could not, as you say, be heroic, but you could present them quite seriously though with the irony that their end casts over them. It is the irony which testifies that the author has faced the present. You will lose it if you write about modern people. Why I should think this I am not certain; it is just an instinct about you. And I have certainly taken a great liberty in going so far.

Edmund's visit—it was his first to the South except New Orleans, and Charlottesville years ago—was very brief, but with characteristic energy he took in all that we showed him, and classified his information so well that he can tell me things I never dreamed of. As you know, he has gone in for Communism—whatever that is—and he was surprised to see a society that still lives mostly on the land. In the East the choice is doubtless debased capitalism or Communism; it is hard to convince a New Yorker that his dilemma is meaningless in the South. I think Edmund is convinced. What alarms me about Edmund's Communism is this: he not only accepts it as a matter of political and economic expediency; he has convinced himself of the philosophical good of Communism. This is bad; for it means that

what is bound to come is good; the will is all gone. If I were an Easterner I would be a Communist in action, but not in belief. Perhaps we shall have a race of convinced Communists here; I can't turn myself into one or pretend to myself. All these matters are settled by the age of ten—three-fourths of them at the embryonic age of two hours. Perhaps this is not true everywhere. Recently we had visitors here named John Herrmann and Josephine Herbst—they are writers, maybe you know of them—and it struck me that they are persons without hereditary directions, absolutely made by environment. They are the Americans. Both are recent American German stock (two generations), but they constantly talked, quite unconsciously, as if I were a foreigner and on the "outside." There was nothing impudent about it; it was rather subtle and very spontaneous. These are the ancestors of the socialized state. Or of some kind of society in which every generation must learn everything from the ground up; in which the environment changes with each generation, which never develops a fixed type except that of the perpetually unfixed. These people, in conversation, give forth vague animal sounds.

How did I get off on that? You must forgive me. We do have a constant and very welcome stream of guests, and somehow they stand out more clearly here than they did in New York. I seem to understand them better.

Glancing at your remarks on MacLeish and Mexico, I must add to some of the discussion above: facing our own past is a way of facing the present. Has MacLeish any Aztec ancestry? It is probably too bad that a man like MacLeish ever received an education, for education is nothing without tradition, and the traditionless educated man will, in spite of himself, work out fictitious and romantic scenes to dramatize his character in, usually in the past. It is a blessing that Ernest never went to a university and took it seriously. . . . Ernest is in Key West recovering from a broken arm. Heard nothing from him since last summer. I am very glad that the Fitzgeralds are improving; remember us to them both. And to Margaret, not forgetting Jonathan and the twins. I send with this a new and for me a long poem.[2] Please retaliate in kind. Yrs as always, Allen

P.S. The Guggenheims turned Caroline down; so we shall not meet abroad as soon as I had hoped.[3]   TLS

1. Tate is referring to his brother Benjamin, a successful businessman, who assisted him financially many times. One indication of Benjamin's generosity to his younger, "impractical" brother is that he provided him with three homes: "Benfolly," an antebellum house and farm near Clarksville, Tennessee; "Benbrackets," in Princeton, New Jersey; and a retirement home in Sewanee, Tennessee, which Tate sold when he

moved to Nashville for reasons of health.   2. "The Last Days of Alice," which appeared first in *New Republic* 66 (May 13, 1931), 354.   3. Tate had held a Guggenheim award for 1928–29. Although Caroline Gordon's application for an award in 1931 was rejected, she received one the next year.

April 6, 1931

My dear Allen: Your news was sad that you would not be able soon to come again to France as Mr. Guggenheim's guest. It's too bad. I suppose they don't believe in twice putting their money on the same family.

Margaret and I both hope to come over toward the end of the summer. But if we both come the trip will doubtless be a brief one. I can't see her staying very long away from the infants.

I have just seen the page proofs of my book[1] and telegraphed a few corrections to [Maxwell] Perkins—this being the arrangement to speed publication. The work I did on the galleys is all to the good, which is a relief. The first tale in particular seems to me much improved.

Your poem, The Last Days of Alice, is one of the best you have ever done. I should like greatly to steal several of the phrases and probably will. I, too, have done a poem, which I enclose.[2] It is addressed as you will gather to the three Fates. I have started several others but they are not as yet fit to be seen.

We went over to England last week, Margaret to get a new nurse, myself to play around. I paid my respects to Donne on the three hundredth anniversary of his death genuflecting before his beautiful nervous face in stone, shrouded and metaphysically thin, in St. Paul's. And I met Richard Hughes, the High Wind in Jamaica man, whose lone book I liked very much. He cultivates a Shakespearean beard and is full of respect for Americans. I put as much into the three days as I could, sleep excepted, and am still feeble as a result and painfully empty headed.

Edmund's going over to Communism is as sad as [T. S.] Eliot's passage to Christianity. Why won't they, if they must embrace a creed, take an enriching one? TSE's book, or rather pamphlet on the Lambeth conference is regrettable by just that much, that it represents an improverishment of his thought, a thinning of his already meagre emotional life.[3] Probably no religion's any good in which you can't have an orgasm at the altar. I can't imagine that happening in the Catholic church of England. And Communism—really! When the situation needs so much the clarification of just such a mind as Bunny's,[4] to have him sink back, wedge himself into that tight machine—Alas! And besides, the only possible way to believe in

Communism is to have been yourself one of the totally disinherited, which EW is emphatically not. He believes as much as I do in the immense heritage of the mind. How can he step out with Michael Gold? No, it makes no sense, certainly not here, nor in Tennessee, nor I suspect in New York.   As ever, John

P.S. I wish you'd be as severe as possible with the poem.   TLS

1. *Many Thousands Gone.*   2. "Ode," *New Republic* 70 (April 13, 1932), 245.   3. Eliot published in 1931 an essay, "Thoughts after Lambeth," in which he sought to justify the Church of England's washing its "dirty linen" in public in "The Report of the Lambeth Conference" (1930). He argued that "some of the best parts of the Report," such as The Christian Doctrine of God, had been neglected in favor of some of the more sensational parts, those with which "readers of the penny press are most ready to excite themselves."   4. Edmund Wilson.

April 17, 1931

Dear John: Your poem is splendid. I feel no need of being severe. I envy your power of setting the emotional tone so clearly that you don't need to keep telling us about it. This is my weakness: I don't know if it is possible for any poet to see the "emotional tone" of his own work, but because at any rate I can't I am always trying to write it in, instead of letting it emerge. I have only one question, and that concerns the strictly expository statement "The three are sisters."[1] There are other expository statements in the poem, and you are triumphant in keeping them subdued or running into a fusion with the "vision." I say you are triumphant because a free rhythm such as you use ordinarily makes exposition stick out too conspicuously, and you avoid this, I believe, except in this one case. By throwing your rhythm into metre you can often subdue the exposition or in fact, by giving it the same pattern metrically as the vision, reduce it to an identical form. (If it weren't for this function of metre we should not have Paradise Lost.) "The three are sisters" is off form, simply because your form depends on the logical nature of your style rather than on its metrical character. This may be obscure; but here is what I mean by vision as contrasted with exposition: "Her least movement recalls the sea" is vision; it is something inherent in your subject and is not simply brought in to define the subject or merely to inform the reader what the subject is about. The second stanza of my Alice poem is pure exposition, but I hope it is disguised by the metrical pattern.

There is a vast logical distinction between the two kinds of statement—expository and visionary. It is the difference between the analytic and the synthetic judgment. All poetry is analytic judgment; a poem simply draws out of an idea what is inherent in it, what properly belongs to it; when this law is violated we call in the charge of faulty taste or irrelevance. But in every poem there is a little of the synthetic judgment, which puts before us the logical framework, and separates the subject from all other subjects. The analytic judgment bores into the qualitative meaning of the subject in all its richness, but the subject must first be limited, set off, and its place and dimensions established by the synthetic judgment, in some form. It is better if the synthetic framework can be implied, and this is why Marvell's To His Coy Mistress is probably the purest form in English; it needs to resort to no subterfuge to establish the subject; it plunges immediately into it.

"The three are sisters" is a synthetic judgment because the noun "three" doesn't at all contain in itself the idea of "sisters"; thus it is a scientific, logical, quantitative sentence that momentarily halts the qualitative exploration of your theme in order to distinguish the theme from some other. You immediately return to the analytic statement—

> There is one
> Who sits divine in weeping stone . . .

I suggest that you revise the passage somewhat as follows, though I urge you not to adopt my phrasing and rhythm:

> There is one, one of the three sisters
> Who sits divine in weeping stone
> . . .

Thus by imbedding the expository element grammatically in the visionary statement it is properly subdued; the mind picks it up as an incidental, though a necessary item; the emphasis is not shifted from the vision, though it is clarified by the expository phrase "three sisters."

This is mighty long-winded; perhaps I could have made the point by merely saying there is something "wrong," and you would have seen it. But I think the reasons why a thing is wrong are as interesting as the wrong itself. It is the only thing wrong I can find with a very fine poem. At first I hesitated over "And of his bones are charnels made," but after some re-reading I really like the literary allusion, for the connotations extend the meaning of your line very precisely.

Well, it's spring here and more: 88 yesterday at noon. I do hope you all will come over and come this far. I don't know if Margaret's family still live in Ohio, but if they do, at Columbus, it is no distance at all down here. By the mid-summer our books will be done,[2] and we can perform many qualitative judgments on the entity which is Tennessee. In some respects Tennessee is the most interesting Southern state. Nashville is still at that point of transition where the mixture of

Old Southernism and modern capitalist ambition produces a kind of vulgarity, which for corruption and stupidity is I believe unsurpassed by any city in the country. Come and see it. We will have a house-party of carefully selected types. I wanted to do this when Edmund was here; as a non-Southerner (he is too good a fellow to be called a Yankee) he would have taken especial pleasure in such an exhibit, and you as an Eastern Southerner would be interested in the western variety. As half western and half eastern, I o'erlook the scene and foretell the rest.

I'm looking forward to the novel.[3] I am much pleased that it has advanced so far as page proofs. And send me more poems.   Yrs ever, Allen   TLS

1. The second verse paragraph of Bishop's "Ode" begins as follows: "The three are sisters. There is one/Who sits divine in weeping stone/On a small chair of skeleton/And is most inescapable."   2. Soon after he completed the biography of Jefferson Davis, Tate began an "interpretative biography" of Robert E. Lee. He expected to complete this book by mid-summer of 1931, but, as he wrote Bishop on October 19, 1932, he had abandoned it because he had come to believe the attitudes he had attributed to Lee were really his own. When he put the Lee project aside, he began a prose piece with the working title "Ancestors of Exile," which later became his novel, *The Fathers*. Caroline Gordon's book is *Penhally*.   3. Tate is referring to Bishop's short-story collection, *Many Thousands Gone*.

May 1st, 1931

Dear Allen: I was more than usually pleased by your commendation of my *Ode*. For it was the first poem I have done for a long time based upon ideas, and consequently I was more than usually unsure of its effect on the reader. Bunny also liked it (with R. Torrence) and it is coming out in the New Republic.[1]

I quite see your objection to the expository line "These three are sisters." It was not in the first version, but I later added it, deliber-ately, as an aid to the reader whom, I wanted as soon as possible, to identify the three women with the three fates. I say identify. That isn't quite correct. For the parrot-eyed goddesses are not identical with the Parcae, though they may well be related to them as to the [horns?] under "the gray ash tree."

I have occasionally meditated on what it was that Christianity freed men from. Certainly, in the beginning, it must have come as a great, supreme relief to have everything denied which up to that time men had painfully recognized as directing their lives. The fatality of character was opposed with the doctrine of grace, the decaying influ-ence, the irrevocableness of Time by the doctrine of immortality (also I suppose in the beginning by the New Heaven and the New Earth) finally, the myth of Christ, born of a Virgin and made one of the Trinity, assails the identity of numbers and the law of cause-effect.

With the decay of Christianity, we are once more faced with these same realistic fates whom, you are kind enough to say, I have realized as (almost) pure vision.

To come back to the flaw: I agree with everything you say. But I still think that at times a simple statement, explicit in its intelligence, can be effective and even, though not poetry, can be made to appear poetry. I am not defending this particular phrase: I trust your taste and judgment on it. But the principle of prefixing or concluding a passage elaborately metaphoric or of pure sensuous vision with a straight logical statement I do defend, not on grounds of pure theory, but practically. Of course it must serve as a point of illumination or, being different in kind, afford a sudden sense of displacement which allows everything that has gone before to be seen again and from a slightly different angle.

I explain this badly being filled to the brain with argyrol and dripping at the nose with a very liquid cold. I think, as I say, that I agree with you. Certainly the fault of much of Bunny's poetry is just that (I reread his book this morning) there are too many lines of direct statement, in which whatever is being conveyed to the reader is conveyed at once and by the shortest cut. Now I can spot this at once in another person, but in one's own work—particularly at the moment of composition—it is difficult to know.

It is to study this question: How to render moral ideas as pure vision that I have been rereading Rimbaud lately and translating some of his poems—one or two I think rather happily. There is something to be said for translation: it enables you to study your own style in slow motion, as it were. For you have nothing but style to consider, everything else being given you.

I have one or two things of my own to send you—but I am morally and physically too feeble to copy them today. I am medicated to the brim, trying to shake off this cold in order to dine with [Ezra] Pound tomorrow. It is a long time since I have seen him, and I hear he is quite pathetically aged.

The nightingales have returned and spring is at its best. Having for the time being deserted prose for verse I find myself indifferent to the sad state of the world. Funny! Thanks for your praise, John

AL

1. Edmund Wilson and Ridgely Torrence were editors at *The New Republic* during this period. Bishop's "Ode" was first published in *New Republic* 70 (April 13, 1932), 245.

May 11, 1931

Dear John: Your book arrived yesterday "with the compliments of the author."[1] I write this letter with the enthusiastic compliments of the reader. I read it from first to last at a sitting, and the effect is overwhelming and perfect. There are a few minor quarrels I have with details, but I have nothing but admiration for the design of the book as a whole and for the symbolic value you contrive to give each story without forcing the symbols. I think much of the book's power lies in that. You have selected the material so perfectly that each story and each character is a facet of a unified mind, which was the mind of wartime Virginia.

Two of the stories I had not read at all. I am inclined to think the Young Death and Desire is the finest in the book. It is richer in all its implications. Dr. Burwell and his daughter and the serjeant[2] very nearly exhaust the Southern mind. There is a tremendous amount of insight in the girl's character—mixture of frivolity and coquetry and with a great deal of courage at bottom. And Dr. Burwell is good too; only I think the matter of his hat is a little overdone; if she had been his young second cousin, well and good. You have done a fine piece of analysis in giving us the serjeant, the only convincing Confederate soldier I've seen in fiction. If Dr. Burwell *is* exaggerated, it is perhaps inevitable; for we can't quite get back to the basis of such a character, without which its surface seems a little strange and maybe a little ridiculous. For example a man like our friend Ernest seems rather monstrous at first, until we know him better and get to his sources. Here is a general commentary on your book: your women characters are much better than the men. Perhaps that can be explained too: the women survived better and in your boyhood were more interesting than the men, were closer to the vital tradition. The style of Young Death and Desire is surer and more concise than any other.

Next best I believe is If Only. In form it is probably better than my favorite, because its subject-matter is more sharply defined, and there is no need to define the action in terms of an external situation which demands description, as you had to do in the case of the confusion over the wounded men in Young Death. I have looked back through the stories for their endings, and I believe If Only comes off better than any of them. It is really perfect. And I am astonished, in view of this, that you let the ending of The Cellar trail off as it does! Given the device of the narrator, it is hard to see how you could have avoided it; and without the narrator you could hardly have piled up enough detail (an impersonal narrator couldn't have had enough omniscience) to make the axe scene come off. This is a dilemma, and perhaps you couldn't have got out of it. I only wish that the most dramatic scene in the book didn't suffer an anti-climax! I think it is the only serious flaw in the book, but the book can well afford it.

There are endless comments that I'd like to make; I'll save them up. I think there is some interesting discussion to be made of your general point of view. For instance, the Southern tradition was not in decay in 1860, but I feel that in the stories all the characters are decayed ladies and gentlemen. This casts an air of melancholy over the book which is just right, and more than that it sets the irony of your treatment at just the right pitch. But there's something about this irony that I want to think over at the next reading. I can't yet tell whether it is produced by your own knowledge of your characters' fate, of which of course they are unaware, or whether it comes from an actual dislike of them. I can't quite make out whether their limitations are inherent or due to circumstances. This is particularly true of Lou and Ellen.[3] Possibly, as in the case of most Southerners of our generation, you have both views at once and are not able to distinguish them sharply. I should like to know your opinions of this question, and to know if you were quite conscious of it in the writing of the book.

There is one distinguished feature that I have failed to remark. There are few books in our day that are written out of a full and settled view of human nature. Yours is one of them. The only American novel, recent American novel of this kind I can think of is Stark Young's "River House." You and Young still have the sense of the social type, and I doubt if either of you could write a book about a society that has no well-developed types. That is why, in a recent letter, I urged you to stick to the past!

I am still struggling with Lee—who was a social type. In odd hours we do a little planting, and a little gadding about. Please let me know if your plans for the trip over this summer are final; I want to look forward to seeing you. Regards to you all,   Yours ever, Allen

P.S. I have caught you in an error of historical fact! The charge of the V.M.I. Cadets at New Market didn't happen till 1864.

I'm sending you some poems about the Past.[4]   TLS

1. *Many Thousands Gone.*   2. Tate is referring to an unnamed Confederate corporal in "Young Death and Desire."   3. Two elderly sisters in "If Only."   4."Emblems."

May 26th, 1931

Dear Allen: I cannot tell you with what eagerness I awaited your letter, nor with what satisfaction I read it. For there is no one of my acquaintance to whom I can appeal on the double count of literary critic and Southerner except yourself; there is therefore no other whose opinion could mean more to me and that it should come as praise rather than blame is in the highest degree gratifying.

I understand your reservations perfectly, having been largely conscious myself of the shortcomings which you point out. You are right—the Southern tradition was not in decay in 1860. But, dependent as I was on my material gathered at a long later date, I could not, in spite of myself, show it otherwise than as I have done. There was one story, which eventually I had to abandon after much labor, which was to show the Virginians flourishing. I could never manage it. Also, it was a similar limitation which makes the women better than the men. First, a child is closer to women than to men, and secondly the reminiscences of the women were more fluent than those of the men. There was one veteran of the Valley campaign with whom from a very early age I was most familiar. He was not so old, having been himself but sixteen at the time of Jackson's flurries up and down the Valley. Having two daughters, but no son, he took to me with an extraordinary affection. Often I went with him into the basement, where he owned a panelled study, and [was] shown his relics of the war. But all he could say was, I picked this piece of shell up on such and such a battle field. Or, This is where the bullet went in my neck, and here's where it came out again. In all wars men are silent or liars.

If, as you say, my corporal in Young Death and Desire is successful, it is largely because I don't let him reminisce as too many have made their soldiers do. The reality of [the] fight, as I say of him, is incommunicable. It must be inferred.

The incident of the hat *is* overdone. But it was not only for a comic exaggeration that I introduced it. I was aware that Dr. Burwell would not ordinarily have made this gesture to his daughter. But for the moment I wanted them to cease the daughter-father relationship. He is meant to see her as a desirable girl at that instant, not as his daughter. This is perhaps too subtle, and only the ridiculous gesture remains.

There is, however, something more to the insistence on failure than I have represented above. It is my theory that, for a number of reasons, literature is concerned with failures rather than successes. The most interesting thing about anyone to me is what they think of themselves, that is the character which they conceive themselves to be, and the divergence between that character and the reality as revealed by the march of events. That divergence is best revealed—and particularly is this true in shorter pieces—at that moment when the pretence falls, toppling either by virtue of its own unstable height, or undermined by relentless circumstance. That moment may be treated comically, elegiacally or tragically. Needless to say, I have for this book preferred the elegiac treatment.

I have tried to be sympathetic to all the main characters and at the same time to condemn them. I think there is here a lack of accent (that is in the stories, not the theory) which I don't defend—but I am pretty sure that it is in some such way that the third dimension is secured in fiction. The ideal attitude on the part of the author—I speak generally now and not at all in explanation of what I have done or not done in this volume—is a full sympathy with the passions of the characters, even, I suppose, with their oddities and vagaries, but at the same time a relentlessness which coldly judges their virtues and condemns their sins. And the condemnation must come through the march of events, neither through comment, nor trickery.

This is why the personages of the Inferno, in spite of the brevity of the scenes in which they are shown, are so terribly clear: there is the fullest sympathy with their passions—that is, with those passions which Dante shared in his own life (I mean by this that Dante is only sympathetic to characters like Francesca and Farinata whose vices he was guilty of)—and at the same time an utterly ruthless condemnation of those passions. The sympathy may be personal, the judgment should seem divine. (This incidentally is why Faulkner fails of the best; his condemnations are just, terribly so, but they remain personal judgments; they never reach the serenity of impersonal justice.)

This is my theory, which I am prepared to defend. My practice is another matter. And I am aware of the fact that I began always with too clear a sense of the ridiculousness of the Southern temperament, an awareness made more acute by the knowledge that I was writing primarily for a non-Southern audience.

As to Ellen and Lou, my clearest idea about them was that they were two persons who ignored the passage of time. This I conceived to be a Southern characteristic from which I am anything but free myself. I meant them to have—particularly Lou, who is the more intense of the two—a sort of comic grandeur. Lou's illusions have such force that only time can destroy them and that only by destroying Lou.

Of course, in this story there is an additional irony in that fact that the Virginia tradition was never as grand as Ellen and Lou made out. Certainly their life had there been no war would have been on a far simpler, ruder and humbler stage than, in their minds, they were able impossibly to conceive it. You must remember that they are natives of the Valley, and as far as I can make out the Valley life was always a rather sober and solid affair that looked with romantic longing toward the Tidewater. There they imagined fantastic dignity, elegance and courtliness. And as a matter of fact there was a grandeur about some of the Tidewater men and women who settled amongst us. I recall particularly old Mrs. Mitchell, Betty Lewis's granddaughter, still with something like awe, and that because of some personal quality, her own and not reflected from a most illustrious ancestry which included all the great names of 17th century Virginia. I attempted, none too successfully, to deal with this quality in my ill-fated novel,[1] which may be one reason why I avoided any suggestion of greatness in the later opus. One must also admit that the time is not favorable for the direct treatment of heroic virtues. I neither deny them, nor disparage them. But for practical reasons, I avoid them.

I don't particularly envy you your subject in Lee. I can conceive of few more difficult. And yet, last summer, I thought I gained some insight into his character simply by spending the morning at Stratford.[2] That landscape, so like the wilderness, that remoteness, so complete, must largely have determined him. A man who could conquer those influences would be daunted by no odds.

But there is something about the nobility of the time which defies recovery. One reason why your Davis was so much weightier than your Jackson was that a divided character like Davis is the more comprehensible than an integrity like Jackson's. And Lee will prove, I should guess, even more aloof than TJ, though to be sure there are moments of outburst which are more revealing than anything I know of in Jackson's life.

I find your poems touching and profound. I like the new direction of your Muse, which seems toward greater clarity—I use the word in all its force, not simply to mean the opposite of difficult to unravel. There was a time when, urged perhaps by your admiration for Eliot and Crane, you sought a too closely packed line. Somehow, I do not think this is right for you; your thought is always enough compressed—you should I think try in your verse for an even flow and for greater weight on the rhyme. At least, contrasting a considerable number of your verses, this is my conclusion: I find those best where the voice is heard in a long breath and not too often halted by pauses within the line. I would not therefore have you lose your cunning disposition of alliterations and assonances, which provided one of the great pleasures of your earlier poems, or fail to allow yourself those liberties in accent which you have shown you know how to use. But I don't think you would be wrong to give a little greater importance to the line, in other words, to consider the pause the rhyme word almost inevitably makes. I am not in this counselling you to change, but only trying to confirm you in what you have already done.

I would in fact alter nothing in *Emblems*,[3] unless it is in the last line of III. Shouldn't this go:

> the burning shiver
> Of August, like a hawk, strikes the crouching hare.

It seems to me as an image clearer so. And yet the minute I put this down, I reread the stanza and wonder if I am not a fool to suggest the change.

I have done nothing for a week or more, having just come back from a tour of the Touraine, with Margaret and Herbert Gorman, one of the best trips I have ever known. Such a country! At least I understand the till now obscure phrase *la douce France*. And what a wine Vouvray is when thirty years have ripened it! We did the chateaux by day and dined by night, alternating a sunny sensuousness with a most delicious intoxication.

I enclose a poem.[4] Many thanks for your letter,   As ever, John

The others (translation excepted) are old poems. I'm wondering whether I ought to include them in a book.   TLS

1. "The Huntsmen Are Up In America," a novel Bishop expended great time and energy on in the 1920s, which was encouraged but later declined by Scribner's. The novel was never published.   2. Stratford is Robert E. Lee's ancestral estate in Westmoreland County, Virginia.   3. Tate's "Emblems" appeared in *New Republic* 67 (September 30, 1931), 182. It is composed of the following: I "Maryland Virginia Caroline," II "When it is all over and the blood," and III "By the great river the forefathers to beguile," the last previously published as "Pioneers" in *New Republic* 64 (September 24, 1930), 152. Tate did not incorporate Bishop's suggested change, for the line in question reads as follows in the published version: "the burning shiver/Of August strikes like a hawk the crouching hare."   4. "Encounter," which first appeared in *New Republic* 76 (September 27, 1933), 181.

[Early June, 1931]

Dear John: Your letter came yesterday just as I had finished a chapter of Lee, and I am given an excellent pretext to take a morning off to answer your message. It begins to appear, I think, that ours is perhaps the only eighteenth century correspondence being carried on at present in the industrial world. I hope that it has some of the eighteenth century virtues, but lacking these it can hardly have its vices either. I very much fear that we both evince a good deal of the Southerner's obliviousness to time—a distinct virtue, or certainly at least a quality of indifferent value, in a civilization that lived without time. But the present civilization lives on time solely. I make no pretense of keeping up with it: I am merely shocked by events into a sort of dumb resistance. Perhaps you, by great deliberate effort, try to evaluate Change; but this is very different from the attitude of a man, say Hemingway, who was born in Change, and can never know that there was rest. Isn't the idea of time as a sensuous fact bearing down upon our sensibilities and limiting our thoughts, a new idea?[1] I mean isn't it new for us, who come directly out of a timeless background without the preparatory stages that a New Englander has had? I suppose that the belief that time is a strictly objective record of events made the grandeur of the old characters you write about; time did nothing to people, it was not a fact of experience. Of course those people never had any experience; they merely had observations. And so I doubt if our correspondence is very 18th century after all.

I had hoped to read your book again before I should write this letter. I haven't been able to do it (for obvious reasons). Red Warren was here the other day, and we had some lively argument about it. He says that If Only is the best in the book, and Young Death the least distinguished. I am now inclined to agree with him. In that story you handle a far more complex situation than in any other, and I was so impressed at first with that, that I assumed that you were therefore most successful in doing it. Assuming that I was right about Dr. Burwell (you don't need to), perhaps he is exaggerated because you don't have time to draw him out; his case is rested on one scene. Yet if you had given him more than that, you would have started another story. And I think in general that is the tendency of Young Death; you concentrate the material on the girl and the corporal[2] only by cutting off short, by a kind of main force, the other motifs of the story. I still think the corporal a splendid character—as I said, the only convincing Southern soldier I've seen.

I agree with you fully about the character of literature; it is best when it deals with failure. But I think that Southerners are apt to identify the great political and social failure with their characters, or if they are poets and concerned with themselves, with their own failure. The older I get the more I realize that I set out about ten years ago to live a life of failure, to imitate, in my own life, the history of my people. For it was only in this fashion, considering the circumstances, that I could completely identify myself with them. We all have an instinct—if we are artists particularly—to live at the center of some way of life and to be borne up by its innermost significance. The significance of the Southern way of life, in my time, is failure: those Southerners who leave their culture—and it is abandoned most fully by those who stay at home—and succeed in some not too critical meaning of success, sacrifice some great part of their deepest heritage. What else is there for me but a complete acceptance of the idea of failure? There is no other "culture" that I can enter into, even if I had the desire—and of course I assume that one needs the whole pattern of life: I can't keep half of it and live on another style the other half of the time. And it seems to me that only in this fashion can a Southerner achieve in his writing what you call the "impersonal judgment"; for otherwise his standards will be drawn from some other equally temporary way of life, rather than from a perception that the old Southerners did not reach perfection in the style that they developed, or the style that they lived up to. I think that your awareness of this situation makes Ellen and Lou very nearly perfect characters in fiction: you judge them by their own idea and they are found wanting. Otherwise, if you had judged them by a foreign idea, you could have treated them from the outside only, and they would have been caricatures. That, I believe, is the trouble with Dr. Burwell; he is a caricature. And he is that for a reason that you indicate in your letter: it was harder in our time to get into the minds of the men than to understand the women.

You may remember that I said that you are one of the few who still understand the social type. Ellen and Lou are perfect social types—that is, they have a definite form that they cannot escape from; your business is to show that they don't achieve the full meaning of the form. That is the right irony for literature, and that only is the meaning of the dogma that literature must be "native" or have "roots" in a locality. The writer must assume that everything he requires is inherent in the subject-matter. The trouble with most Southern fiction of the [Ellen] Glasgow and [James Branch] Cabell school is this: their characters are condemned for not being New Englanders or cultivated Europeans, rather than for being imperfect Southerners. This is what you call the personal judgment. And it is, of course, as you say, very different from Dante's kind of judgment, which becomes impersonal for the very fact that Dante himself had the virtues and vices of the people he condemned. In this, it seems to me, there is a general lesson for writers; they must never attempt to judge characters outside their own "culture," except at the risk of making the judgment trivial. (We see in The Awkward Age how [Henry] James failed miserably in dealing solely with Europeans; so we must infer that his success with them in his other books was due to the fact that he could understand them only as they were brought to life in a clash with his Americans whom he understood profoundly.) I suppose the thin and sensational quality of much contemporary literature, European as well as American, is due to the general collapse of all bases of judgment, the disintegration of the old exclusive and self-contained societies. It is pretty obvious that the more intensely local literature was in that sense, the more impersonal and universal it became. The comic spirit particularly in its satirical aspects can survive under modern conditions, but I doubt if we can have tragedy. Your Charlie Ambler[3] is probably a genuine tragic character: you judge him by a standard that is entirely inherent in his own character, a standard that is both his own creation and the measure of his deficiency. Compared to the moral pattern that guides an Oedipus it doubtless has certain limitations, but the point is, that it is perfectly relevant to Charlie's situation. One trouble with most American fiction, fiction of the Mid-West mainly, is that the characters never have a chance; they are given no relevant issues; this is as true of Miss [Willa] Cather as of [Sinclair] Lewis.

There is one respect, I believe, if you will let me point it out, in which you give your characters, chiefly Dr. Burwell (I can't let him alone!), what I call an irrelevant issue. Why did Dr. Burwell show excessive politeness to his daughter? Now compared to the behavior in a like situation of an equally perfect gentleman in another society, his gesture is fantastic. I am now inclined to think that it isn't the gesture in itself that makes him a caricature, but the lack of a context for it: you simply imply that he is ridiculous where his peer elsewhere would not have been. (I am aware of the technical service of the scene, which shows the girl as physically attractive and has its effect in the scene with the corporal.) Will you let me indulge in a little gratuitous speculation? I think the gesture, and most of the Southern code, grew out of the people's relation to the land. You seem to miss this, and to judge him from a viewpoint which itself has become far removed from the influence of the land code. In general I should say that our excessive politeness to women was due to the realization that they were the material medium—philosophy makes us use strange words—through which property is perpetuated, and while we had no respect for them as individuals, we had an exalted respect through them for the land. For this reason Dr. Burwell's gesture is not in itself ridiculous in the sixties. (That's why I said that the Southern tradition was not in decay in 1860.) So I fear you've judged him by a personal and external standard, without showing that circumstances alone have made his code fantastic. I am very curious to know what you might have done with him had he been given a full-length portrait; he is the single instance of external treatment among your male characters.

Probably this is all due to the fact that like most of us you are both inside and outside the old tradition, that in a word you are a modern and divided mind. You are right in this matter; the Davis book was relatively a success, but the Lee is a failure.

I must go back to that failure, and bring this to a close. As to the ridiculousness of the Southern temperament, you are right, if you don't grant its origin, which was the land. Now that we are removed from the land, it seems to have no base but social habit that hangs on and dies hard. I understand this quite well; I share some of that temperament's most ridiculous features. There is a recent example of this that you know something of. You remember my controversy with one of the Humanists?[4] Well, I had an impulse that must seem comic to most of my contemporaries. I wished, I still wish, to do the man violence. Now there are two kinds of violence; one is reserved for those who participate in our own code, the other is for those below it. The latter kind I thought suited to the occasion. I know this is "ridiculous"; I know also that the social system that such conduct was meant to defend has largely passed away; and I know that "people" no longer do such things. Perhaps too I have a clearer conception than most persons of the changes that have come about since the decay of the land code, and the meaning of those changes. Nevertheless, I had the impulse, and I still have it, and I will not feel that my title to full self-respect is clear until I satisfy it. What can we do about such things? Of course I should submit to circumstances, but circumstances for me include my own sense of the difficulty. I took some pleasure in my opponent's statement to my brother that such things were done nowadays only by people in the underworld; it seemed to me an unconsciously profound criticism of modern society. Here is an example of the ridiculousness of the Southern temperament, but it is one of those irrational, irreducible factors of character that one can do nothing about. I can't think it away, and I can't rid myself of the foolish belief that not to feel so is a mark of inferiority. What again can we do about such matters. I can only suggest that you write a short story about your friend Allen.

I am greatly impressed with your poem Encounter. It is the best by far of your recent work. Only to a less degree I like the Elegy for a Young Girl.[5] I have the feeling that it isn't long enough. The speed is too great for the complexity of the emotion that you establish in the first stanza and elaborate in the second. Shouldn't we be permitted to linger over it a little longer? Take Browne's "Underneath this sable hearse / Lies the subject of all verse"; there is a simple emotion that can be swiftly presented, upon which thought lingers after reading it. The process there, for the reader, is to complicate the emotion later. Your poem starts a complex emotion, which engenders the opposite process, that of simplifying the emotion after reading the poem. You might well give it a fuller treatment. I like tremendously the translation; it has an enormous amount of style. I hope you will send me your other Rimbaud pieces. This is about the only decent translation of Rimbaud I ever saw, except a poem done by Sturge Moore. I don't know about the piece done back in 1920. It seems to me fundamentally obscure, though I think I see clearly the intention. Let me look at it a little more. And so, my dear John, I salute you once again, from the banks of the Cumberland to the hill in Orgeval.   Yrs, Allen

TLS

---

1. Tate develops this idea in his "Aeneas" poems and in his essay "The New Provincialism." It is also, of course, a dominant theme in his "Ode to the Confederate Dead."   2. The "serjeant" referred to in the letter of May 11, above.   3. The protagonist of "The Cellar."   4. In Tate's essay "The Fallacy of Humanism," *Criterion* 8 (July, 1929), 661–81, he had attempted to demonstrate the weaknesses of the arguments of the New Humanists. One of their number, Robert Shafer, responded to Tate's essay with a heated, almost insulting article, "Humanism and Impudence," *Bookman* 70 (January, 1930), 489–98. Tate then retaliated with "The Same Fallacy of Humanism: A Reply to Mr. Robert Shafer," *Bookman* 70 (March, 1930), 31–36.   5. This eighteen-line unpublished poem was expanded, at Tate's suggestion, into a much longer poem, "October Tragedy."

June 24, 1931

Dear Allen: Your letter, happily for the reader, but unfortunately for
the one who would answer it, brings up many questions of import.
But let me say only to begin with that it has always seemed to me the
most difficult, as well as the most important, matter to know how one
is to judge one's characters. You say, and rightly, that the standard of
judgement must be relevant, and yet I am not sure that that tells the
whole story. For instance, I cited Faulkner: Faulkner's judgement of
his Mississippians is sound in so far as he judges them not as New
Englanders or Europeans, manques, but always as Southerners, acting within the Southern scheme of things. They fail to measure up to
their own conception of themselves—and horribly and cruelly they
fail—but this is not the full force of his horror in considering them. He
seems to hate them as human beings, and that not because they fall
below his own conception of human nobility. Rather he rages at some
essentially human trait in them—above all that they are not perfectly
intelligent and that their sexual activities are not pursued on some
high and impossibly pure plane. There is, as one of his French critics
said, a center of bad idealism there. And besides, he seems also to
have failed to purge himself in writing of nearer and more personal
irritations. Thus, in *Sanctuary*, his best book, he is sound in having
the young small-town cockteaser raped by an impotent man with a
corn cob. It is a form of judgment, cruel but essentially just. It is what
should have happened to her. But, beyond the Swiftian rage, there is
also in the book a purely personal resentment at her (and her type) as
though he resented not only what she was and had done, but also
that on certain occasions she had failed to come through for him on
the back seat of the Ford. The resentment is not pure. Nor is the
judgement.

   Now, to me it is always the most interesting thing about a man
what he thinks of himself. That is to say, what is the form he has
conceived through which to live—next, the disparity between that
form and the actual person as I see him. Or, supposing that he
achieves that form (as doubtless Lee did) then the criticism of it
through events. Many of Shakespeare's men are completely inte-
grated, yet always he places them in those circumstances which alone
will defeat them.

   With Lee, you have a most difficult subject. There seems to be no
drama, no conflict within the man. Of course, I don't know the material as you do, in fact, know it but slightly. And then, our attention
has always been fixed on Lee in his maturity and age. There must
have been a conflict necessary to achieve his apparent success (in
fulfilling his form) and even in maturity he must at moments have

revealed the incompletion of his character. Otherwise, or so it seems to me, there is no human interest, a phrase needless to say which I deplore, but which here means exactly what I want to say.

He came from failure. His father's end was his beginning. And the landscape of Westmoreland is a background of struggle; nature gives nothing or next to nothing; it is lonely and it is barren.

And yet, of course, he loved Stratford as he loved Virginia. Perhaps it was that very love which undid him, limiting his vision to the Virginian battlefields. That would be, I should think, the starting point for a Shakespeare who was after treating him with irony, and how else can one treat a character but with irony?

For if we approve of our characters, they flatten. Mary Johnson[1] is a perfect example of this: she deals only with virtue or small attractive failings and her characters are cut out of paper washed over with water colors. We must judge, if not as gods, then as poets and historians. The poet must provide an ideal of conduct, the historian must correct the ideal bringing it within the range of the humanly possible. For only the historian knows what nobility and what depravity the race is capable of and knows a wide enough range of cultures to guess what the particular culture his character knows can provide.

I think one feels this about Lytton Strachey. Strachey has great human limitations; he is a pederast and a scholar. The wholesome eludes him: his Elizabeth and Essex remain distant if not vague, whereas that other fine old bugger F. Bacon is perfectly done. But as a scholar Strachey has a sense of at least two periods, the French XVIIIth and the English XIXth centuries. He knows something of the limits to which the race can aspire. He does not judge his XVIIIth century personages from the standpoint from which he judges his Victorians. Nevertheless, his knowledge of more than one culture aids him in dealing with any particular representative of any particular culture.

Personally, I think the Southern culture was too limited and too short-lived to provide all the points of comparison we need. It is not a question of judging it in immediate opposition to, say, the English squirearchy of the XVIIIth century. Rather, I should say, it should be seen, first against the whole American background and then against the whole European background. I say the whole, but of course my whole is not the cosmopolite's. I mean rather what can be intimately assimilated as one's own and regarded, not as an acquisition, but as a heritage.

I speak for myself, because this is what I must do. Hemingway, who has no historical sense (and has derived great advantages from its complete lack, for most people have an ignorant spot of it), nevertheless manages to give a pretty sound judgement on his characters.

Morally the man is simple but on the whole sound. He sticks to a few herioc virtues and is able to dispense with complexity. I cannot do that.

To go back to Dr. Burwell, who seems to worry you, I admit he is seen and judged from the outside and that he is consequently a caricature. But I saw him as a very minor character: I was interested in him only because I had to supply some sort of familiar background for my girl and had to arrange to have her left alone with the corporal at night. Her father was determined by these narrative exigencies. And because I wanted speed, I resorted to caricature to place him quickly. I don't think this is necessarily reprehensible; even Shakespeare was willing to use the method for very unimportant characters, as for example, the fairy courtier in Hamlet.

As to what made the Southerner ridiculous—I don't think he was as long as his system held. It was when he fell from power into poverty that the manners of a firm landed aristocracy came into disrepute. So you are right in saying that the elaborate courtesy was not ridiculous in the sixties.

Nor do I think your desire to do violence to one of the Humanists ridiculous, because with you it was a personal thing and not a class gesture. That is to say, you wanted to provoke RS [Robert Shafer] to fight, not to preserve a tradition of your class, but because you found your own honor assailed.

I had done a little parody on that episode before your letter came, but I don't know whether I want to send it. You and Bunny are both caricatured in it—though I hope sympathetically—and the Humanists are, I hope, successfully derided.[2] But you are seen in a bawdy posture, as you demolish the Humanists. But that, me dear Allen, was not unkindly meant. My greater hesitation in sending it is (O vanity!) that I don't find it above reproach as a parody.

Best luck with the Lee. Think over what I've said above and reread Coriolanus; it might provide your point of vantage for tragic treatment. John

P.S. I have left many things in your letter untouched which I would like to discuss in detail with you. But as EW says, I cannot do justice to them in a letter. At any rate, not in this letter! JPB   TLS

1. Bishop is apparently referring to Mary Johnston (1870–1936), a writer of southern historical novels.   2. The New Humanists included, among others, Paul Elmer More, Irving Babbitt, Norman Foerster, Stewart P. Sherman, and Robert Shafer.

July 7, 1931

Dear John: Alas, I too can't do justice to yours of the 24 ult. I have just finished nine sonnets,[1] from first to last occupying two and one half days; and I am flattened out. Perhaps the sonnets after all will in a manner answer your letter; they will be grist to the Bishop analytic mill, which as an ironic instrument will be pleased to separate the real Tate from the version of Tate that he expresses in the poems. This is certainly the best opportunity I've given you; the sonnets are the most personally forthright poems I've ever written. Aside from this, which doesn't really worry me, is the style they're written in. It is perfectly spontaneous; I just started fumbling with a pencil, had no idea I was going to write sonnets, even a sonnet, had no definite theme in mind, and before I'd written the second one the others came crowding so fast that I could barely get each preceding one done in time. I don't know what to make of this; two of them are fair sonnets in the pastiche of fake Shakespeare, but I've never even done that well with a sonnet before. I explain this because I would like your better explanation. I enclose two other poems[2] which are more like me. (?)

Now that you've mentioned the parody, you've got to send it on. Did I send you a burlesque (rhymed) on the poets, our contemporaries, which is done in imitation of Edmund's imitation of Joyce? You are a handsome figger in it.

Your discussion of the Point of View particularly with reference to Faulkner is perfect; I stuttered all through my letter to say it, But as I've hinted I can't do justice to it in this letter. Next time.   Yrs. Allen

P.S. I decided not to let Minton, Balch bring [out] my next book of poems, and Perkins has agreed to publish it in January.[3] I'm damned if I can decide whether to include the sonnets. I want your advice— very severe if necessary.

By the way, I rewrote the Ode to Fear, adopting most of your suggestions.[4] I hope you're getting as much out of our correspondence as I am.   TLS

1. "Sonnets of the Blood," *Poetry* 39 (November, 1931), 59-65.   2. Not identified.   3. *Poems: 1928-1931* was published by Scribner's in 1932.   4. "Ode to Fear: Variations on a Theme by Collins," *New Republic* 70 (February 17, 1932), 10.

[July 1931]

Dear Allen: I am sending you the parody I spoke of.[1] I hope it will not offend you. You are portrayed in caricature (which you distrust) with gargantuan exaggerations, brobdignagian anatomy and gulliverian attitudes. If you don't like it, tear it up and forget it (if you can).

I began it after receiving your poem on the same subject and composed in the same vocabulary. It was more or less spontaneous, devised in a taxicab and on a full bladder. Attribute its yellow complexion to that circumstance.

There's a question I want to ask you. Remembering your criticism

of my recent opus, I suddenly began wondering whether by the anti-
climax of the Cellar you meant the nonexistence of the sixth soldier.
Was that what bothered you? Or is it that the story trails on too long
after the demolishing of the others. I'm simply curious.

In the meantime, I am, as ever,   Your friend and admirer, JPB
                                                          TLS

1. This parody has apparently not survived.

                                                      Shout Shix
Chusty [July] 13, 1931   Clarkswill, Benny's Bee

Beer Bonne: Your farrowdy meases and teases this holed Confeder-
feit gentletone like piped and pickled periwinkle, and he show is
tightly prateful per mit, persnicularly in the pipus and nipus, which
fallus him astore and ashearn, whether he slobber in Hurope, Irop, or
Syrop, or smearly passes Slidell hours with the bonely flute, the
boned benny. It's like bonny, he is, this ole Jishop, and like Jonny this
beminguished bold desplendent of the Vringian landed gentian. Ah,
the maze that were! In Trance, my old blend Abysm's gate. Ah, Gism!

It's prism, I mean, the Beller and Cellar.

But I'm tired and must lapse. I was going on to say that the
reader, this reader of the Cellar hated to see the narrator come back at
the end, preferring the clear and overwhelming picture of Charlie at
the end to remain timeless. That is, the return to the narrator *times* the
killings, after you had raised the whole action above place and time. I
may be wrong about this, and I certainly don't see how the story
could otherwise have been told effectively without a narrator. It is a
dilemma, and it means I suppose that to achieve certain values in the
story you had to sacrifice others. Without the narrator you couldn't
possibly have amassed the tremendous and necessary detail; you
couldn't have gone so deeply into Mrs. Ambler. You see then that my
remark wasn't criticism, for to be that my remark should have pointed
out some alternative kind of construction.

The parody is superb, and I am delighted with it. I am a little
puzzled that you feared I might be a little offended. That—that, my
dear John, comes nearer offense. . . . That fine old Southern Gem-
merman, Spark Young, has been here for a few days—left this
morning—and being tired I will send this off to you. Stark is a great
fellow. He wished me to remember him to you.   Yrs. ever, Allen

P.S. Having read the parody now three times, and discovered new
beauties each time, I must amplify my appreciation. It is really tre-

mendous! Caroline no less than I is charmed. I've never seen myself in such heroic lineaments. Both characters are astutely and accurately done.   TLS

[July 1931]

Dear Allen: Like yourself on the last two occasions I am tuckered out. The enclosed poem will tell the tale.[1] It is really much harder revising than composing anew, but there seemed to me enough good stuff in the old one not to lose it.

I can already see some changes as I read over what I had meant to be the final version, but they are mostly in the lining—that is in the division of lines—and in the manner of connecting one passage with another. I shan't put any more work on it now.

I'm glad you liked the parody. I didn't really think you'd be offended, but here alone I have to remember that everybody does not like the ribald as much as I. Also, I didn't want you to think that I considered what you had deluged More et Cie with was so much piss. I meant only—as you doubtless perceived—that that was all I thought they deserved.   Until the next time, John   TLS

1. "Portrait of Mrs. C," a revised version.

[July–August 1931]

Dear Allen: You must by all means include the sonnets in your book.[1] They are in themselves excellent and besides, for some I reason I could never discover, the critics are impressed by nothing so much as a sonnet sequence.

I have ventured to make a few notes, since I understood this was what you would like me to do. I wish you would seriously go over the punctuation, which to me seems excessive. I think one can trust the pause at the end of the line to take the place of an occasional comma and commas within the line should, unless the rhythm halts intentionally, be omitted when the sense permits. My own rule is derived partially from a regard for the Elizabethan practice (which conforms to elocutionary, rather than logical pauses) and partially from a study of Yeats' very meagre use of dots, curled and tailless. Generally speaking, I believe in punctuating poetry in conformity with the sound, pausing more or less, as the rhythm dictates and unless absolutely necessary for clarity leaving out all logical punctuation.

It is VII and VIII which seem to me to need a little going over. My impression is that you probably began to flag not in inspiration but sheer physical strength about this time. They are not so clear as their predecessors in the series, and by clarity I mean poetic, not logical clarity.

My emendations are only suggestions, made where I felt some change—not mine—should be made.

I have read I'll Take My Stand,[2] with whose program I was astonished to find myself in almost complete agreement. I had, from other data, come to much the same conclusion as the assembled twelve: that there is no economic, no social health where agriculture is allowed to succumb for sweet industry's sake. The example of France is pertinent.

One other thing. It might be possible in the South rather than elsewhere to get the intelligent young men into politics. And that is the only hope for the survival of the Republic in the Etats-Unis. The government, in large measure, should stand against money, not, as we have supposed these many years, back of it. Any speculation as to ways and means of bringing about an improvement must, for a long time, be academic. That is what the New Republicans will not see. And what Edmund will not see is the identity of [Henry] Ford and the Communists. (I am not so mad as to think the identity absolute, but *mutatis mutandis,* that is to say, Russia and America, I can see no great difference in the effect on the worker.)

It is the end of the day, and I am tired without having accomplished much. I am again, after a pause for a story, revising poems. And lethargy seems to hold my mind. I wish I could get these odd jobs over. I'm pretty clear now on my projected novel and want to start.   Tout a vous, JPB   TLS

1. "Sonnets of the Blood," with the exception of number V, were included in *Poems: 1928-1931.*   2. It is surprising that Bishop was not asked to contribute to this symposium; neither is his name mentioned as a possible contributor in Tate's letters to Davidson and Ransom, in which he assists in every stage of planning the project.

August 10, 1931

Dear John: I am delighted that you think the sonnets are good. That helps me think better of them; though lately I had begun to view them more favorably. They are so fluent (for me, at least) that I suspected them. I am convinced that a sonnet sequence entails some unavoidable commonplaces, a good deal of conventional phrasing; otherwise one's performance is likely to be too violent, and the most accurate kind of perceptions tend to look mannered. It's different with isolated sonnets—for example, Meredith's Lucifer. Your marginal notes are extremely helpful; I think before I am through I shall have adopted them all. And you are quite right, too, about excessive punctuation. I'm going over the poems and cutting out semi-colons and commas.

Portrait of Mrs. C I have always liked, and although my memory of the earlier version is dimmed by several years, I think you may have improved it. It is a beautiful poem, and I can find no criticism of the tone and atmosphere, upon which it chiefly depends for its effect. I have made some notes; but they are all concerned with minor points . . . . There is certainly one great improvement in arrangement where you postpone the exact place of the lady's birth from the very beginning to the third page. Didn't the poem begin "The house where I was born stood in Albemarle," etc. That made the beginning an announcement, instead of a reverie as it is now, and better so. On reflection, I think even your present way of putting it might be improved—made more casual, somewhat as follows:

Down where I was born in Albemarle
I have seen the soldiers there

Or perhaps you might leave it as it is, omitting *in;* that would accentuate the sudden turn of her thought to the soldiers. I may seem too fastidious, but that is a crucial passage, since it follows the highly difficult and highly successful bit of abstraction about pride, etc. You start a new theme, and you can't be too careful.

I am hard at it with Lee, and I hope to be through by the end of the month. Three of these books in four years have done me in: the old Confutterate wunderbusser is about petered out. (No pun intended.) The trouble is that I can never resign myself to the job, but keep going off into poetry. I am much pleased to hear that the novel is about to begin. I thought Warren's review of Many Thousands Gone very intelligent,[1] but I don't think he discussed the positive qualities of the book enough; he seemed chiefly concerned to point out that you are an intelligent writer and so couldn't make the usual mistakes.

I've had some flaming controversy with Edmund. I reviewed his book in the current Hound and Horn, and simultaneously he wrote a piece (N.R., July 29th) about our symposium entitled "Tennessee Agrarians,"[2] the tone of which was superior wisdom before our mere ancestor worship, which is after all, of course, all that we have to offer. I scored Edmund on two points: first, his irresponsibility (he evidently hadn't read the book) and secondly his lack of alertness—which is evident in his failure to review the book and in his falling back on all the prejudices he has ever heard about the South. In general, he accuses us of day-dreaming over the past, i.e., of non-realism; I answer that we are simply calling on the traditional Southern sense of politics, which was eminently realistic, while his

Planned Economy, seen through the whiskers of Professor [John] Dewey, is the most fantastic piece of wish-thinking I've ever seen. As you say, they have no sense of actual economic structure, which invariably rests on the land, but think of economic organization as a matter of boards, commissions, controls, etc., which are purely arbitrary, and unless backed by some powerful and interested motive, like practical communism, are merely a liberal's dream. Well, this diatribe of mine crossed Edmund's reply to *my* review in the mails. Really—and confidentially—I fear something is happening to a good man. He says that I don't understand him because I refuse to take at his own evaluation his belief in social justice, whether it represents economic realism or not, and his humanitarian belief in human perfectibility. He has gone over to that school without reservation. It seems to me that he has succumbed to all those degradations of values that are tearing society to pieces. For example, he says that art and science are the same thing—instruments of social adjustment toward ultimate human improvement, and that a thousand years from now men will be as great an improvement over us as we are over the stone age men. This is the doctrine of Mill and Taine which has done so much harm: when the fundamental distinction between art and science is lost, the pure motives of both are lost, and they are destroyed in the uses of a purely secular program, which seems to me pure barbarism. But Edmund, sensitive and fine as he is, has always been very innocent philosophically, and now I begin to think he is an irresponsible child turned loose on things he doesn't understand. In support of this, I refer you to his recent articles on the strikers;[3] Lord knows they need protection; but society as a whole, of which they are a part, doesn't need sob stories which stir up undirected action. He is now convinced that we must have high hopes for "humanity in general"—whatever that is—and when men have such hopes, I'm suspicious of them; I suspect that they have no specific task to perform, and spread their ambition over man in the lump—which is irresponsible. When all is said, I can't see that there is such a thing as humanity; there are millions of men who have a society in which they agree to the protection of individual values. There is no humanity; there are only individuals.

I didn't mean to go off on this, but there it is. Write me how things are going, and what is happening in Paris. Yrs ever, Allen

TLS

1. *New Republic* 67 (August 5, 1931), 321.   2. Tate's review of *Axel's Castle* appeared in *Hound and Horn* 4 (July-September, 1931), 619–24; Wilson's article on *I'll Take My Stand* is in *New Republic* 67 (July 29, 1931), 279–81.   3. "Frank Keeney's Coal Diggers," *New Republic* 67 (July 8, 1931 and July 15, 1931), 195–99; 229–31.

August 25, 1931

My dear Allen: Your letters are a constant delight to me, and more, a vast help. I can scarcely tell you how valuable your encouragement was in the beginning; it came at, for me, a most difficult time. It is still grateful. And your remarks on the Portrait of Mrs. C are exactly the sort of thing I wanted. Most of all I am grateful for the suggestion of changing South (in the abstract passage on pride) to Green Spring. I knew South was wrong, but stupidly could not think of the obvious remedy of making the substitute even more local than Albermarle.

The other changes I shall ponder. One or two of the words which to you have not a local enough sound were words of my mother's (rapscallion for instance) and I shall probably retain them. But in every case I recognize the justice of your criticism and its extreme nicety.

I am more and more depressed by Edmund's direction of heart. I cannot go into it now, nor do I want to until I shall have seen him, which I will do soon, since we are sailing, Margaret and I, in a week, landing at Baltimore on the very cheap line which goes there from Havre, on the ninth of September.

But I will say this: first that I flee humanitarianism as the very devil of all sound thinking *and* proper feeling. One has no right to try to think politically without being willing to think, when need be, ruthlessly. And as you say, the recent thinking of EW and the other NR writers is a mere twittering of excited swallows flying in and out of these tiresome old whiskers of that dull old man John Dewey.

It seems to me that in America we have never understood the use of compromise, which is the only word we have for what I should call tension. In a healthy society there are various tensions opposed. There is a continual effort necessary to maintain equilibrium which must be (this the Americans will not admit) an unstable equilibrium. They want it stable. They want everything finally settled. Whereas nothing should ever be settled.

Now the great service of the South was to provide a proper tension in two directions. First it gave a pull toward agriculture, the land as against the machine; secondly, one toward the past, traditional living as opposed to progress. And this was good. With the destruction of the South as a political force there was no strong political force to oppose industrial progress. It has gone on, unopposed, to the dire results we are at present witnessing and which EW is deploring. And yet, one knows that he would, in the beginning, have been all on the side of progress and the machine. Even now, he is unwilling to put the blame where it belongs.

Personally I feel there is no hope for us unless we are willing to go back, examining our mistakes and admit them. To go on the way of machinization and progress to their ultimate destination, some American form of communism, is simply to applaud and hasten death. For death it will be, make no mistake. The Russians may well survive, for they are the beginning of something non-European; we are the end of all that is European. With us Western civilization ends.

I wish, when you finish Lee, you would undertake a political and social history of the US. You have the knowledge and the philosophical training (which I have not); you also have, as I believe I have and believe EW has not, the historical imagination. I don't mean, of course, a factual history; but an account of the essential ideas and forces that have made our life, a concentration on the important decisions, a revaluation of the conventional historical values. American history has been, at its best, treated only from the libertarian point of view; it should be treated simply from the point of view of, shall we say? a poet and a gentleman.

Of course, I want like everything to see you in America. I shall be at my sister's in Charles Town, a week or so and mail will reach me there. The trip will have to be brief and conducted with the most scrupulous economy and whether I can venture as far as Tennessee is a question. Both time and money will make it difficult. We'll be there altogether about six weeks and are trying to do it on a thousand dollars for the two. You haven't by any chance some research to do in Washington?　As ever, John　　　　　　　　　　　　　　　　TLS

November 5, 1931

Dear John:　I'm rushing your poems back. I've made brief comments throughout, which of course are only hints here and there, in the poems I veto, for you to reconsider. What pleases (it surprises me also) is that I was prompted to make so few detailed criticisms. I am immensely impressed by the ms.[1] My expectations are borne out in full. Perhaps your poetry is better than your prose for this reason: you have a *feeling for rhythm by phrases,* but not sentences, and your whole interest is *emotion not action;* and your interest in the emotion is its immediately perceived value, not for the sake of a dramatic situation but *morally.* I'm inclined to think that the trouble with the hat scene between Dr. Burwell and Cecily is [that it is] not good because it is a misplaced poetic impulse: you can't resist putting the emotion where it belongs—right for poetry, but exaggeration in a story. I don't mean to underrate your prose, but it simply doesn't touch your poetry. The ms. is one of the two or three finest I've seen since I began our trade, and if you've no objection I hope to say so publicly when the book comes out.

We got home a little bewildered, not knowing just where we'd been or what we'd done.[2] The best single piece of news we heard at Charlottesville was from you—your plans about coming back to America. It will be hard to decide where to live, but I hope you will get within, at most, two days' drive from us—not farther off than Virginia. We should be the only society for you at first in this section, and yet the reasonable prices of the comfortable country houses hereabouts are to be considered. You can pick up a mansion for a song. Don't settle near New York—*near* is commuting distance. As to the "conference," I'm like Morse Phelps, who writes me that he never knew what it was about. But it prompted me to write a N.R. article called "Sectionalism and Regionalism" which you will doubtless see.[3] Let me know how France looks, and then return.   Yrs. ever, Allen

Evidently we were mistaken about the character of the fellow who crashed the gate, for Faulkner liked him so well that he went to visit him in North Carolina![4]

I've read Cummings' new book—very thin stuff indeed.[5]   AL

1. Tate is referring to Bishop's *Now With His Love* (New York: Charles Scribner's Sons, 1933).   2. Bishop and the Tates had attended the Southern Writer's Conference October 23-24 at Charlottesville, Virginia, along with some thirty other writers.   3. "Regionalism and Sectionalism," *New Republic* 69 (December 23, 1931), 158-61.   4. Following the Southern Writer's Conference, Faulkner motored to New York, sailed to Jacksonville, Florida, and returned to Chapel Hill in the company of Milton J. Abernethy, a senior from the University of North Carolina who had "crashed" a dinner party for the Conference participants.   5. W. (1931).

December 11, 1931   21 Square de Vergennes/Paris (15ᵉ)

Dear Allen: I am infinitely grateful to you for your comments and eliminations in my book of poems.[1] It was just what I wanted and has been far more helpful than any advice received from other quarters. MacLeish gave me adulation which was grateful, of course, but very little useful counsel.

The quandary is really a simple one—my taste and that of the rest of you had changed in ten years. And the attempt to include poems written that long ago, unless extremely well done, is dangerous. I'd like, for private reasons, to save some of them, which then didn't seem so bad. But I can see that it is unwise except for a very few. Your eliminations were, I thought, much sounder than Edmund's.

I may also say that I found your analysis of my literary qualities very just. I suppose it needs no saying that I'd rather excel in poetry than in anything else in the world. But it is a hard trade. You can't put yourself to work as you can in prose, and more than that little below the best counts at all.

Speaking of prose, I thought Caroline's novel the very purest prose.[2] It had that evenness of tone that James so earnestly sought after and the handling of time (to me so difficult even when there's not a hundred years to cover) superb. So many people have tried to write that novel—a century of American life as included in the chronicle of one family, but all that I know of have fallen down on the literary problem of time. Caroline's people not only age themselves, preserving their character meanwhile, but they also convey the impersonal changes of time. It is really wonderfully done.

I've been doing nothing but journalism since I got back and am horribly bored with it. I want to do a long-short story on Americans in France for the Scribner contest. Not, of course, that they can give me the prize again, but I would rather like being in the competition. Besides, it will be a not too ambitious attempt to paint the colors of the 1920's as in Many 1000's I did the 1860's. We'll see how it turns out.

I am also meditating some changes in the poems, particularly in Beyond Connecticut, Beyond the Sea which was never really finished; I'll send it to you.

I was greatly impressed by your poem on the wolves in Harriet's little monthly.[3]

Do write me, for the winter begins to look lonely and I have great need of spurring.   As ever, JPB   AL

1. *Now With His Love* (1933).   2. *Penhally* (1931).   3. "The Wolves," *Poetry* 39 (November, 1931), 68-69.

February 1, 1932

Dear Allen: I have just received your letter of the 14th of January[1] and hasten to send you a crop of poems, none of which have appeared in periodicals.

Of the long ones I'd prefer the Venus and Mars one to be used.[2] The short ones represent those which from your comments I believed would find your approval. The choice is yours to make. None have been published.

There is one which you have not seen, *The Truth About the Dew*. It is the only southern one of the lot, for it grew out of a conversation I had with [Malcolm] Cowley on the confused and divergent views held about the South even by its natives.

I also enclose for your perusal a revised poem of the sonnet on the Jew and a revision of the Bishop poem.[3] (I am sending "Beyond Connecticut, Beyond the Sea" elsewhere.) I wish you'd tell me if you think they are improved.

I have done little but hack work since I have been back but am trying now to settle down to a bit of fiction. I have one very good (if successful) story which I am about to set my hand to.

I read all sorts of good things about Caroline's novel. I am so glad that it has been received well and hope it sells no less well.

Our plans are still rather uncertain. It's a bad time to sell Tressancourt and I think we should do it if we are to come back. But the whole thing involves too many perplexing questions to go into it now.

I have missed your letters. Paris is more than ever lonely and intellectually sedative.   As ever, John

P.S. I think Max is all right. Scribners are vague still about publishing the volume.[4] The Portrait of Mrs. C. is being held by Ridgely Torrence for the N.R. though he was unable to assure me they could use it. I left it there on the chance.   TLS

1. This letter is missing, but apparently contained news of Tate's appointment to edit a Southern number of *Poetry* magazine and a request for unpublished poetry by Bishop for inclusion in that issue.   2. "And When the Net Was Unwound Venus Was Found Ravelled With Mars."   3. "This Is the Man," and "Beyond Connecticut, Beyond the Sea."   4. *Now With His Love,* originally scheduled for publication in the spring of 1932, did not appear until September, 1933.

February 11, 1932

Dear John: The poems have this moment arrived, and I've barely had the chance to glance at them. I know that you will be my chief support in the Southern number; in fact, you have saved the day.[1] With the exception of Saville Clark, a good poet who is practically unknown, the material I had already received was depressing. There will be about 30 pages of poetry; you and Clark will take up over half that space. I will let you know in a very few days just what I shall use. It occurs to me, since Scribner's are vague on the date of your book,[2] that The Hound & Horn might publish some of the poems. They have recently appointed me their Southern Contributing Editor, on an assumption which of course met with my hearty approval—that the South, like France or Germany, required some distinct representation. By maintaining a very judicious course in my recommendations, I can get them to publish just about anything that I recommend. This part of it, of course, is confidential.

I have begun two letters to you in the last month, but had to lay them aside. I've had the grippe off and on since Jan. 5th, and Caroline is now in bed with fever. I've done nothing, and a particularly bad attack of poverty at the same time has hardly improved affairs. I hope to resume correspondence when Spring comes, and the signs are that it will be here before the month is out.

Although I've finished the page proofs of my own book of poems,

I fear it may not be out for several months.[3] Perkins wrings one's heart with his recital of adversity, and one's heart, being so wrung, is not equal to the task of pushing him. Alas, Caroline's book[4] will do well if it makes back the advance—about eight hundred. She has just written a juvenile story in the hope of immediate cash. I've put aside Lee for a new project which will take less time to complete than to put the finished strokes on Lee.[5] I'm taking my own ancestry, beginning with Robert Reade in Va. about 1638, and bringing it down to my brother and myself, who are fairly good types of modern America, absolutely different but motivated by the same blood traits. The mechanical, or external form, will be that of the regular genealogy, much epitomized and foreshortened; there will be two chief figures to a generation, who will be dealt with simultaneously for contrast, and each generation will get a chapter, about eight in all. Although each chapter will introduce two new figures, each of them will continue what his father stood for, and I think the continuity will be preserved. The fundamental contrast will be between the Va. tidewater idea— stability, land, the establishment—and the pioneer, who frequently of course took on the Va. idea, even in Tenn., but who usually had some energy left over, which has made modern America. My brother and I show these two types fairly well. Most of the names will have to be fictitious, especially those near me in time, and I will have to make some imaginative leaps in the dark where there are only records of birth, death, and marriage to go on. But that, I think, is legitimate. I believe the idea is almost wholly new, outside pure fiction. Tell me what you think of its possibilities. It all depends of course on how I do it; yet there are some ideas that won't work out under any treatment; I hope this is not one of them. I expect to finish the book by early summer. It's all in my head, and I need only to begin writing.

I hope you go ahead with that story, but I hope even more that you are getting down to your next novel. I'd like to hear about it.   Yrs. ever, Allen   AL

1. Tate is editing a Southern number of *Poetry*. The issue included two poems by Bishop—"Hunger and Thirst," and "The Truth About the Dew"—and two by Tate— "The Anabasis," and "Brief Message"—as well as others by such contributors as Robert Penn Warren, Donald Davidson, Saville Clark, James Palmer Wade, Merrill Moore and John Gould Fletcher. Davidson also contributed an essay, "The Southern Poet and His Tradition," as did Robert Penn Warren, "A Note on Three Southern Poets."   2. *Now With His Love.*   3. *Poems: 1928–1931* appeared in March (New York: Charles Scribner's Sons, 1932).   4. *Penhally.*   5. Tate never completed the biography of Lee. The "new project" is the unfinished "Ancestors of Exile," much of the material for which ultimately found its way into *The Fathers* (1938).

February 11, 1932[1]

Dear John: I'm keeping the Mars & Venus poem, Colloquy in a Garden, Hunger & Thirst, and The Truth About the Dew—which will run to about six pages in *Poetry*. The Truth About the Dew is very fine and, of course, a perfect answer to Cowley. The others I already knew and admired, chiefly Hunger & Thirst. The Mars & Venus piece is, in itself, superb, but not so good as your other long blank-verse poems. Beyond Conn. is greatly improved, though I am unable to recall the details of your revisions. It is easily one of your best poems. I believe you revise your work better than any one else I know.

Since Beyond Conn. is not available, there remain with me three poems—the two untitled stanzas, This is the Man, Wish in the Daytime. I have decided to return these to you, and not send them to the Hound & Horn. Why don't you send them one of your long pieces?—if there's time before your book.   Yrs., Allen   AL

1. This is the second letter to Bishop on the same day—after Tate had looked over Bishop's offerings for the "Southern" number of *Poetry*.

February 24, 1932

Dear Allen: I must tell you that I have just received a check—munificent to the point of two dollars—from the New Republic for *Colloquy in a Garden*. I did not know they had it. E.W. showed [Ridgely] Torrence the mss of my poems and he wrote me that he was holding *Portrait of Mrs. C* with no word of any others. Since it has probably been sent to press that rules it out for Poetry. However, it is short and will not leave a large space by its omission.

I'd like very much to send some poems to the Hound and Horn—despite the fact that I have just had returned to me the one mss I sent them—but, if it's not asking too much, would prefer their going through your hands. I have also a story, fairly short and unsalable commercially, which I think they might use.[1] I want to change a paragraph or two at the end, after which I'll mail it to you.

As to the poems, there is—if the N.R. publishes what they have—only one long poem left—October Tragedy. If you think it worthwhile, I'll make a fair copy and forward it, with such short ones as remain unsold.

Your own two poems are very fine, particularly the Anabasis, which is noble and grave and pure. At first, I was inclined to think that the rhythm halted in one or two places. Now, I am not so sure. But I will put down my comments for what they are worth. Line 2—Dash instead of comma. l. 3—Substitute O for A or qualify "woman" with an adjective of direct address. l. 5—for, l. 8, "unstudiously" for "unstudiedly"; l. 12 ⊙ for , ; l. 13 avoid accent on "that" (it shall—. that shall, possibly) l. 19: is "The" right? l. 22, 23, 24 Obscure.

Your idea for a book on your ancestors seems to me very good.[2] Indeed, I thought of it once myself. The difficulty is to deal with those who are but names and dates. I shouldn't hesitate to invent, or indeed to incorporate incidents from the lives of their contemporaries. Each life must be at once particular and a symbol of the age. But you know that. Possibly, you might interspace the chapters with a brief and rather grandiloquent paragraph on the general characteristics of the time, placing your figures thus against the great background of the western world.

The winter has not been pleasant. We have had as almost everyone to face a great financial uncertainty. And Margaret has a domestic care since her sister and brother-in-law split with much venom and tears—after 11 years of married life. At the moment, however, I am able to feel my solar plexus in its proper place and not, as for some months, wandering all around my center. If we can manage it, we'll stay over this summer and come back permanently in the fall. I'd like to do a novel before returning, but intend to keep to shorter pieces until we are back in the country. My attempts at journalism have not been very successful—articles are old or useless when they get there. So, I am now doing stories. I have quite a few I'd like to get behind me before undertaking a long work.

It's too bad about Caroline's novel not selling more—though she beat me by some 1400.[3] Books are the first luxury the American dispenses with when he's cutting down, and I gather that nothing has sold well except possibly Faulkner and I am told W. Cather.[4]

Rereading your letter, I am struck with the necessity (in your projected book) of treating the feminine line as well as the masculine. That would add to your difficulties, but it ought to be done by someone—trace the gradual modification of women in America and the changes from generation to generation as they come from the 17th century to our own day.

I hope things go better with you, physically and financially. As the Queen of Spain remarked, it's a hell of a life we lead.   As ever, JPB
AL

1. Bishop is referring to "Toadstools Are Poison," which appeared in *North American Review* 233 (June, 1932), 504–510.   2. See Tate to Bishop, February 11, 1932, above, containing Tate's plan for "Ancestors of Exile."   3. *Penhally* outsold *Many Thousands Gone.*   4. Willa Cather's *Shadows on the Rock* (1931) was a bestseller.

March 23, 1932   Chateau de Tressancourt/Orgeval, S & O

Dear Allen: I seem to be in a most horribly sunk state intellectually—and alcoholically—and I can't pretend to do justice to your Poems.[1] But let me say, that all your changes are for the better. I have seen many of the poems and while I could not put my finger on every emendation, I am aware now of little but perfection in their finish. Then, too, as is always true with an authentic poet, they gain by collection. One poem adds emotional force to another. (I remember that while I picked out Eliot's poems from the Harriet Monroe anthology[2] in 1917, I had no conception of their richness and profundity until I procured a copy of the Knopf edition of the *Poems*.) I am particularly struck by the religious poems, *Alice* above all,[3] which I had seen before, but without I am afraid full appreciation of its subtlety and profound accuracy.

If I have any criticism it is this: That you should constantly labor to make things less difficult for the reader. Now, I am aware of all the arguments for obscurity. But in your case, I feel that you could retain all your present complexity of thought and emotion and *by adding something*, bring it all one point nearer that final intensity which is greatness. It's just the one more word, the one all clarifying phrase, that I miss in your poetry. I do not think one need be afraid of the most homely expression following a complicated elaboration. It is the "Pray undo this button" that caps the long anguish of Lear.[4]

I am, of course, delighted at the prospect of your being here this summer and will try to briefly answer your principal questions.[5]

First: bring the Ford by all means. You get a tryptich, I should guess through the American Automobile Association which allows you to bring it abroad without paying duty. The freight charges are not, I believe, high. And travelling by automobile is an economy if you make any distance.

England is probably cheaper than France now—outside of London. But living has gone down some here and I should guess that you could name your own price in the hotels of the Riviera this summer. If we can rent Tressancourt advantageously, we may go there ourselves for a while and possibly later to the neighborhood of Salzburg, which is delightful and very cheap. I've investigated prices and it is much less dear there than either France or England. It's what we'd like to do. Tressancourt is expensive to run and very uncomfortable without a goodly staff of servants, which we can ill enough afford. I'd sell in a minute, if to sell didn't mean a sacrifice now. On the whole, France is in much better shape than the rest of the western world and will undoubtedly recover.

The best passage for the money is 2nd class on the Bremen or the Europa, though with three in a cabin the Baltimore Mail Line runs a little less and is quite good though slow. You'd save railway fare by embarking at Norfolk. But you and possibly both of you might work a little graft with the German line's magazine. Anybody in New York can tell you about it. I got my passage free by doing three short pieces for them (dictated in one day). Don't use my name, as I promised not to give away the secret. But [Robert] Benchley was my sponsor. I can't at the moment remember the name either of the editor or the sheet. We came back for $175 (taxes included) with a large cabin and excellent service and meals. The passengers are awful, but the time is short.

I am sorry to hear that you have had physical ills to deal with. They always come when money is short. Well, the world clatters and there are times I'm glad I'm no younger. But I still haven't gone communist.   More anon, JPB　　　　　　　　　　　　　　　　AL

1. *Poems: 1928–1931.*　　2. *The New Poetry: An Anthology,* edited by Harriet Monroe and Alice Corbin Henderson, was an annual selection of the best new verse from *Poetry* magazine. The initial volume appeared in 1917, published in New York by the Macmillan Co.　　3. "The Last Days of Alice."　　4. Tate's correspondents, Davidson and Ransom among others, often comment that Tate's poetry seems unnecessarily complex.　　5. Tate left for France in June, 1932, with his wife, Caroline Gordon, who had been awarded a Guggenheim fellowship.

19 May 1932

Dear Allen: I feel I must write you once more before you embark, though I have not been in a communicative mood for some time.

Your note telling me that Miss Monroe had declined the erotic poem depressed me greatly, though I of course understood her fears.[1] I blame neither you nor her. But it was just one thing too many that had been returned—with praise. It leaves me bewildered.

If I thought I were that good, then I might make out an attitude. But I can't think that, nor can I think my work so bad. I am, as I say, bewildered and a bit flattened.

I thought your own poems much the best in the May issue of Poetry.[2] My own things practically always leave me uncomfortably cold when I see them in print, so I can't judge them. But I have seen nothing better of yours than the revised Anabasis. It is very beautiful. And I like the epigram addressed to Warren.[3]

I rather think we'll be here this summer. We are asking a high rent for the place; if we get it, we'll go elsewhere. But it will hardly pay us to move unless there is a fair recompense.

I look forward to seeing you very much. You are not only a pleasure but a moral stay. And I need one.   My bes' to Caroline, John
　　　　　　　　　　　　　　　　　　　　　　　　　　　TLS

1. "And When the Net was Unwound Venus Was Found Ravelled With Mars."　　2. Tate's contributions were "The Anabasis" and "Brief Message."　　3. "Brief Message."

June 19, 1932

Dear Allen: I had somehow thought of your arriving earlier than you actually are; hence the farewell tone of my last letter.

First, as to our locality. We are in all probability remaining here for the summer. I'd really much rather be here, as our winter in Paris taught me how difficult it is in small quarters with three children. And a slight windfall removes some of the financial worry. Lorna Lindslay has asked us to Antibes for a brief visit, which we will undertake if we decide we can afford it, but in any case we will go childlessly and not stay long.

The weather is as perfect as occasionally it is in the Ile-de France. And we all go around half naked, the children entirely so.

I have at last done the essay for Barr.[1] I wish I could show it to you. It needs your revision. I have also turned out quite a lot of poems, which I rather think I'll put in the book, extracting the more romantic verses of twelve years ago.

By the way do you know the poem Cino da Pistoia wrote on the death of his mistress. I have discovered it anew, first as a most beautiful thing, quite up to Cavalcanti's famous farewell, and also as the source of much of Eliot's Doris's Dream Songs.[2] In fact, I begin to see that the later development of TS has the Italian lyric poets (including Dante in his Canzoni) as masters.

I sent off a bunch of poems to the Hound and Horn, but have not heard from them. I wrote what I now think was an unfortunate letter to his publisher (whom I know) on [Lincoln] Kirstein's book.[3] I really should have been more dainty. I thought it frightfully confused, though not for the same reasons as Granville Hicks. By the way, why doesn't somebody catch him and castrate him. He's the worst in a bad lot of New Republic writers. The American Marxists give me a deeper and more excruciating pain in my conservative (but not Greek) bottom every day I live, or at least any day I catch a glimpse of them. Nocturnally and hence sleepily yours, John   TLS

1. Stringfellow Barr edited the *Virginia Quarterly Review* at this time. Bishop's article "The South and Tradition" appeared in the *Virginia Quarterly Review* 9 (April, 1933), 161–74.   2. Cino da Pistoia (1230–1337) was a contemporary of Dante. The poem Bishop refers to is a sonnet, "Io fui 'n su l'alto e 'n sul beato monte" ("I was on the high and blessed mountain"). Guido Cavalcanti (c. 1230–1300) was also a contemporary and friend of Dante's. His "famous farewell" is a poem of parting to his beloved, "Perch'i' no spero de tornar giammi" (Since I do not hope to return ever"). Bishop is referring to Eliot's "Sweeney Agonistes," an unfinished work.   3. *Flesh Is Heir: An Historical Romance* (1932).

Villa Les Hortensias/Chemin du Fort

September 20, 1932   Capbrun/Toulon (Var)

Dear John: Here we are, but alas in moving I lost that copy of The Return[1] which I meant to send back to you, and also a letter I'd written to accompany it. We lapsed, or rather relapsed into the most incredible boredom after you and Margaret went north, and I almost regretted we had gone to Monte Carlo, it seemed so abysmal when we got back. So I broke the habit of a lifetime and began a story, the first I've ever attempted;[2] it is now about two-thirds done and shortly you will receive the completed, but perhaps not finished copy. I am determined to bring it to an end, though it is so involved that it will require heroism.

Before I lost The Return I had another crazy inspiration about it. Isn't the last line this:

The sea unfurled: and what was blue raced silver.

We thought that *what* was the wrong word. I am now convinced that it is perfectly right. The trouble is the word order. How does this sound:

Unfurled the sea, and what was blue raced silver.

That seems to me to fix it up.

I've never yet answered MacLeish's letter.[3] I suppose the reason why it is a little cantankerous is explained by your news, that he hasn't done any work for a year. I've been nearly insane recently, and the story seems merely pretense at work.

You and Margaret must come down to see us this fall, before the shadows get too thick around Paris. I have just this moment had a notion—let's send a joint manifesto to the Southern Writers Conference. We could say something about the South, a great deal about the literary Communists, and in general turn the Conference into a warm affair. How about it? Caroline sends love to Margaret.   Yrs. Allen

TLS

1. Bishop had sent Tate a copy of "The Return." inviting comment and criticism.   2. "The Immortal Woman" appeared in *Hound and Horn* 6 (July-September, 1933), 592–609.   3. Macleish had written Tate privately in response to Tate's article, "Hart Crane and the American Mind," *Poetry* 40 (July, 1932), 210–16.

I am sending story under separate cover.

October 2, 1932

Dear Allen: I think the story has decided possibilities. I started making notes in the margin, but after more thought, would rather you disregarded them. As I see it, your story takes place on three planes: the narrator's mind (his reminiscence and comment) his eyes (what he sees of the old lady) his ear (what he overhears Mrs. Dulany saying). The story is not long and the action is essentially single. There is, therefore, a good deal to be said for putting it all in one scene. That is, begin say with description of the old lady in the street (street or lady first as you choose), present her as *seen:* then as remembered, giving along with the recollection as much of the narrator's character and surroundings as necessary to immediately understand, then place Mrs. Dulany: then back to sight of old lady, etc. In that case begin with the street before she appears. (I think this is right.) Or you could make the story in two *present* scenes. (1) The first appearance of the old lady for that year; (2) The last appearance of the old lady forever. This recommends itself to me as the better of the two; but I think the whole action of the story as it unfolds, or rather the action of unfolding, must be definitely dated. I think you can do this in such a way as not to destroy the impression so admirably created of days all alike. It would make for vividness.

Also, I think you must do something to assist the reader in unravelling the complicated family relationships of the people in the big house. I shouldn't be afraid of repeating names and relationships whenever they are reintroduced. And somehow the identity of the three people, or four rather, actually seen must be accented in Mrs. D's narrative. The tone of her narrative is absolutely right. But the relationships the reader is interested in are those the "I" of the story has seen. They must be so accented in Mrs. D's account that we relate them *at once*.

In short, all that I have suggested about recasting the order of events is unimportant. The story can stand as it is now. But the relationships which the narrator sees (I mean with his eyes) must be made clearer, at least more readily comprehendible. I have now read the story three times, and it is only on last reading that I have been able even to guess who these people are. That, I think, is putting too great a strain on the reader.

I have just been reading *The Insulted and Injured,* and there you have something of the same thing, that is a relationship which is not to be fully explained until the end of the novel. But Dostoevsky admirably reinforces the reader's suspicions at every crucial point so that he is always in a position to *guess* truly what these relationships are. Julian Green's *Christine* is another good example of a story where the truth is never stated. Nevertheless, he makes it quite easy enough to divine as we go along and what we do not definitely know is exceedingly provocative.

I think you ought by all means go on writing stories. But I also think, knowing what I do of your mind, that you ought very thoroughly to plot them, so that the action alone carries the burden. Everything else would, I am sure, come by the way. But a good story is one whose deepest truths lie in the events, not in the words.

Your style is perfect, for what you are doing. Though in the early parts you once or twice allow your narrator to use sentences which would not stand parsing. I think this is wrong. First you want a contrast with Mrs. Dulany's rambling style; secondly you have allowed his perceptions, which do not accord with looseness of structure in the shape of his thought.   As ever, John

Eliot returned The Return,[1] but MacLeish writes me that the H[ound] & H[orn] want it. I also sent them Perspectives are Precipices. I have had a fine long letter from Bunny from Provincetown. He likes my new poems and makes some very sound criticisms, notably of the metaphysical spiders in Easter Morning.[2] He also thinks The Return falls into MacLeishishness in the middle stanzas: what about it? AL

1. T. S. Eliot was associated at this time with *The Dial,* to which Bishop had apparently submitted "The Return."   2. Bishop is referring to ll. 15–17 of his poem "Easter Morning": "Truth is a sepulchre, dust is not justice, / Nor will the metaphysical toil of spiders / Conserve the shroud that hides decaying bones."

October 6, 1932

Dear John: Your splendid letter and the two volumes of the Endless Adventure[1] came this morning—the best day's mail I have had since we came here. I am immensely pleased with the books, and will read them immediately.

Your analysis of my so-called story is penetrating and exhaustive. You have had enough of it; so I will not talk about it at any length. I am not sure yet whether I will try to rewrite it or will go on to something else. If I do it over, I will adopt your radical suggestion about making the whole action in two present scenes—the first appearance of the old lady for that year, coinciding with her last appearance forever. Mrs. Dulany's monologue worried me vastly, mostly in point of credibility. Now I see that I did not think enough about its being comprehensible: I thought that the reader wouldn't take it all in, but would let it sink into the general atmosphere of time and change—except at the end, where I wished to emphasize the old lady's connection with the crazy woman, Jane. But, since you felt that you *had* to get the connections all through straight in your mind, they must be made clearer: for if the reader demands that, he must have it, or else the writer must keep him from demanding it, which I didn't do. I am ever your servant for the vast amount of time you put on my virgin effort. I may, however, ask you to take me apart again, if I do another story.

I enclose a little N.R. article,[2] which you need not return. It is along the line of some of your recent talk. I wish you'd write one backing me up. By the way, I have proposed to MacLeish that he and I write essays, for simultaneous appearance, perhaps in the Hound and Horn, on the meaning of craftsmanship and its relation to the contemporary scene. I mean in poetry. Why don't you write one too? We could get Bandler to publish all three together.[3] That is the thing Bandler and I have been trying to work up—joint discussions of all kinds of problems.

I am delighted that Kirstein took The Return.[4] I think Eliot is pretty hopeless about contemporary poetry, at least so far as my part in it is concerned; he took five poems of mine in 1929, but not one of them ever appeared. They're now in my book. I don't think Edmund's criticism of The Return is quite just. There is no MacLeish in it. There are armies and sacking of cities, but MacL. has no monopoly on that. Don't worry about that. The rhythm, the feeling, and the intention are all your own.

I hope to come up to Paris before Christmas. Meanwhile you and Margaret keep on thinking about coming down here whenever you can. Love to Margaret from us both,   Yrs ever, Allen   TLS

1. *The Endless Adventure,* by Frederick Scott Oliver (1864–1934) was a three-volume work published between 1930 and 1935 dealing with British politics during the era of Walpole, 1714–1745.   2. "There Ought To Be a law," *New Republic* 70 (May 4, 1932), 326–27. In this essay on the relationship between art and society, Tate responded to a speech by William I. Sirovich, congressman from New York, entitled "Motion Pictures, Theatres, and Dramatic Critics."   3. The proposed symposium was never published.   4. Lincoln Kirstein accepted Bishop's poem for publication but the poem never appeared in *Hound and Horn.*

[Early October, 1932][1]

Dear Allen: I am glad to have you reassure me as to "The Return." Bunny, incidentally, thinks *Conquistadors*[2] "lousy." I suppose the praise of war is too much for him. I do think myself that "lewd" I'd not have used without Archie's having done so, but it has the connotation I wished my "narrator" to give this activity of the years before the end.

I should be glad to engage in your poetic controversy. In fact, if I go on with this idea of a book on Picasso, Stravinsky, Eliot, etc., I'll want to take up the question of what truth poetry (and other high art) is qualified to illuminate. And the essay you propose might serve as a first draft. I'd call it something like Poetry and Time, and deal first with what Time is to the poet (as opposed to the scientist, this being an idea common to both), go on to the temporal and the eternal (or subsisting) values in poetry, and (probably) finally deal with that now thoroughly ridiculed notion of the poet as prophet, i.e., as one outside the time-scheme of the journalist, the recorder of daily happenings. I fancy with some such scheme as this I could cover the notion of "poetic truth" with some completeness.[3]

I liked your essay,[4] particularly when it most approximated your talks to me. Bunny seems to me more and more confused. Did you see his article on Lytton Strachey?[5] It shot so wide of the mark. In fact, it didn't even aim at it.

I have been wanting to tell you that you ought to go ahead with your Lee.[6] To modify your judgement, to extenuate his conduct, is, once you have seen the truth, to betray your function as a writer. You must not let any considerations of family feeling or local pride allow you to deviate from what in your mind you have determined to do. Besides, to elucidate Lee as you propose, will illumine a general moral issue and that is what a character study should do, particularly if as happens with Lee, the facts of the life are largely familiar.   As ever,
John   AL

1. This is the "half-finished answer" referred to in the next letter.   2. *Conquistador,* by Archibald MacLeish, was published by Houghton, Mifflin in 1932.   3. This proposed essay was never done.   4. "There Ought To Be a Law."   5. This piece is either "Lytton Strachey," *New Republic* 72 (September 21, 1932), 146–48, or "An American Critic on Lytton Strachey," *New Statesman and Nation* 4 (September 24, 1931), 344–45, both by Edmund Wilson.   6. Tate had abandoned his biography of Lee early in 1932 to begin work on *Ancestors of Exile,* an unfinished work that provided material for *The Fathers* (1938).

[Near Oct. 19, 1932]

Dear Allen: In spite of Toulon and Antibes, in spite of stripping to the sun and lying half the summer naked to Phoebus' amorous pinches (Shakespearean influence) I am tucked in bed, running at the nose, but otherwise painfully immobile. It's disgusting. And, as far as that goes, so am I.

Downstairs is a half-finished answer to your letter,[1] written in ink on my best green paper. So I will not attempt to say much in response to your epistle, or comment on your paper on poetry. Speaking of Poetry (advt.),[2] I spent the morning reading aloud Antony and Cleopatra and have rasped my already sore throat. To think that I once turned down an offer (doubtless insincere) from Mrs. Pat Campbell[3] to play Antony to her Cleopatra! At the time I thought only of how my arms would look in Roman armor. Now I think I made a great mistake. No one who heard me recite would remember my arms, and besides I could have relied on drapery. And my legs were good in those days. However, it is certainly a great piece of writing— all those unemphatic monosyllables at the ends of lines and the monstrous shifting from one part of speech to another—"boy my greatness," etc. Under the influence, I am sending you a poor effort, partially my own.[4] You are probably the only person who will understand it, though I don't expect you to particularly approve of it, as I don't rate it among my best. But it's pleasant to write a poem at all, having been in a drought of Arabia Deserta since returning.

Let me speak once more of your story. You really ought to finish it if only for the sake of discipline and technique. And Mrs. Dulany's monologue contains a nice technical problem. You succeeded as far as credibility is concerned. The tone is exactly right. But the problem becomes how, without changing that unaccented gabble to paint the characters and situations that have weight in your (as opposed to her) story. The reader need not understand all the relationships: nor would he try to, granted her gabble, if you at once allowed him to see what was pertinent and when it was done to grasp the identity of *all* the characters in the main narrative. You get the crazy woman. Somehow I think you should get that earlier—for surprise is not permissible there. But as the Mrs. D monologue unfolds, the reader should get (in the midst of the cousins and the sisters and the aunts) more and more salient points about her. All in fact that counts is *her* story. I would do this by interrupting Mrs. D's monologue at the right moments (1) by gestures on the part of the crazy woman actually seen through the window; (2) by interior comment from the narrator. I don't think building up her story will weaken the meaning of the house (which is, I take it, what you were most interested in conveying) but on the contrary reinforce it. My own conviction, which I have a hard time putting into practice, is that the story should be capable of being read by a person indifferent to symbolism and still interesting him as a straight narrative. And even the intelligent reader should be more taken by the meaning, as conveyed through symbols, after he has read it, than while he is reading. I am having a devil of a time working that out in my novel,[5] where, as a matter of fact, I still have not found my symbols. And I know that my narrative must depend upon them for its unity as well as for its meaning. But then, as I say, I have had a period of secheresse [drought] since coming back.

I have been looking into Ramon Fernandez' book on Gide.[6] It's excellent, not only on the announced subject, but in its discussion of various literary and moral problems. I particularly was interested in his description of the state of mind of the young French intellectuals at the time the war broke. I have (in bed) composed a little poem:

> Ode to Andre Gide
> M. Andre Gide
> Is queer indeed:
> A bugger
> That's not bugger-mugger.

As you perceive, my rheums and vapors affect my head. I am glad you are coming to Paris before Christmas. We'll probably be in town by then.   As ever, JPB   AL

---

1. See letter above.   2. This phrase is the title of one of Bishop's poems.   3. Beatrice Stella Campbell (1865–1940) was a British actress who made several American tours.   4. "The Ancestors."   5. Bishop is mapping out his novel, *Act of Darkness* (New York: Charles Scribner's Sons, 1934), the writing of which will occupy him for the next year and a half.   6. *Andre Gide* was published in Paris in 1931.

October 19, 1932

Dear John: Couldn't you preserve your cold a little longer and write some more poems as good as The Ancestors? Or rather poems like it. You are very much mistaken if you suppose it is not one of your very best. It isn't quite up to The Return, but then few poems are; however, you will write for many years without surpassing the two middle stanzas of the new poem. The last stanza, I think, falls away a little in the final line. I feel that the reflection there should continue the general train of images. "Great-grandfather" is a little frivolous just because it is so particular. Here is what I mean—but I don't suggest it as a revision, I merely offer it as an example of the kind of imagery that seems to me to be necessary at the end:

> What calm to send the mind on the stone ease
> Of time, the early settlement of the tomb!

As your lines stand, the "stone ease" and "marble tomb" are tautology. "On nights like these / Whose spacious wars living and dead exhume" is quite magnificent, and perfect.

You are right about the problem of Lee. I have worried about it in precisely the terms you speak of it in. I have a few gray hairs behind my ears which even now begin to show in the prevailing blondness. I am not really concerned about the effect of the book on our sensitive compatriots, except that I should vaguely hope that it might do them good. The whole Southern incapacity for action since 1895 is rationalized in the popular conception of Lee. It is time this was broken down. I have been greatly impressed by Oliver's treatment of Walpole,[1] whose love of power was at every moment controlled by a profound conception of his role as a patriotic statesman. Lee did not love power; my thesis about him, stated in these terms, is that he didn't love it because he was profoundly cynical of all action for the public good. He could not see beyond the needs of his own salvation, and he was not generous enough to risk soiling his military cloak for the doubtful salvation of others. I personally feel very much this way; but then I am not at the head of a large army and I have no political position. You know Lee pretended all along that he had no connection with politics—a fiction that won him applause because it seemed to mean that he was above intrigue; but no man should be above the right kind of intrigue. This is what I feel about Lee. Yet is it true? That is what keeps me awake at night. I can't "prove" a word of it. Of course, the facts do not in the least prove the current notion of him: they don't prove one thing or another. But the facts have got into an emotional association with a certain conception of his character which will be very difficult to break down. That brings up a formal problem.

To be most effective my treatment should be direct and cumulative, not argumentative; yet I am obliged to show that the popular notion is not inevitably true. I can't just assume that it is false. But I could go on forever. And I always ask: Is it true? On what ground do I think so? I can't answer that, and it worries me.

By the way, Miss [Ellen] Glasgow asks me to give you her best regards. And that reminds me to urge you to read her new book, "The Sheltered Life," which is not only her best but very nearly anybody's best. She had told me she was sending me a copy, and I felt very nervous; I had not admired her work at all. But the nice old lady, nearly sixty, has pulled herself up and written a good novel. She has some horrid vices of style—"the spring was singing in her blood" sort of thing, but even that is reduced to a minimum. I suppose her deafness explains her poor feeling for rhythm.

As soon as I hear from MacLeish I will take up the question of the joint discussion with The Hound and Horn.[2] On second thought, I will take it up with Bandler right away. We can go ahead without MacLeish; but all the better if he comes in.

I don't think *Conquistador* is lousy, but it is not as good as most of the critics thought. I wrote about it at length in the N.R. so I won't go into the question here.[3] However, there is a great deal of steam up in it over very little emotion.

I enclose some verses, committed to your critical eye unrevised.[4]
Yrs. Allen   TLS

1. *The Endless Adventure* (1930–1935), by Frederick Scott Oliver.   2. See above, Tate to Bishop, October 6, 1932.   3. "MacLeish's Conquistador," *New Republic* 71 (June 1, 1932), 77–78.   4. Not found, but apparently limericks.

[19–26 October, 1932]

Dear Allen: A thought occurs to me which I must set down at once. Proceed with your Lee! If it is not true to the facts of Lee's life, it will be true to you. And that is more important. You are, alas, a poet. Remember, a work you may despise, Renan's Life of Jesus. Now it appears that it is not a life of Jesus but of Renan. Strangely, that does not detract from its value. Many people can write us lives of Jesus. Even Bruce Barton. But only Renan could write the life of Jesus as Renan. So, if you write the life of the Southerner (yourself, myself, all of us) in terms of Lee, so much more it will be than a life of Lee. I feel this now as a moral problem, and I urge you forward. The technical terms we can discuss later—if I can in the least assist you there! But the popular conception exists. You need not I feel mention it, so present is it. But give us your Lee! Let him be Allen Tate in a white beard (as well as with white hair creeping in prematurely behind the ears) but let him *be*. Allons! Lose no more sleep! Remember Yeats and the stricture made as to the historical truth of his memoirs. Allons!

I had not meant to touch on myself in this letter, but I must thank you for your comments on *The Ancestors*. You are a grand person, Allen, and but for you I should probably have committed suicide some three years ago. If not in the flesh, still in the spirit. I only hope I can keep to the level you are generous enough to accord me. *The Ancestors* (which I should not have sent you in a "fluid" state) began as one poem and wrote itself as another. I was thinking of Unamuno's statement that man is an animal that guards its dead and wrote (in two minutes) the first and last stanza contrasting the living in this leaky house and the dead in their marble tomb.[1] Then the two middle stanzas added themselves as I started to copy the others on the typewriter, and being better they forced a revision of the first sketches. The final lines (which I knew wrong) are still in the transitional stage from version No. 1 to version No. 2. Originally I had the living preparing to go to "repair" the tombs damaged by the storms. This is not right. But I'll arrive at something as soon as I can see what I have actually written. This is to take too long on a poem which only your praise gives value. But it illustrates what nearly always happens when I write verse at all successfully. I must *see* what I have written before I can prepare a final version and between the first draft and the last there is always great labor.

Please don't misunderstand my quoting Wilson on *Conquistadors*. I do not think it "lousy." On the contrary, I think as I told Archie that it keeps a higher poetic level than any narrative poem of its length done by an American in our time. (The W[aste] L[and] is of course not a narrative.) For some reason Bunny despises Archie and the other way round.

Your own enclosures are fine. I particularly relished the comparison with the canvas back duck. Do you know D[orothy] Parker's poem on the Sitwells:

Mr. Osbert Sitwell
It seems doesn't shit well
And his brother Sackerville
Thinks that he never will.

Which is worth all her published volumes. I have been reading 18th century verse. How Pope stands out! The only one with speed. Ode to Evening is good and so's a lot of Swift (in a very different way) but the real trouble with practically the whole century is the slowness. Go from the poets of the 17th or Webster and above all else it's the speed that takes one. By the way, what I was afraid of in The Ancestors was that the stanzas you liked were too-too John and William. Wind by Mr. Webster, poem by Mr. Shakespeare. Paper's out, but not desire to scratch on.   As ever, JPB   AL

1. Miguel de Unamuno (1864–1936) was a Spanish philosopher and author.

October 26, 1932

Dear John: I have done about four lines on my book this morning—enough for plausible virtue—and I take my typewriter in hand to suggest that we should either form a suicide club or a club against suicide. We could be charter members; a letter from MacLeish yesterday convinces me that we might pledge him by mail, and initiate him at the first opportunity. His letter urged me to undertake the Defense of Poesy; it wasn't in those terms precisely, but rather a plea that I should try to make up a vocabulary which would enable us to judge the poem by and for itself. He is led to this by the facts that we discussed here—the revolutionary and heretical attacks on poetry. We stand with our backs to the wall. Of course, the truth will prevail in the long run, but we don't live in the long run; we live now. On the whole I think the club should be soldalicium contra mortem voluntariam. It is a nice question whether, if we committed suicide, it would be voluntary; I think not; so we must live. This is logical enough—but living isn't the whole question. I have got to the place you seemed to occupy a few years ago. Perhaps it is the crisis of the early thirties. You probably know something about that. It is very difficult for me to convince myself that what I am doing holds together; if it does I can afford to starve occasionally to get it done. These are complex questions. For some reason I never doubt that I know what the truth is; I doubt my capacity to state it. We all of us get into these hollows of the spirit; I think I was due for one and the upheaval of this trip to France landed me in it.

I think our first official considerations should be concerned with nothing less than some sort of organized attack on the enemy. If you will write that essay you spoke of, I will write one, and send them off together.

I hope you will favor me with the final draft of The Ancestors. I enclose some rugged verses that I wrote off at breakfast.[1] It is very difficult to write good doggerel; this is only fair. Among our numerous projects for the vindication of the truth, the book of limericks must not be lost. Those I sent you were a little too moral and serious—which came of setting the theme in advance. A limerick should be complete in itself, a careless rapture. I will enclose a new one if I can round it off.

I hope you are writing more poems. I seem to do nothing but get into tempers, and write a little on my book,[2] and get into another temper. But this will pass. We at least have the sun here all day long, every day. I wish you and Margaret would drive down; choose your own time. Caroline suggested this splendid notion this morning.   Yrs ever, Allen

P.S. Have you a copy of the Joycean parody celebrating my prowess against the Humanists?[3] The *ladies* here wish to see it.   TLS

1. Unidentified limericks.   2. Tate is working on "Ancestors of Exile."   3. This parody has not survived.

[October 26–31, 1932]

Dear Allen,   I am sending you a revised version of *The Ancestors*. (You brought this on yourself. Beware of future flattery!)

I changed the first stanza because of the *floor-door* rhyme, the poem being too short (I think) to support the reoccurrence of this rhyme in *poor-store*. I didn't consider the second line quite right. But "glut" with "rain" is I think a *trouvaille* [lucky find].

I keep "stone ease" for the sake of the antithesis (or what you as a rhetorician will) of soft and hard stone—sculptured vs. ease-ruining. I tried to work out something on a contrast between "mind" and "[illegible] in its sculptured tomb." But it doesn't seem too hot.

I'm still in a state of sterility. But look for some kind of fecundation from the gods soon.

I looked up New Republics at the library yesterday (with great depression resulting) but failed to find you on *Conquistadors*. What's the date?[1]

Today was Jonathan's 5th birthday and we had quite a nursery celebration, sending all three to bed with cheeks alive with champagne. I'm trying to wean them from gin early.   As ever, JPB   AL

1. See above, Tate to Bishop, October 19, 1932.

October 31, 1932

Dear John: I never flatter anybody but women, so you must be aware that what I say about your poetry is the truth. I am glad that you have sent me the new version of The Ancestors. I suggest that you restore two words from the first draft. Restore *planks* in the second line, for *floors*. In line four, restore *to*, thus: "We sit to shudder in the rising wind." I'm not sure about the parenthetical "(O house!)."

Nor about the adjective "ghastly." That word seems to me to compromise your restraint; ghastliness is one of the effects of the poem; and the word gives it away. The last line is just right; but think of the possible effect of *bodies* in place of *corpses*. The imagery in the three or four preceding lines makes them the living dead; and *bodies* might well keep up that fine ambiguity better than *corpses*. Altogether this is one of your very best poems.

I enclose one which is not one of my best, but it has a few nice phrases.[1] I've tried to keep it direct and classical, suppressing the dramatic irony that usually I try to put in. I go to town this afternoon to buy a copy of Vergil in order to locate the exact quotation that prompted the poem.

By the way, since you don't mention it, I assume that you haven't heard of the death of Edmund's wife.[2] Ford got a letter day before yesterday from Edmund—about the Pound pamphlet[3]—in which he casually mentioned it. I don't know when she died, nor where Edmund is; so we just sent a cable to the NR.

By the way, if you have time right now, you might do that brief eulogy of Pound. Ford wants to get them all off to Farrar and Rinehart in the next ten days. About five to six hundred words.   Yours in haste, Allen   TLS

1. "Picnic at Cassis," later entitled "The Mediterranean."   2. Edmund Wilson's first wife, Margaret Canby Wilson, died in October, 1932.   3. Ford Madox Ford was attempting to compile a pamphlet of tributes to Ezra Pound from various contemporary writers. The project was never completed.

November 2, 1932

Dear Allen: I am writing at the end of the day and without a very clear idea of what I mean to say. In other words, I should prefer to be sitting with you somewhere over a glass.

I liked MacLeish's poem in the N R[1] and can't help but think he has said most that we need to say. Which, of course, doesn't prevent our repeating it in prose. I have an idea which may be worth nothing, particularly from the standpoint of strategy. But after putting through the essays, we might get up a manifesto.[2] I think it would need the three of us. And my idea would be to erect a standard to which others, particularly the young, might repair. If the idea appeals to you, I suggest that we proceed as follows. Make out a list of subjects on which we think it desirable to state our position, war, religion, Marx, etc., let each meditate these, adding any articles of faith he feels sure enough to put down for himself, each expression to be as brief as possible, a sentence if possible, otherwise a series of sentences, or at most a short paragraph. All this to be done independently. Then, if there was enough community in the various points of view, we could combine them into a single manifesto.

Of course Archie believes that a poet should not have political opinions, and it may be that as a poet he is right. I myself have always been very suspicious of manifestoes.

I have a fairly long poem underway.[3] It was in a way suggested by Crane's *Cape Hatteras,* which is one of the most intellectually deficient of his poems. It was to supply the proper ideas for an aeroplane flight that I undertook to write it. I include also an admonition to an astronomer and conclude with a statement of their mutual incapacity to make a moral judgement on man. The whole concept may be bogus. The description of the flight is pretty good, but I think the astronomical section needs a better basis, which I am now attempting to supply. Perhaps what I really wanted to do was to write a rhetorical poem with a good deal of ornamentation. I have been afraid that I was perhaps getting my style too bare, too gray, and wanted to see if I could still turn out a purple patch. I'll send it to you when done.

You mustn't think of committing suicide. The brother of a very good friend of mine walked into an armorer's shop day before yesterday, bought a revolver and put a bullet in his head. I can't tonight do more than say *Don't.*

I like the idea of your Epitaph,[4] but think it shows signs of haste. I'll presently send you some limericks. The great thing is to present a combination of fantasticality and logical development. It's best to start not with an idea but a difficult and ingenious rhyme to a person's name or place name. This should suggest the situation which develops through the small interior couplet and comes to a climax in the last line. The best limericks are little anecdotes and should be treated as such. The young lady from Niger is rightly famous. Of course the whole should be very neat, use no little alliteration and be perfect as to accents. I have written a lot, but don't get one good one out of five.

Please thank Caroline for her suggestion that we come down. I wish we could. If I get any money I'll come alone later, but it's out of the question now. I'll look up the Joyce parody.   As ever, JPB

P.S. I have left much out of this letter I meant to say. I'll try again. But I don't want to tackle The Defense until I get a little further on my novel, which goes better.	AL

1. "Invocation to the Social Muse," *New Republic* 72 (October 26, 1932), 296.   2. Tate, Bishop, and MacLeish were contemplating a program of essays on poetic craftsmanship and the function of poetry to be published in *Hound and Horn.* See above, Tate to Bishop, October 6, 1932.   3. "O Let Not Virtue Seek," which first appeared in *Virginia Quarterly Review* 11 (April, 1935), 260-263.   4. A limerick, which apparently has not survived.

[Autumn, 1932]

Dear Allen: You're wrong. *Picnic at Cassis* (Title?) is not one of your best poems. It is *the* best. Margaret, to whom I've read it aloud several times agrees with me. It is—I hesitate, but it is—a great poem. Never, I think, has the feeling of the Mediterranean from one of Northern blood (which you are) been so well expressed. Maybe The Mediterranean or something vague like that would be better [as a title].
[*marginal notes*] I feel I should wreathe this card in laurel. *Se mai contiga.* Is "power" a dissyllable? I mean in speech?
    There are three things in it I don't like. They are "feckless," "affecting our day of piracy," and "stuffless." The first two are not sensuous enough—they should add to the sense of the scene by the actual Mediterranean. I don't know what "stuffless" means here, so won't say more. I suggest that "air" be left without an adjective and preceded by a short phrase to fill the line. "us up" is a little hard for the tongue. But make no mistake. You can't commit suicide. The poet who writes this has no right.
[*marginal notes*] There was a strange creature from China / Apprehended corrupting a minor. / There was a young fellow from Mercer / Who was partial to Venus aversa. / I am grateful for your comments on The A[ncestors]. I'll send you version no. 3 after your emendations. Ara vas prec to you.
    I salute you—John

P.S. You can't imagine how your poem cheers me up, despite the news of your letter. I'll cable E.W. I didn't know.   AL

November 7, 1932

Dear John: In the end I can't be very sorry that you took my discourse on suicide a little more seriously than I expected you to; nor am I too inquisitive about the motive for your high praise of my Mediterranean poem. I think affection is as good a motive as one can have. Still I am believing a large part of your praise, thinking what a fine fellow you are and what a good poem I have written. I am sending you new versions of the two poems, and a new poem besides[1]—not that you are to comment on them; I always feel nervous when an incomplete copy is in your hands. I will be satisfied if you just lay them on your table. In the new version of Cassis I have tried to meet most of your objections, which were very well taken indeed; but the first stanza does its work without throwing the particular emotion off the track; I felt that something like that was needed for exposition.
    I am very much interested in your aeroplane poem.[2] You are right

about Crane's effort on that theme; it is horribly muddled and contradictory. Did you see my In Memoriam?[3] I made a point about that poem to the effect that the aeroplane was, in itself, no better a symbol of truth, or of salvation, than the subway, which in The Tunnel is his symbol of damnation. The more I read Crane the more I believe that some trace of intellect is necessary for a poet; or at least a poet must thoroughly understand two or three fundamental ideas.

I think your notion of a manifesto is excellent. We might work it out, and then forward it to MacLeish. The accomplished fact would probably make him sign it (with a few additions and emendations perhaps); but he would be sure to say no if we ask him to collaborate directly. In the next few days I will make out a statement such as you suggest, and send it on; we may take out time.[4] Meanwhile I hope you get something done on your novel.

By the way, isn't Arnold's feeling for the Mediterranean nearly perfect in the last two stanzas of The Scholar Gipsy? I don't think I have anything quite that good. Perhaps the idea underlying my poem is a little more realistic—less committed to the illusion that there was ever a paradise; but my writing is not so good.

What do you suppose poor Edmund will do now? I wish he might be brought to some notion that would save his soul. Keep on planning to come down. Today is the first cloudy weather we've had since September.   Yrs. ever, Allen   TLS

1. "Aeneas at Washington" is the new poem; the other two are "The Mediterranean" and "The Meaning of Life."   2. "O Let Not Virtue Seek."   3. "In Memoriam: Hart Crane: 1899–1932," *Hound and Horn* 5 (July–September, 1932), 612–19.   4. This project was never completed.

November 11, 1932

Dear Allen: I have been hard at work on my aviation poem and have been too feeble at night to undertake a thorough examination of the three versions of Picnic at Cassis. I am now able to sit up and take, let us hope, poetical notice.

Well, I am convinced that the first version is the best. My enthusiasm for this was in no small measure due to its dramatic character. And that is, I think, destroyed by the invocation to the Trojans. The stanza is good in itself, but it interrupts the realization of "a scene."

It is my belief that the poet, no less than the prose-writer, is obliged to secure credibility. In prose, credibility depends upon an accumulation of familiar detail, but also upon the strict preservation of the limits of the character described. Caroline's story exemplifies this admirably. She has ornamented her tale with a number of small details, which we are convinced were true of that life (i.e. the pioneers') and which, taken all together, could only have been true in that life.[1] There are also some visual touches which our experience or imagination tells us to be true (the firelight falling far through the trees). But more than anything else we believe because Caroline never, for one tiniest phrase, departs from the consciousness of her imagined figure.

Now credibility in poetry is another matter. But, if the utterance is to carry conviction, and that intensely, we must believe that there is someone to whom this utterance applies.

I suppose in a lyric it is enough to speak out. The reader supplies the poet in his own person. He may speak in any quality, as a lover, a warrior, a mortal. It means much that his speech is felicitous and if it is sufficiently so, I suppose we are often ready to suspend belief. This is more or less what happens in say, the Restoration lyric, which no one believes for a minute, but which is sufficiently charming to hold our attention.

On the other hand, I think that the poet should speak in a time and place. True the movement from time to another time, from place to another place, so that we are simultaneously conscious of a change, or rather are made to feel a change in consciousness, is one of the great excitements of poetry. Consider Keats' admirable last Sonnet, where we move from a position of the earth to one above it and from the time of the poet, which is limited, to that of the star, which is eternal. This comparison between two times is a great theme, and not discovered, as Edmund Wilson thinks, by Flaubert and Eliot. It is present in all Shakespeare's sonnets.

Now, after this, I may seem to be wrong in condemning your shift in time. But I don't think so. You describe in your poem a place—the shore of the Mediterranean. The time is continuous with the progress of the verse. But behind this time is the arrival of Aeneas on these same or similar shores and this carries you to another arrival on other shores. You make the reader aware of Trojan time. I don't think you need devote a stanza to it. The information contained in it—the prophecy from the Aeneid—had better be put in your motto. What that should be is the Latin for your first motto, or perhaps better, your translation of the Virgil.

Aeneas is better than hero, ceased than undid, vine than field. The extra rhyme produces an inspired effect. You were wrong to change it. I still don't understand what you mean by stuffless unless it is a way of getting around empty.

There is a good deal of confusion in my analysis above. There is a

deep fog outside, the children are all indoors and at my doors, Mrs. C
is packin and my mind cannot collect itself. I feel like Byron when the 8
little Hunts came to Pisa.

Still, what I have said may make it clear why The Meaning of Life
seems to me an inferior poem. It is good of its kind, but it is definitely
an inferior kind. You ought, it seems to me, have shown the old men
(who perhaps were not then so old) killing for luck. Then your comment could have concluded. But as it is, the sense seems to me too
explicit. [2]

I don't know quite why I find Aeneas at Washington unsatisfactory. [3] Line by line it is beautiful. But in the light of what I have written
above, I think the whole trouble is Washington. It reminds me somehow unfavorably of Christ in New York. Or Satan on Broadway. The
juxtaposition is too easy. Leave him in Rome. That would be enough
and would I think preserve that credibility of which I have not very
eloquently spoken. The poem could be so written that the comparison
which you make explicit would be implicit and therefore all the more
convincing. Aeneas could then be, both himself and Allen Tate the
ghost of a XVIIth century settler in Virginia. As it is, he is half one,
half the other. The figures should be superimposed one on the other.
They seem to me now like Siamese twins, rather awkwardly and
monstrously joined.

After this, you will not think that my affection and admiration for
you as a man determines my admiration and affection for your
poetry. I am glad I do admire your poetry, for I have friends whose
writing I cannot tolerate. It is pleasanter when you like both man and
author.

You may soon have your revenge. I have pretty well completed
the part of the new poem devoted to flying. I make the aeroplane
exactly what it is, the consummation of an ancient dream of flying, a
remarkable instance of the increased powers of movement which
mechanical science has given man. But nothing more, not salvation,
nor anything like it.

The astronomical portion I am about to set about writing seriously. I have a draft, but it does not contain what I want it to
contain, the conception of space-time and of astronomical time, that
is as a one-way continuum. I may be able to get it, but wish I knew
more astronomy and did not have to labor for the purpose of the
poem to acquire a clear sense of what an astronomer does.

The first section should contain all the conquest of space which
man as an animal is capable of; the second all the conquest of space
and time his mind is equal to; the third the conclusion that there is
still a something called man whose conquests are of another order

and whose virtue depends upon his domination of the microcosm, not the macrocosm.

We move to Paris Monday. Hotel La Perouse 40 Rue la Perouse. Yours, John   TLS

1. "The Captive," *Hound and Horn* 6 (October-December, 1932), 63–107.   2. "The Meaning of Life" first appeared in *Hound and Horn* 7 (October-December, 1933), 42.   3. "Aeneas at Washington" first appeared in *Hound and Horn* 6 (April-June, 1933), 445–46.

November 12, 1932

Dear John: I'm just back from a fatiguing afternoon in Toulon to find your very fine letter. We are in France and I shall answer it more at length in the French manner in a few days—in person! We are coming to Paris forthwith—as soon as we can get results from an American cheque. I simply can't do my work here without books. We shall live in dire poverty somewhere at least until January; every cent we have got hold of for four months has gone home to creditors. But it is better to be in Paris poor and working than in Toulon idle and poor, but living beyond our means.

The trouble and thought you have given the Cassis poem cannot be sufficiently acknowledged. I am going to adopt your leading suggestion about the shift of time; I resorted to that expository device chiefly because I dislike a motto that carries part of the poem—that is the poem must explain the motto, not the other way about. I thought the internal rime in the final line somewhat inspired but I let Ford talk me out of it: I shall restore it immediately.

By the way: when we get settled in Paris I intend to store the car away for the winter. I know from recent experience that garage rent in the city is high. Do you know of a cheap space that I might rent in Orgeval? I recall sadly that your garage has space for only one car.

Caroline is simply overjoyed with your praise, and now that you have uttered it I am sure it is proper for me to say it is deserved. You know she entered the story in the Scribner contest this year. If you will look at the September Scribner's you will see what they preferred; they thought so little of the story that they wouldn't even print it. Edmund, being one of the judges, explained to her that "you don't know how amazing the life of a jewelry salesman is"—that's what Herrmann's story is about.[1]

Well, my friend, I look forward to long talks over the glasses before many days, and I hope the first one will [be] entirely about your new poem. Be getting a copy ready, up to date. I know you don't let any personal question affect your judgment, but then you

see you must allow me to blush for a moment by dallying with false
surmise. Love to Margaret.   Yrs. Allen   TLS

1. "The Big Short Trip," *Scribner's Magazine* 92 (August, 1932) 65-69, 113-28, by John
Herrmann was one of two winners in the Scribner Prize Short Novel Contest for that
year; the other was Emmet Gower's "Hill Idyll," *Scribner's Magazine* 92 (December,
1932), 338-42, 375-84.

[Late November, 1932]

Hotel La Perouse
40, Rue la Perouse/Paris

Dear Allen: This is to make you sure of the address. I shall welcome
you both to Paris.

I hope the check comes soon and that the reception committee
can start soon ordering music, plays and lemonade. Let me know
where you'll be and have dinner with us as soon as you've dropped
your bags.

I had such a nice letter from Caroline this morning. I think we'll
have to abandon Edmund. And for exactly the reason she specifies—
the lack of historical imagination. That lack vitiates all his recent writings.

I am doing no work today, trying to rest my eyes after a change of
glasses. I have rewritten my poem on the benefits of science to include a burlesque of the American communists.[1] That may be foolish. I
think they'll vanish almost as quickly as the Humanists. And then
where will our band-wagon-climbers be?   We'll discuss all this at
length and liquorishly—John   AL

1. Possibly "This Dim and Ptolemaic Man."

March 23, 1933

Dear Allen: I want only to say how I have missed you. Since you
and Caroline went away, France is another country and I am desolate.

I have been working pretty well on my novel but I feel terribly the
lack of actual contact with the people I describe. Harriet (M's sister)
has offered us her house for the summer, but I don't see how we
could pay the passage over. And as far as I can figure out, the extra
cost of servants compensates for lower costs in food. We've brought
our expenses way down here and will probably be able to make it for
the present.

I'd really like to be in America now, but think I'll try to stick it out
until I finish this book. [Geoffrey] Grigson sent back my works, but I
have made a second effort. [Morton Dauwen] Zabel is taking three
out of five poems.[1] And [Richard] Rees at The Adelphi has bought the

Montmartre poem.[2] So much for the muse. She has had a menopause and is not producing young just now.

I see the H & H is publishing Aeneas at Washington and (I guess) the story.[3] I am delighted.

I read *Western Values*[4]—a good book. It upset my article in the Va. Quarterly less than I feared it would.[5]

Stravinsky had a swell concert the other day and the primroses are in bloom. That's all the news for those without a social conscience. As ever, JPB AL

1. "Beyond Connecticut, Beyond the Sea," "My Grandfather Kept Peacocks," and "The Ancestors," were all published under the group title "Forbears" in the July, 1933 issue of *Poetry*. 2. Bishop's "Martyr's Hill" appeared in the May, 1933, issue of *The Adelphi*. 3. "The Immortal Woman" appeared in *Hound and Horn* 6 (July-September, 1933), 593-609. 4. Bishop is referring to Edward Westermarck's *The Origin and Development of the Moral Ideas* (1906). 5. "The South and Tradition," *Virginia Quarterly Review* 9 (April, 1933), 161-74.

April 7, 1933 Merry Mont/Trenton, Ky.

Dear John: It is nearly two months since we left France, and this is my first backward glance at Europe. It is very far away, remote, and unattainable; I have really never been there. All the emotions of this country clicked back into place, and life now goes on. We are barely settled here, having stayed with Phelps in Maryland two weeks; when we crossed the mountains Nashville detained us another two, and I have made two trips there since. We have been having some excitement of our own. Perhaps you will have heard by the time you receive this of Seward Collins' conversion to Agrarianism.[1] He has changed his magazine from the ground up—even the title, which is henceforth The American Review—and the Tennessee group will vie for the honors with the English Distributists, Belloc and Chesterton. In fact, we are his American support.

So Nashville has indeed claimed most of my time. Collins came down last week-end to map out his program and to assign to us our parts. I was astonished to learn that the Distributists, with some minor differences of terms, have precisely our point of view, which of course is briefly: the dole must be capitalized and its beneficiaries instead of remaining idle must be returned to the land. The big basic industries must be broken up and socialized, and the small businesses returned to the people. The Distributists differ with us on this in no respect. The end in view is the destruction of the middle class-capitalist hegemony, and the restoration with the material at hand, not a literal restoration, of traditional society. Unless I am much mistaken there is more chance of this being realized in the next generation than at any time in the last seventy years. Indeed capitalism as

we know it is at an end, but the answer is not Communism or anything like it. This is the first time I have felt any real enthusiasm over
social ideas—I mean the kind of enthusiasm which goes beyond private conviction.

In helping Collins draw up his program I took the liberty of mentioning you as a thorough-going reactionary—at the very word reactionary Collins beams—and of putting you on his list of active sup-
porters. There is one thing that he must be made to see. In spite of his
conviction of the truth, of his conversion to the light, he has reached it
in an heretical manner which makes the terms of his conversion
largely accidental. He has come to our position abstractly, just as
Edmund reached Communism in some tortuous abstract path. He
therefore cannot see that the creative arts are essential to his program.
One of the faults of the liberals and Communists is that their art has
not gone beyond the most naive propaganda. It is our view that the
most powerful propaganda that any social movement could have is a
mature literature which is superior to propaganda. We have talked all
this over, and you would be surprised at the unanimity with which all
our group here is at present confirming our own conversations
through the winter. Collins can't see the need of representing the arts
in his magazine. He wants to confine it to propaganda. What he
doesn't understand is precisely what he failed to understand about
the Humanists—that morality for example has no validity unless it
has a physical background in which morality, economics, religion and
art are simply different expression forms for the total mentality of
society. He thinks it is all morality, and that moral ideas of themselves
are capable of doing work. He is a perfect New England fanatic who
has no sensuous life, and he can't understand the backgrounds of
ideas. But whatever path he may have taken to arrive at his present
position, we join him there; and we may eagerly put up with his
limitations for the sake of having a magazine, for once, that is
thoroughly sympathetic to our views. I will let you know more about
this in a week or so. Meanwhile start furbishing up your essays. I
think in the end we shall be able to overwhelm him with the aesthetic
phase by means of sheer weight.

You will be glad to learn that the cast of opinion around the New
Republic is changing. I suppose you saw Edmund's article on the
inaugural parade—folly could go no lower.[2] Stark [Young] created an
issue with it—said that in a time of crisis that Greenwich Village
wisecracking had no place in a great weekly. It did seem to me like a
little boy pissing on the schoolhouse door to spite the teacher. Well,
Stark says that the NR is getting very shaky—has no point of view
that can put them in touch with affairs—that they are disarmed by a
President who is just as critical of the abuses of capitalism as they are

and leaves them nothing to say. It is amusing that Malcolm [Cowley] has overwhelmed me with suggestions about articles. I fear the worn-out cat, who has jumped so many ways in the last ten years, is about to jump again. It has always been my belief that if the NR had known its own mind it would never have permitted me to write a line for the sheet. Or you either.

This is about all the news. We came right here from Baltimore; so my New York items are second-hand, or came by mail. Please write me the news from France. And please tell me how you all are getting along, and what your plans are. It might be well to come to America for a while. It is a more congenial country than it has ever been in my lifetime. Americanism is thoroughly discredited. Even business men see that "recovery" must be in new terms. An era has passed them by. The racketeer in business, his twin brothers the messiah in litera-ture and the parvenu in society, are about to go. Come over and look at it. Caroline joins me in love to you both. And remember us to Esther [Strachey]. Yrs. Allen   TLS

1. Seward Collins, owner and editor of *The Bookman,* had abandoned his alliance with the New Humanists in favor of the Agrarians, and changed his magazine to *The American Review.* It became an organ for the Agrarians' polemical essays.   2. "Inau-gural Parade," *New Republic* 74 (March 22, 1933), 154–56.

April 23, 1933

Dear Allen: Get thee glass eyes
               And like a scurvy politician seem
               To see the things thou dost not.
This is a personal admonition, not just a little thought for Shake-speare's birthday. It seems that now the politicians are beginning to see. Two French papers, L'Intransigeant and L'Humaniste have pub-lished photographs of workers in the Bureau of Engraving with cap-tions *Comment on Fabrique les Dollars.*

It was fine to hear from you again. Your absence left a great and desolate silence. But in the meanwhile I see you have not been inac-tive on my account. I heard from the Lion and Crown. I am giving them *O Let Not Virtue Seek!* and some other poems, about ten in all.[1] Max P. is at last bringing out my other book, but wants me to subtract nine poems to shorten the volume.[2] His list of omissions includes Perspectives are Precipices and one or two other of the best. Fortu-nately, he leaves the final selection to me.

I want to ask you about *The Senator* piece.[3] Rereading Eliot's *Difficulties of a Statesman* I am very dubious about the advisability of publishing my poem now. It's enough like T.S.E. for all the critics to pounce on it. For the rest I'll cut out the feeble works following your previous suggestions.

As to Collins, I had a nice letter from him and will communicate directly. At the moment I have nothing on hand but the Manet piece which will need some recasting. When the Picasso came back from [Stringfellow] Barr—unsurprisingly—I sent it in desperation to Leippert.[4] I'll write him at once if he doesn't want it to give it to Seward. If you can think of any thing *particular* I could do for his Review I'd be grateful. Our minds are so agreed on essentials that I don't think I'll find trouble in fitting in with your plans. But it is terribly difficult for me, so far from the so rapidly changing American scene, to know what starting point to take. I flatter myself that I have ideas on all the matters you touch, but one needs a hook and not a rusty one. It's the rust which, from this distance, I can't see.

Besides, I am pretty heavily engaged in my would-be novel. It's going quite well. I've got to stop this week to amplify one or two passages in the Fortune article on the [Major-Lit].[5] Needless to say, I'm glad to do this, for I think their check will be what saves the situation.

I never wanted more to be in America and for once Margaret agrees with me. We even had a house offered in Connecticut. But it's unavailable for winter and while living would be a little cheaper there, it would not cover the passage for six people. Of course, if the dollar goes far down, we'll have to fly. But, due to Margaret's energy, she has cut expenses here unbelievably (to her) and besides is actively engaged. As a consequence, she is much happier than last year.

I don't in any event want to wait much longer. If I get anything out of the novel, we'll go then. But I'm scared with three young to move from under our three-hundred-year-old roof with no provisions, no surety of a newer one.

Esther [Strachey] is in great form. She has her divorce which clears up her personal life. The only bad effect is she has (according to Dickie Ames) acquired a weakness for breaking wind. I haven't heard it. And anyhow she's a great girl. I now unite with her as once with you to denounce the Communists. Her latest proposal is that Roosevelt, speaking for American capitalism, broadcast to France, beginning,

> Darling I am growing old
> Silver threads among the gold.

I haven't seen E.W.'s inaugural address. But I did read his very pale little account of Roosevelt with that impossible expression occurring again "enlightened opinion of our time."[6] I'm reading Trotsky's *Life* with a profound feeling that it is a waste of time. And speaking of reading—look again at Dante's Sordello passage. I bawled my eyes out over it the other day. It's the greatest piece of patriotism ever done—the real thing. I weep over it and have for years.

Margaret was no less delighted than I to have word of you and joins me in affection to you and Caroline. John   AL

1. None of Bishop's poetry appeared in *Lion and Crown*.   2. *Now With His Love.*   3. "No More the Senator."   4. Barr was editor of *The Virginia Quarterly Review;* Leippert was editor at *Lion and Crown*.   5. Bishop's handwriting is totally illegible here, and he published no articles in *Fortune* after 1932.   6. Bishop is referring to Wilson's article "The Hudson River Progressive," *New Republic* 74 (April 5, 1933), 219–20, a review of several books by and about Roosevelt.

May 3, 1933

Dear Allen: I am sending you The Return and Aliens. I have come to think more highly of the latter since its composition. The use of both in your poetry section is contingent upon its appearing before Scribner's publishes my book. The date for that is, tentatively, August.[1] If that does not fit with your plans, I'll try to find something else for you. I understand the Lion & Crown series is also due in autumn.

Dickie Ames was here over the weekend, and was invaluable, due to his long experience with concerts, in helping me make the final selection and to arrange the included pieces. I've got forty-six poems, and have weeded out the obvious weaklings. What's left is, I think, pretty good.

I have several things which need some work before they can be sent out. One I worked on today. It is not for S. Collins. I am dubious as to its value myself, but its tone forbids its appearing in the A.R. But something I'll have for you if you put off publication till fall, which I hope you don't.

Archie is here and has read me his Phi Beta Kappa poem.[2] It brings up the very questions I raised over *Aeneas at Washington*, which it strangely resembles. My instinct is, the metaphor ought to be preserved. But the generally *fade* [?] quality that ensues—in my own work, for instance—is perhaps an answer. But somehow it ought to be able to keep the metaphor and make it tell vividly and immediately.

Now that Malcolm has deserted the New Republican (I have read his piece postponing the revolution for forty years, the Marxist one forever), can't you persuade him, as a final gesture of disdain strangling, garotting, gutting or otherwise eliminating Granville Hicks? America deserves a great deal that it got during the depression. But not all its sins since the Civil War warranted having Granville Hicks and V. F. Calverton thrust up her anal column. For enter through the intelligence—that they cannot do. Poor country! Poor roadside whore! I love her still, mais j'ai les mains froides. Love (of another kind) to Caroline—JPB   AL

1. *Now With His Love* appeared in September, 1933.   2. MacLeish's poem "Elpenor," originally titled "1933," was the Phi Beta Kappa poem at Harvard that year, and first appeared in *Yale Review* 22 (June, 1933), 49–55.

May 5, 1933

Dear John: I am mighty glad to get your letter and its news. It is good to hear that the novel progresses and that Perkins is bringing out the poems. Don't let him talk you out of Perspectives are Precipices; though I might be inclined to aid him in talking you into a new title for it. I am sure that Margaret would assist us in this cause. I have no absolute advice about The Senator. I suggest that you omit it if the book will really be small, but that you put it in if Perkins changes his mind and issues a larger book. A small book usually means or should mean the highly selected best; and I don't think The Senator one of the best.[1] It is the kind of poem that is quite good enough to support other work, and to provide some sort of documentary material for the high moments. And of course you are putting in The Return. If you have sent me that poem for the project with Collins, please let me know when Perkins intends to publish the book. If Collins lets us have the poetry exhibit, it is possible that we will not have it ready before the September issue. By the way, do you happen to know whether MacLeish has written anything good recently that remains unpublished? I don't want to ask him unless I am sure of the quality of the work in advance. I don't want any more difficult situations; increasing years do not necessarily bring wisdom, but they do bring a desire for peace.

I have an idea for an article that you could certainly write for Collins. Why don't you analyze the liberal mind for him? Particularly the liberal implications of the idea of social justice? I suppose you would have to attack poor Edmund—a task too easy—but perhaps you could direct the argument chiefly against other people. My notion is that the more justice of the liberal kind that the working class receives, the more that class receives a status of recognized servitude; so that the liberals are only aiding, instead of correcting, all the tendencies in that direction. There is certainly an article there, and I think you are the man to do it. I will be writing to him shortly, and will mention it; meanwhile you might write him yourself, proposing this or some other notion. By the way, I was astonished that Collins has the same idea we have on the Jewish nature of liberalism and on the Old Testament character of Das Kapital; so with the fierce, literal, Yankee logic of his, Collins has worked himself into a great froth over the Jews. Let us not discourage him.

I've got to start off for Nashville; I seem to be always doing that; and I must end this. I hope that you and Margaret find some way to get back over here. I imagine you will; the House has just passed the inflation measures, the Senate will probably follow suit; and the Dollar will probably shrink greatly in France, so that you'd better spend it in America.[2] It is too bad you paid your debts in the last few years, that is if they were American debts. I am feeling very contented; though I did waste about $600.00 by paying $1200.00 last year. . . . You must tell Ames not to be upset by Esther's wind; it is only the wind of sound doctrine, and highly inflammable. Affectionate regards to you all, Allen   TLS

1. "No More The Senator" was not included in *Now With His Love*.   2. Tate is referring to Title III of the Emergency Farm Relief and Inflation Act approved by the "Congress of one hundred days" on May 12, 1933. Commonly known as the Thomas Inflation Amendment, it was a deliberate effort to inflate the national economy by increasing the amount of money in circulation and expanding credit.

June 20, 1933

Dear Allen: Thanks so much for the photographs of your house. They made me very homesick for the South.

Well I may be there shortly. We've about decided to progress westward in September unless the franc collapses in the meanwhile. If I were sure of having my novel through I'd be happy about it. I have been extremely sterile lately. I can't even write letters.

Well, so Collins goes. Alas, all the editors are going the way of Hoover. Fortune is trying to cheat me out of some hundreds of dollars. I'll write Perkins about the proof. I've seen galley, which looks pretty well.

Lincoln Kirstein has been here and surprisingly I like him very much. The Russian ballet he revived with Massine; Dali has had another show full of limp cocks in crotches of olive wood and at least two stiff ones (very miniature); Erskine Caldwell has written a book glorifying cunt-lapping;[1] Cummings qualified the Emilio [Terry][2] exposition as objects found in a vagina. Sex is the word. Get out your old symbols and start painting. Esther is here and magnificent, lectures at libraries and Women's Clubs, very well. Our friends swung in a fine bistro party on the eleventh anniversary of our marriage which concluded 6:30 AM at Les Halles with les Cummings and Esther and miles of vegetables. The first time I'd seen the markets in nine years. I'm beginning to feel like D. Ames who says he doesn't like living in interesting times.   Best to Caroline, John   AL

1. *Tobacco Road* (1932).   2. Bishop's handwriting is nearly illegible here; Emilio Terry remains unidentified.

	Valley Forge Road
October 14, 1933	Westport Connecticut/R.F.D. No. 2

Dear Allen: Here we are on the banks of the Saugatuck, rather tired and more confused. My sister-in-law offered us this house rent free and it seemed rather mad not to accept it. It's charming but summerish (which means *not* sound proof) and I've rather got the idea of thirty children rather than three. However, I suppose we'll shake down. Next week I hope to return to the attic to work.

Scribner's has done a nice job on my book. I have one copy only as yet.[1]

By the way, have you heard anything from the Lion and Crown man? I forget his name. Do you have it? I sent him a heap of poems in June without response. If he's bankrupt I'd like to peddle them elsewhere.

I like Mr. Rockefeller's buildings[2] but my God, what was happened to the American looks? I never saw so many ugly people.   My best to Caroline, JPB   AL

1. *Now With His Love.*   2. Rockefeller Center, in New York City, was built during Bishop's residence in France.

October 30, 1933   Route 6 Clarksville, Tenn.

Dear John: I am glad to hear that you are at work so soon after the trip; it usually takes me one to four months to settle down. But it is bad that Perkins is holding back your book. It is amazing that the best of publishers are superstitious. But maybe there are people who pay them (blurbs) some attention. I felt that I couldn't review the book half so effectively if I wrote a blurb too. In spite of the delay I don't see why Perkins doesn't send me a copy.

I've been in a crisis. I have out a heroism or cowardice (take your choice) thrown over the ancestry book forever.[1] The agony was great, but the peace of mind is greater. It was a simple problem that I could not solve. The discrepancy between the outward significance and the private was so enormous that I decided that I could not handle the material in that form at all, without faking either the significance or the material. A couple of years were wasted, but I learned a lesson, how valuable depends on whether I made the same mistake again. I feel a great release of spirit, but for the moment at least a good deal of sheer exhaustion.

Aunt Harriet's prize money buoys me up, and I need all the props I can get after a long siege of troubles.[2] But I think these are over for a while. The climax was the death of my father two weeks ago up in Kentucky. I have just got back. He died after a taxi accident—or rather he was knocked down by a taxi and his hip broken. He would not have walked again. His heart failed him. He was seventy-one, died in poverty after a reckless life, but gallantly; with his last words he rallied the nurse about her good looks.

I have finished a series of three articles on poetry for the N.R.[3] I appreciated Stark's defense in the current issue; but I don't think [Horace] Gregory worth the trouble.[4]

Finish the novel, and start travelling—in this direction. We are rebuilding the office in the yard—a perfect place to write. Come and occupy it before I do. Love to Margaret,   Yrs, Allen   TLS

1. "Ancestors of Exile."   2. The November, 1933 issue of *Poetry* carried news of the award to Tate of the $100 Midland Author's Prize for a group of poems published in the November, 1931, issue of *Poetry* under the title "The Rooftree," including "Sonnets of the Blood," "Message from Paris," and "The Wolves."   3. "Three Types of Poetry," *New Republic* 78 (March 14, 1934), 126–28; (March 28, 1934), 180–82; (April 11, 1934), 237–240.   4. Stark Young, "Poetry of Defense," *New Republic* 76 (November 1, 1933), 334–36; Horace Gregory, "A Defense of Poetry," *New Republic* 76 (October 11, 1933), 235–38.

Nov. 26, 1933

Dear John: Your letter and your book (from the NR) arrived yesterday.[1] I am on the book today, and hope to begin writing tomorrow. Your four best poems are easily Ode, The Return, Perspectives Are Precipices, and The Ancestors. In the Dordogne and Young Men Dead are very fine too; I would add To His Late Mistress except that it is a little literary in framework. October Tragedy is among the best, but I can't believe that the narrative quite comes off; your interest is chiefly moral. (Who read the proof on the lyric in O.T.?)

Cowley asks me to write about 800 words only; so I suppose I'll have to do it in that truncated form. He suggests an essay later on poetry in the last two years, and says I can do justice then. But I'll try my best in the 800 words.

I am delighted that the novel goes so well. Go on and get it out this spring.[2] Perkins wants Caroline's new book for the spring list.[3] She put her novel aside in October, and began a book on the hero of Old Red. She has seven chapters done, three more to write. I think she will have it ready. I want very much to read your ms. If I had known that my father's remarks had documentary interest, I am sure that I could have thought of many more of them.

Your historical commentary on your poems is extremely interesting. Your four best poems were all written in the last four years—which shows, among other things, that you have just got a good start. I hope that can be said of me at forty (or is it thirty-nine?). I wanted this chronology because I thought I was doing a long piece, and wished to see how many times you had anticipated one of our esteemed contemporaries in the use of certain technical effects. But now I don't know whether I can work that into the shorter review.

[Stephen] Spender has written two or three fine poems, but it is all in familiar materials. I can't see him as the great pathfinder, as his admirers in London seem to do. (I wrote a review of him for New Verse: that he was good, but simple-minded, and that his Communism was pretty stale stuff.)[4] He has a nice mixture of buggery and radicalism that seems to give his friends great hope of saving England. I couldn't make head or tail of MacLeish's review in H & H,[5] until it suddenly occurred to me that it was really a covert attack on me: the young critic with the two or three thin volumes, the pompous tone, the grudging praise, etc. Who fits that description better than myself? The only fault with the picture is that my praise of MacLeish has been spare, but not of several other people. Why his private letters should be as consistently laudatory as his public utterances, spoken or written, are the reverse, baffles me; I don't get him, though I admire and respect him enormously.

I am warned that I must bring this to a close. John Gould Fletcher is due to arrive in a few hours for the week-end. He has returned to the South for good. Another amazing fellow. Interesting and of great qualities, but the rudest human being on two legs. Sir, I assure you that I am not so narrow as to think there is only one kind of Southern gentleman. I am undecided how I shall spend Thanksgiving—the football game in Nashville or the cock-fight in Hopkinsville; I think it will be the latter, since I've not seen one since I was a boy. The challenger's stake is one thousand dollars; the seating capacity of the arena five hundred. The fight opens the season.

You'd better come on down here when you get to Charlestown. It isn't far, and the fare is cheap at the present. Love to Margaret. Can you give me Esther's address?   Yrs ever, Allen   TLS

---

1. The letter is missing; the book is *Now With His Love,* which Tate reviewed in the *New Republic* 78 (February 21, 1934), 52–53.   2. *Act of Darkness* appeared in the spring of 1934, two days after Wolfe's *Of Time and the River,* causing, Bishop felt, a loss of sales. See below, Bishop to Tate, June 7, 1935.   3. *Aleck Maury, Sportsman* (New York: Charles Scribner's Sons, 1934), was not published until fall, 1934.   4. Tate reviewed

Spender's *Poems* in *New Verse* 3 (May, 1933), 21–23.   5. "Stephen Spender and the Critics," *Hound and Horn* 7 (October-December, 1933), 145–47. In describing contemporary poetry critics, MacLeish wrote: "Young amateurs in writing, with a few of the regulation slim volumes of the period to their credit (or the opposite), emit god-like judgments which a Dante would hesitate to sign."

[Late November, 1933]

Dear Allen: If I have a literary success, I shall owe it to you. As it is, whatever meagre accomplishment is mine is much in your debt. There are times, of which today is depressingly one, when I doubt if I should go on if it were not for your aid and encouragement.

My peculiar gloom is not due to your letter, but to having been rewriting a particularly weak chapter in my novel. I believe I'm doing something with it, but it was God-awful looking at the first draft. And it most horribly occurred to me that maybe it was all like that. There are certainly some flabby places in it. I hope I'll have time to tighten them up. The trouble is I have to get something on paper before I can begin to see the form of anything so long as a novel. I can't work it from a strict plan. Which means a great deal of wasted effort.

The mistake in the October Tragedy lyric is the printer's.[1] So is tall seven sons in Beyond Connecticut, which ought to be seven tall sons and the "the" chopped out before "hand" in the charlatan stanza of Hunger and Thirst. Affrontery is my fault.

I agree with you on the whole about the best poems, though *Ode* no longer excites me and I prefer two of the romantic lyrics to To His Late Mistress. However, anything you say will have my approval.

I did feel pretty bitterly about the H & H suggesting that I learned assonance from MacLeish. He was writing a composite of Meredith and Masefield when I met him and with the exception of The Return all my assonantal verse dates from 1923. I did what Archie calls distributing accents in Princeton circa 1917. I got that sort of line originally from Dante, though later there were other poets, notably Yeats and Eliot, who influenced my use of it.

Your opinion of Spender is about the same as mine. But I think that both homosexuality and communism are now played out as subjects in poetry.

I can't understand Archie's attack on you. I haven't seen the last H & H, but I know him capable of it. Lincoln K[irstein] whom I have just lunched with tells me he is full of rancor about everybody. He has absolutely no sound reason to have a grudge against you. But he may have. I am privately inclined to think that having achieved the position he's been after all these years, he's finished. His latest poems are a great let down.

Esther's address is 155 E 52nd.

I am planning to go to Charles Town in January, possibly for a month. I'm going down for court, as I have to see a trial there for a scene I'm doing. Also my sister's having a baby and I may stay for the birth. What I would like to do is to get off the mss of the novel, Feb. 1st and then run down your way. Lordy, I'll be glad to get the opus done. It's my last venture into the past for a long time. My present existence is the most boring I've led since the Army days in Chillicothe, Ohio. And that was a bore! Give my love to Caroline, John

AL

1. The printer's error was "o" for "of" in the lyric.

December 1, 1933

Dear John: I write this note in a rush, but I am very much pleased with your letter, and moved by it. I am sure you exaggerate my good effects, but it is better to do that than to deny them. I can heartily return to you the same thanks. As a matter of fact, I think that among men of letters who achieve a certain degree of excellence, encouragement, even when there are no warm feelings of friendship, is absolutely necessary, and that its absence is a kind of treason to the craft. MacLeish's general attitude is incredible to me; it is so incredible that I can't even take it seriously. (As to MacL., I hope what you say isn't true, but such an end is possible with a mind of the instrumental type, which does or can do many things well, and loses the incentive to work when it has gained a certain end. Better to do one thing well with great difficulty!)

I began this to say that Fletcher stayed longer than we expected, and that I've got to leave in the morning for Baton Rouge. We'll be gone until Wednesday, and I must postpone the review until then. But I've got it worked out in my mind, and I think you'll like it. Love to you all, Yrs, Allen

P. S. What novel doesn't have bleak spots? Go on through it and worry about those spots later. TLS

December 10, 1933

Dear Allen: I have only just read Archie's essay on Spender in the Hound and Horn. I think it probable that we have both done him wrong and that the critic of the slim volumes does not refer to you. But aside from that it is a shamelessly bad attitude to take and one that can only do him harm. He ought never to write criticism, even declaiming that he's not writing criticism. For he can't do it without getting rancorous and obtrusively personal.

I have lost a week's work. Went in for the repeal celebration and Margaret, at five AM, developed an abcessed ear which was lanced the following day. She's still deaf, but I hope won't stay so.

I don't think I repeated to you from Bunny that Eliot when with E. W. put you and [Howard Phelps] Putnam down as the two best American poets.

Horace Gregory had given me a very good review in the *Herald Tribune*, aside from a few Left-wing cracks at social superiority and Southern ancestor worship.[1] I wrote him a very polite letter explaining that The Ancestors were everybody's and not my private progenitors.

Tell Caroline I liked her story in Scribner's very much and retract what I said a year ago.[2]

For the first time in 11 years, liquor is rare in New York and still very high in price. But the nightmare is over.[3]   As ever, JPB   AL

1. *Books*, December 10, 1933, p. 8. Gregory asserted in this review that "Mr. Bishop's verse has a genuine feeling of caste behind it, a real conviction that Bishop blood is superior and that worship at ancestral shrines is a means of restoring strength to bones and tissue."   2. "Old Red," *Scribner's Magazine* 94 (December, 1933), 325–32. The comment of "a year ago" was apparently oral, for both were in France then.   3. National Prohibition had ended on December 5, 1933.

December 14, 1933

Dear John: I am sending you a carbon of my review. It is the third version, but I fear it is very cluttered up. The whole trouble was the limited space; I had to try to say a good deal more than 900 words will carry. What I regret omitting most of all was quotations from the poems, and some definite comparative criticisms. But I couldn't do that and what I did, at the same time; so I had to choose.

There are some things that I want to say that the proprieties of reviewing would not permit. For one thing you are second to none in this generation. You are so much better than MacLeish, for example, that I begin to feel sorry for him. I could say this publicly in a longer article, where I could prepare for it and let the illustrations make the point; I intend to do it yet. The thing that both Warren and I—Warren has reviewed you for Poetry[1]—think is certainly true, that you have the best equipment known to us, and the fact that you have gone slowly, taking your time and mastering each stage of your development, ought to preserve you at very nearly if not on the head of the age in another fifteen years. I won't say that you will be the best then; nobody knows anything about that; but there's a great chance that you will be if the hard fate that attends upon poets does nothing extraordinary. . . . I suppose this is the best way to congratulate you upon your book.

I haven't seen Gregory's review, but I know the line he would take. It is nonsense. There's something cagey about that fellow, and of all qualities that I dislike I hate most caginess. MacLeish's rancor is much better.

I had heard Ole Marse Eliot's opinion of the poets. (I call him Marse because he wrote me some letters in his conception of Southern dialect: my God, is the whole world coming South?) I don't know what to make of it. I may be a stick to beat somebody with.* That is ungenerous, of course, but remember that he accepted but never printed three of my best poems. We shall not look this gift-horse in the mouth. Amen.   Yrs. Allen

*Does this indicate it? I first heard it this way: Putnam and Tate, good; Cummings, fair; MacLeish, no good.   TLS

1. "Working Toward Freedom," *Poetry* 43 (March, 1934), 342-46.

December 14, 1933

Dear John: I forgot something in the other letter.

Collins has definitely turned his April issue over to us for a poetry number, and the crowd here have selected me to edit it. I only wish The Return were still available. But there is time for you to write one of your best poems; so set about it, please. You've got to be in this number.[1]

Now what about some other poets? We are asking the following persons: Eliot, Auden, Yeats, Baker, MacLeish, Putnam; these, besides yourself, are the only ones who have passed the meeting, as it were. Your friends here are not kind hearted. Can you think of anybody who ought to be included? If there's some one young, unknown, and very good, we want him, or even her, although there is a distinct prejudice against female poetry in this region.

Write me about this. There will be about four or five pages available to you, or about 100 to 125 lines.   Yrs. Allen

P.S. We don't intend to argue the politics of poetry, but we think there will be some healthy political effect in getting out an exhibit of fine poetry backed by some aloof criticism. There's been nothing like a special poetry number of a general magazine since I can remember. And incidentally strategy calls for secrecy. We want this number to take 'em by surprise.   TLS

1. The "poetry number" of the *American Review* appeared in May, 1934.

[December 14–23, 1933]

Dear Allen: Do you remember the evening in the Rue Mignard which you and Warren spent with me over a bottle of Scotch? Well, it was probably pleasant enough and casual enough for you both. But it was from that evening, from the comment that you two made on the verses I most shyly showed you that I conceived that it might still be possible for me to make a place for myself as poet. I do not think even you, who have been so much in my intimacy since, can know upon what despair and forlornness your words came. The confidence I had had in youth was gone with youth. I saw myself with little done and that little had not only had no recognition that I was aware of, but I had almost convinced myself that it deserved none.

When, since that time, I have written you with what may possibly have seemed to you exaggerated gratitude for your aid and encouragement, it has always been with the knowledge on my part that I did owe what is little less than my life to you. If, as I say, my thanks may have appeared excessive, with only your most recent letter in mind, you must not think them so. For always I have known that but for that evening, when your comment was mild enough, much milder than the praise you have since so generously accorded me, I should not now in any real sense exist. I want you to know this. It is not entirely easy for me to say it. But ingratitude would be worse than immodesty and silence here is ungrateful.

That I should now seem to you to have justified your confidence gives me great joy. I had hoped for a good review of my poems from you, I could have expected no less after your conversations and letters. But the praise you heap on me in your essay confuses me with happiness. Or perhaps I had better say joy, for I am overjoyed with all you have said. And the curious thing is that you have so well trained me, I now can quite well feel I deserved no less.

There are one or two points of your essay I would like to comment on. First, the question of style. I believe that Baudelaire was the first modern to understand this. That is, the practical problem faced by the artist at the present time was already present as soon as the middle class had obtained power. I have an essay on Manet which no one has ever been willing to publish (Manet is not news) in which I made a beginning of a study of this problem in its historical aspect. But Baudelaire believed that the correct style for any work of art (as I remember he is discussing painting at the time he says this) must be dictated by the subject, must in short arise out of the subject. Ingres, he felt, imposed a classical style on his bourgeois patrons in their portraits, which to Baudelaire was quite wrong.

This problem has been enormously aggravated in the century that has followed Ingres. I don't want to defend my own practice, but to recognize a condition. I think, for reasons that are still in part obscure to me, that we are forced to construct a new style for each new piece of work we undertake. A consideration of Picasso's career is very much to this point. At the same time, I know there is a great loss of energy involved, even when one is as vigorous as Picasso. I know that I feel whenever I sit down to a new job as though I had never written before, that everything is still to be determined. This is hard. And probably it is also wrong. But I doubt if the fault can be laid to the individual artist. He simply must take things as he finds them and work as he can. The most that I hope is that a constant sensuous equipment will end by imposing some sort of unity.

And you are quite right in saying we are now all moralists. But the poet is aloof. And he must criticize prevailing moralities, either communist or conventional by living acts. As I said to Cummings last summer in a remark which he greatly approved: The communists, and with them I include all writers like Edmund whose sense is explicit and whose intelligence is critical, wish to criticize life through ideas, while we must constantly criticize ideas through life. Poetic morality can do nothing more: Dante opposes one after another great and essentially good man to the damnation of Aristotle's ethics. And the only moral system sufficiently living for us to oppose is now probably the communist. Against it we must erect such figures as we can and wish that they could have the splendor of Farinata, holding Hell in great disdain.

Of course, here I am merely corroborating what you have said and in no way contradicting it. But I cannot but think that my reading last summer of Baudelaire's critical writings helped enormously to clarify my own mind. You know what he says of philosophy in poetry: that all poetry is inherently philosophical, but poetry being essentially *une chose fatale*, the poet must never set out deliberately to construct a philosophy in his poem. That phrase seems to me very great and just. Unless what we say comes with the finality of fate, then it has not been said with that conviction which is proper to poetry. But all that in practice is very hard. We can, a propos of the bandwagon boys, only keep in mind what Gertrude [Stein] said to Hemingway. Remarks are not literature.

I am deep in my novel which goes very well. Today I am tired from my single debauch since returning. It was worth it, for Saturday I laughed more than I have for two years. I also drank not a little liquor, and had one glass of champagne sold openly at dinner, which was a pure delight. What a load off it is to have repeal!

I have more or less agreed with Nicolas Nabokoff to do the lib-
retto for a short opera with his music. It is a rare chance to attempt
poetry on the stage and I mean to seize it, inasmuch as the subject
which interests him is one into which I could put a good deal of
private emotion. I shall of course write it in such a way that it will
stand poetically alone.[1]

As to your poetry number of Collins' Review. I have had no
response from Leippert, my letter to him at 1124 Amsterdam Avenue
being returned by the Dead Letter Office. So I will send you the
whole lot of poems I had given him, as well as the others I have done
since and not included in *Now With His Love*. I would like to see you
use *O Let Not Virtue Seek!* and would be willing to have you emend the
punctuation and spacing to bring it within the necessary limits of
space.

I regret to say I have no young poet for you, though Nabokoff
spoke to me the other day about a young American in Paris whose
poems he thought remarkable. He is now about twenty, but the
poems in question were written at sixteen. Nabokoff's judgement in
general is good, but it is always a question with a foreigner when
judging poetry in a language not his. I'll see if I can get hold of these.

With many thanks for you public and private praise   I am, yours,
John

It's good news that Warren is doing my book for Poetry.   TLS

1. This project was apparently never completed.

[December, 1933]   Westport 5892

Dear Allen: I am sending you a copy of *O: Let Not Virtue Seek*, which
I don't think you possess. Also *The Mothers*, which I don't believe
you've seen.

If the American Review could use the longer one, I'd be glad. For
because of its length, it will be hard to dispose of elsewhere. Will you
consult your colleagues?

If they are not satisfied, I have enough shorter pieces to fill out the
space you have allotted me. I think *The Mothers* pretty good as a piece
of contemporary myth-making. It might be called Male and Female if
Cecil deMille hadn't got there first.

My calendar says "Au jour d'hin l'est l'hiver." My God among
the French. It's been winter here since I could remember.

Well, a Merry and maudlin Christmas to you all, and a Happy,
Hangover-less New Year—John   AL

December 23, 1933

Dear John: Yes, I remember the evening in the rue Mignard, but I could not understand all its implications at the time, though I must confess that something in your response to what Warren and I said led me to reflect, a little later, on the kind of friendships with which you seemed to surround yourself. In fact, I became a little impatient though secretly with your suicidal disinterestedness. You remember the circle of that winter; there were other people who didn't appear on the scene just at that time but I got them related to it; and I decided that your generosity and real love of craft had permitted you to surround yourself with the most unmerciful crew of bloodsuckers it had been my luck to observe. The really bad part of it was that they were nearly all highly gifted people, who in a sense deserved the attention you gave them; but because you clamored for little or no attention yourself you got none. If I have played any part in your history, you may derive its outlines from this analysis of your life as I saw it four or five years ago. If it is true that I have trained you so well (!) that you are now convinced that you deserve the praise, it is also true that one effect of the training, which is inevitable in every other case I have observed, is missing; I mean the ingratitude. This is especially pleasing because I've done nothing to deserve gratitude; I saw some fine work, said it was fine, and thereby only did my simple duty by the republic of letters (which is the only kind of republic I believe in, a kind of republic that can't exist in a political republic).

You are quite right on the matter of style versus styles. I have not said much about this, and I'm not sure I saw its significance till I had got the process under way; but I have been struggling with the problem since 1928, when I began the later work which I think, with the exception of the Confederate Ode,[1] is my best. I still feel that every poem is the last, and the interval of agony will make me prematurely old; for these intervals are long since I will never be a prolific writer of poetry. But I have been trying to write in the First Person, from the point of view of an Ideal Self; I find that this gives me the possibility (unrealized as yet) of greater sensuous range, since it permits me to exceed my personal observation. But I don't think it solves the problem of style, the solution of which seems to be this: that every phrase and line, in every poem of an author, implies every other phrase and line, and takes its place with reference to the whole body of his work.

Dec. 29. The onslaught of Christmas halted this letter. I will leave the discussion where it stands, and resume it a little later. Your note and the two poems have just come, and I want to speak of them.[2] "O! Let Not Virtue Seek" will run to about 145 lines in make-up, or six pages; so the question of publishing it will first of all have to wait upon the other writers, to see whether they fill the space allotted them. As a matter of fact, Collins has decided not to give us a whole issue of 128 pages; he's expanding to about 170, so that he can run some of his regular stuff, leaving us 96 pages. That cuts down each poet's space to 3 pages, or about 75 lines. Moreover, both Warren (who is here) and I agree that The Mothers is the better poem (one of your best), and while we want to publish the long one, knowing long poems are hard to place and that you can easily sell The Mothers elsewhere, we are naturally loath to give up what we think is the superior poem. What do you want us to do about it? The Mothers will take at least two pages, perhaps run over to the third. I think we should prefer to use it, and another poem even if the two poems together ran over your allotment.

I think the trouble with O Let Not Virtue Seek lies not in the style or the quality of the writing, but rather in the difficulty at present of writing such a poem without making it didactic. That is, your imagery is bound to be primarily illustrative. (In The Mothers the imagery *is* the poem, and likewise in your and anybody else's work at its best.) You've never done anything better than the closing lines (Coriolanus) but it is a poem of fine passages.[3] I didn't see this so clearly last year in Paris, but I see it now very distinctly right after my recent close study of your book.

I will get this off to you, and when I get your answer I will return to your longer, and very fine letter. Tell Margaret that I hope she will take care of herself. I almost ran off a thirty foot embankment last week. It is because our teeth have been set on edge. Love to you all.   Yrs. Allen   TLS

1. Tate's concern with style can be seen in his numerous revisions of the "Ode to the Confederate Dead," which did not reach a finished version until 1936.   2. Tate had just received Bishop's letter, above, containing "The Mothers" and "O Let Not Virtue Seek" as Bishop's additional contributions to the poetry issue of the *American Review*. Tate's selections of Bishop's work resulted in "The Mothers" and "Your Chase Had a Beast in View" being included in *American Review* 3 (May, 1934), 248–50.   3. The lines to which Tate refers are as follows:

> Now take
The height and shadow of our man, our noble
Coriolanus, who still armors the earth,
Albeit dead and never but a man,
And tell us once again what stature his
And what his stride, who nothing asked
Even of a god but his eternity!

January 3, 1934

Dear Allen: I am hurriedly sending you another work,[1] which may be just the right length to fit in after The Mothers. I think you may like it. For it is a little erotic allegory that nowhere deviates from the image. And being erotic it might be well to have it with the other piece.

I dare say I can send O Let Not Virtue Seek! to old Aunt Harriet. She likes things about aeroplanes. And the present poem is sufficiently obscure to put it out for most editors.[2]

The last line troubles me. Would

Confusing shame, confounding bone

be better? Also 'deep tendrils,' but I can't get anything better at the moment.

If Warren is there, he might consent to give me a criticism of O Let Not Virtue Seek! Not that I can do anything about that opus. But I want to do some other long blank verse things which will also carry opinions and if there is anything I can learn from this I'd like to do it. My guess is that it lacks organic form, the structure being intelligently imposed, but for all that imposed. Or maybe it's the material that is at fault. I've got a rough draft of a projected work probably to be called Timon and Alcibiades which needs dramatization.[3] And any hints I can get on it from a consideration of the faults of this other work will be grateful.

I won't attempt seriously to answer your letter. I am too disabled by New Year's festivities. When I get down to see you I'll bring a book by Boris de Schloezer on Stravinsky which has the best definition of style I have ever seen.[4] I really think it helps to get outside literature in trying to arrive at practical conclusions. For almost inevitably we confuse diction in some measure with style and naturally the fact that people write not only poems but newspaper articles in words makes it more difficult to see our medium unembarrassed of all but essentials. But of this more later.

I hope the year makes you rich and famous. If not, may it console you with lots of work and plenty to drink. John

You can make your choice of variants [to "Your Chase Had a Beast in View"].   TLS

1. "Your Chase Had a Beast in View."   2. *Poetry* did not publish "O Let Not Virtue Seek!"; it was eventually published in *Virginia Quarterly Review* 11 (April, 1935), 260–63.   3. This project was never completed.   4. *Igor Stravinsky* (1929).

243 North Potomac Street
[January, 1934]   Hagerstown, Maryland

Dear Allen: Will you do whatever you think fit about the poems? I trust you completely.

I have been in these parts some weeks with great profit to my novel. I am working, quality and quantity, in an unprecedented way. I am beginning to think it will be pretty good. And the end is in sight though I think there's another month of steady work.

Has your review appeared in the New Republic? I haven't seen it.[1]

I am too feeble to write more now.   As ever, JPB   AL

1. Tate's review of *Now With His Love* appeared in *New Republic* 78 (February 21, 1934), 52–53.

[May, 1934]

Dear Allen: I was just about to sit down to compose you a letter, when your own arrived with the check from Collins. It comes gratefully; I must buy some underdrawers and a bathing suit this afternoon in preparation for the summer.

We raced off with the [Gilbert] Seldeses ten days ago to look for a habitation—we are being put out here politely the 15th—and found one on Cape Cod. My address will be The Ford Cottage, South Harwich, Cape Cod, Massachusetts. We start moving Monday.

It belongs to a professor at Yale and is nicely placed in the pine woods, about a mile and a half from the village, between a small lake and the six mile beach. I wish you and Caroline could come up some time during our four months there. My recollection is that there is a guest room, but we saw so many cottages that I am a little vague.

I got slowed up on my opus when the date passed for spring publication. And also when I got into some very personal emotions at the end. I don't think this is the new novel you are looking for; but one reason I wanted to do it was that I thought if I could get down to certain emotions experienced in adolescence, I should not again suffer from too great pideur in writing. For I suppose that it is always in adolescence that we encounter our greatest shame.

Well, it is all written now, though I have quite a bit of revision to do.[1] The narrative is, of course, fictitious; nothing, except minor incidents, actually happened to me; but it is as near as I can make it an account of the true emotions of that period, seen with as much maturity as I could dramatically manage.

I look forward to seeing you before too long; we must manage it some how. I can't think of any more ramblings than are necessary until I get my proof corrected. Margaret and I are vaguely planning a huge motoring expedition in September and October, to start here and end up on the Pacific coast. I hope we can pull it off. I want to see this country.   Affectionately, John   TLS

1. Bishop did not finish revisions of the novel until late summer, 1934. The trial scene in the last section of the novel presented the most difficult problems of censorship and bulk.

June 4, 1934

Dear John: I am glad that I made it possible for you to buy the drawers and the swimming suit, and I only wish you were wearing the latter here every day with us in the river. Perhaps I am wishing that you could suffer with me the early summer lassitude of the South in which the merest effort wins one's highest praise. I am trying to get my work done so that we can take a trip this summer, in August, as far as Washington anyhow and maybe to New York. You and Margaret must not start west until September, so that we shall be here to provide a stopping place. But I shall probably not get the work done; we shall not take the trip; and we shall be here any time you all come by.

Did I tell you about our wreck? It happened on the first of April. I had just bought a new V-8, driven it 1800 miles, when a colored gentleman, who had just bought a second hand Pontiac, drove out of a side road through a stop sign and crashed into us. We were going fifty, he thirty. We turned over one and a quarter times. But miraculously no one was seriously injured. My car was ruined; the repairs would have cost as much as a new one. So I got the second new car, on credit of course, like the first, making my new Ford cost eleven hundred instead of seven. There is a tale of woe. I should add that the member of the oppressed race who did the damage hired a smart shyster lawyer who got [him] out without paying me a single cent, though he was absolutely to blame. You might write a New Republic article about it.

Have you seen Edmund's essay, The Canons of Poetry, in the April Atlantic?[1] I am glad to see that he is restoring his powers through legitimate criticism once more. It is a good piece of writing and a sound piece of criticism. One thing he misses: he seems to think that the modern breakdown of the conventions that upheld the departments of literature is necessarily permanent. He arrives at this by the historical argument; but another historical argument would hold that such breakdowns are strictly temporary, and that the normal sequence is not logical but rather up and down. I suppose the wing of K. Marx has cast a very deep shadow on Edmund. The most debatable point in his essay seems to come out of this. It is all very well to say that new experience breaks down old forms and conventions, but we have now almost reached the point where the new experience, if it is to be communicated, must instinctively impose limitations, and thus accept formal limitations, if it shall be expressed at all. I think Edmund's fallacy here lies in his failure to distinguish between science and literature. From the *logical* point of view any experience can receive some kind of treatment, but the imagination has no logical history, and there are times when [it] ceases to function in spite of a possible continuation of the scientific impluse. The continuation of this impulse Edmund thinks of as only another expression of the mind, and hence as "literature" like any other kind of literature. But his argument is based on an assumption of the very thing he wants to prove: he assumes that everything is literature, and then uses that assumption to prove that everything is literature. But the incidental observations throughout the article and the descriptive parts are quite sound. I would write him congratulations on his return to criticism, but I'm sure he would think I was twitting him.

I wish we could come to Cape Cod; we shall probably devoutly wish it if the heat here gets worse. But I fear we can't. It is an instance of limitations to live in one place.

I hope the last-minute work on the novel is done. I wish you would write some poetry now. Caroline is on the last lap of her book[2]—at present she is in East Tennessee with her father, in mountain solitude, writing the last 5000 words, where chickens, dogs, cows, and the rest of the farm cannot reach her. Love to Margaret.   Yrs. Allen   TLS

1. "The Canons of Poetry," *Atlantic Monthly* 153 (April, 1934), 455–62. This essay was reprinted in a slightly revised form as "Is Verse a Dying Technique?"   2. *Aleck Maury, Sportsman* (1934).

June 11, 1934   Ford Cottage, South Harwich Massachusetts

Dear Allen: It was nice to have a good long letter from you. But what a rotten accident yours was! To have a new car broken up by a darky and be defrauded of your rightful claims by a shyster lawyer—I should think you'd be sick and angry, those terms being rather synonymous in my make up.

I haven't seen Bunny's essay on Poetry in the Atlantic, though I made a tour to the free library here to sample it. (The library is only open on Saturdays, I discovered.) But I know that error of his. It's an old one. He thinks everything that's well written and that runs a chance of getting eventually into the manuals for schoolboys is litterature. He has never made the most necessary distinction between litterature as an art (I seem to have introduced a French spelling) and writing as a means of persuasion.

I was struck by the same thing in M. Josephson's article in the NR on Literary Life in Russia.[1] His modern novelist with the zipper pockets is doing what is undoubtedly a politically fine and economically necessary thing, quite as necessary as advertising was in America in the boom period. But why call it literature? It has exactly nothing to do with literature.

The trouble is that all the critics in this country (with very few exceptions) have to become journalists to live and they are affected not only by the trade they practice, but their feeling of inferiority and shame at practising it. Because journalism is not really *doing* anything; it is reporting, or occasionally forecasting acts done or to be done by others. Whereas, creative writing is very definitely doing, making. But Bunny won't see this.

And there is so much need for a critic in this country with just those gifts which Bunny is endowed with. If it wasn't for the ghost of Cotton Mather plowing under his conscience like a mole!

I will confess to you, though I must now say it privately, that I think this whole Marx rot stinks. I was quite impressed for some months after reading Das Kapital, but the longer I reflect on it, the more irrelevant Marx seems to me to any intelligent thought. And Socialism, as Wells very aptly says is a label on an old valise, representing a voyage that is accomplished. I am convinced that Socialism died the hour the German socialists voted the war credits.

Bunny would perhaps agree to that, but would suppose that Communism is its successor. Ils crient et je n'ai pas peur.

You'll be surprised at my quoting Wells, but I picked up the World of William Clissold here the other night and was amused by his description of Marx and also of the prewar socialists.[2] A good bit in an unspeakable book.

I was sorry not to see any other signs of your activity in the American Review than that of editor of the Poetry section. You have it so far over your Southern contemporaries that I cannot, when reading them, but compare them unfavorably with you.

I thought The Mothers good, the other opus punk. Publication helps discrimination, says author of own work. However I bought a most lascivious bathing suit, but so far it's been so cold up here that I have been the only one excited by it. The children went in the ocean today, however, and I plan to go down tomorrow.

I have done little but work on my novel, revision as always with me going more slowly than composition. I am now once more in my trial scene, which I think is going to be good. Then I'll have the final chapter to rewrite and I'll send it to Max Perkins. By that time I think I'll have to have proof, in order to get a fresh view.

I think I've been able to get around the obscenity in the court records I am working from, though there's one Molly Bloom gesture

I'd like to keep, where the lady is made to put her hand on the gentleman's cock. It's really very important in the evidence, but I can't quite see it getting by the Scribner office. As a matter of fact, it might be more effective to merely imply what happened, if I could do that. After the seduction of Wazemmes in the new Jules Romains opus* which no one has complained of in the courts, such a gesture ought to be possible. But I should like to get an effect of horrible obscenity without using any but the chastest words.

I like it here very much, aside from the fogs and clouds which almost all month have covered the sky. Most of the people are Bostonians returning to the Cape each summer, some are here the year round. There is certainly much in them preferable to the same class in New York and in most aspects of Cape life I find a fundamental and ancestral decency which I can only approve of, so unspoilt is it, and so perfectly in accord with the landscape.   I wish I could see you. I miss your talk. John

Have you read this? The best novel in years.[3]   TLS

1. Matthew Josephson, "The Literary Life in Russia," *New Republic* 79 (June 6, 1934), 90–93.   2. H. G. Wells, *The World of William Clissold: A Novel at a New Angle* (1926).   3. Felix Wazemmes is a character in Romains's *Les hommes de bonne volonté*, a series of twenty-seven novels dealing with early twentieth-century French life. The seduction of Wazemmes figures in volumes one and two, both copyrighted in 1932.

July 15th, 1934

Dear Allen: I have been sunk in a haze of laziness for the past ten days and now am getting around to answering your letter.[1] The sun and an active life have been too much for me. I suppose I'm storing up reserves against the winter, but the dear old mind simply ceases to function. I have got to get back a little while into the introspective rut and finish up my work.

I congratulate Caroline in all envy at completing her novel.[2] I have more or less promised mine to Max the 1st of August. Two weeks of good work will do it, but not such work in spare hours of loafing as I have lately done.

I like the Meaning of Death very much.[3] But, in line 11 I dislike *in to at*: line 14, shouldn't 'would' be 'should'? I like the sound better. I would think about the end of the following line and beginning of the next (which I see starting on the word 'yesterday.' Those five little words together bother me, particularly "it."

In the next paragraph I don't take to the little Lord Fauntleroy line. And I'm not sure about 'at home.' Where else would a small boy live? The idea is right, but 'at home' falls a little flat. And Lord F seems to me localized in the wrong way. That is, the connotations are too many beside the right one. I think the line could be dropped altogether without harm. I'd cut out "tupping in the public square." It stops the movement of the paragraph as a whole.

If these are flaws, they are small ones in an excellent poem. The later Ivory Tower gets off to a good start, but I am not sold on the prostate.[4] Can't you get some word that will imply the whole sexual activity? I know the prostate is the mainspring, but I would suggest a less definitely physiological word. And I would end the poem on "food is set." The crack at Bunny is misplaced.

I am glad to hear that John Herrman is to be dismissed. God! what a depression that was! I wish Edmund could be brought round. I expect to see him soon. He is supposed to arrive on Cape Cod (Provincetown) circa today. The Walkers are, I hear, at Well Fleet. I suppose they will all three suffer together. I don't know why they choose that desolate end of the Cape unless to afflict their souls. It is a real Waste Land: sand dunes and neurotics creeping slimily through the vegetation, which consists exclusively of eel grass.

We live here odorous with pine and sea, the small houses at the moment embowered pink in roses. I like it very much, lie in the sun, bathe, and occasionally sail, a sport at which I am most ignorant, but can hold a tiller if somebody else sets the sails. I have even tried a bit of deep sea fishing, which left me exhausted for two days.

You can see from all this that the social problem weighs on me very little. In fact I don't let myself think about anything but the moral problems involved in my novel, which, the sun being what it is, I find quite sufficient to hold me. I have read a few books, Malraux's Condition Humaine (very good) but not at all what the revolutionists consider it, a Chinese Testament and Mann's Joseph, which I hold to be quite a remarkable exposition of the religious mind.

I can give you a poem for the Westminster [Review] if you'll take one already achieved, such as The Senator. But I can't undertake to write a piece just now.

I have finished up all the revision of my trial scene except the speeches of the lawyers. I wish you were here to help me with those. I have them written, but I am afraid of weighting the book too much with legal verbosity, particularly as my hero's statements on the witness stand run to thirty pages. They took me almost a month to write, but I don't think they can be cut much. The trial is really over before the speeches get under way, but since my hero is condemned, I think I have got to give some of them, particularly the speech that sends him to the penitentiary. But even in the Brothers Karamazov, which is the best criminal book I know, the lawyer's speeches are almost intolerably boring. However, I expect to come to a final decision on this tomorrow and then start revising my final long chapter.

This place would be almost as good as the Riviera could we only

have you and Caroline hereabouts. I find a great respect for the literary here (a relic of the Concord movement I suppose) but no one with
sense enough to talk to on a practical subject. My friend, Henry
Chapin was up last week with an epic on Leif Ericson for me to look
over. Maybe that was what broke my labors and sent me for the last
ten days into a wholesome sensual life.   My best to you both, John
TLS

1. Tate's letter has not survived.   2. *Aleck Maury, Sportsman* appeared in the fall,
1934.   3. "The Meaning of Death" first appeared in *New Verse* 2 (March, 1933), 9–10,
and later in *Hound and Horn* 7 (October-December, 1933), 42. Tate apparently considered but rejected Bishop's objections and criticisms.   4. "The Ivory Tower" was
collected in *The Mediterranean and Other Poems* (1936), but never published separately.

October 9, 1934   2374 Forrest Avenue/Memphis, Tenn.[1]

Dear John: I am very much annoyed. I have just reached the place
where Aunt Maria has arrived to see what the hullabaloo is about,
and cetera desunt.[2] I want to go on, and I hope the rest of the proof
will arrive very quickly.

I am returning what I have. I have gone through it pretty carefully, marking whatever places I though ought to be changed just as if
I were reading my own proof. You can see immediately what I have
marked. There are no great changes that I thought necessary. In your
letters this summer you spoke of a lot of possible cutting in the first
part of the book. You surely have done it already; I don't see how you
could drop large sections, or small ones, in Book I. It is very closely
written; but of course, not having seen the end, I can't tell whether it
anticipates too much. In itself Book I is just as it ought to be.

You will see that I became a little alarmed at the change of
viewpoint with the fornication between Charlie and Ardista. Of
course you've got to change the point of view, but I wish it could be
done less violently where the scene is not so conspicuous. It may be
that the non-technical reader will be so absorbed with the event that
he will not notice the change; if so, all right. It is impossible to decide
for whom novels are written.

That is the only technical criticism so far in what I've read. I have
one other major criticism, however, and that is the character of Miss
Lillian. She is absolutely the only character who doesn't come off
beautifully. I think she is a little overdone. You want to show Charlie
there—that is your purpose—but she runs away with the scene. She
isn't convincing. I believe you could still improve her by cutting her
part in the conversation to about half. The young whore who takes
John upstairs is good, and so is John there too; you don't want to ruin
an otherwise good scene.

I thought I would postpone my general reflections until I shall have read the entire book. But no. It is a very fine piece of work, and in places magnificent. Your mastery over your characters is much greater than in Many Thousands Gone. You have gained a great deal of power with your greater restraint. You may remember that I mildly criticized the stories for the external judgment that you passed upon the action at times. There is none of that here. Your dialogue is very fine; I am astonished at it when I remember that you've been away from it for years. If the first duty of a novelist is to create characters and let them create the action, you have succeeded wonderfully. Every character is a recognizable type, but only secondarily. The grandfather and Aunt Maria are splendid, perfect in fact; I doubt if you could have done them five years ago. (I was amused to see my father's advice in your grandfather of the novel; it was given me a little more abruptly, but with a good deal of your implication).

One reason why the characters represent their generation in the South is that you've resisted the impulse to make them represent anything. Charlie is perfect for his generation, and of course Aunt Maria's diagnosis of his trouble is exactly right. Charlie is the generation of transition from planting to politics to business; the transition was pretty bad.

The amount of social and human insight that you've put into this book vastly exceeds anything else I've seen from the South. If we're going to have novels about degeneracy in the South, it is well to have them written by persons who know (1) the South and (2) what degeneracy is. The worst kind of degeneracy—if the word means what it ought to, a decline from race—is that which misrepresents it. That is why so much of the social literature of degeneracy is boring; it is more depraved, with all its moral purpose, than the evil it attacks.

There's one other difficulty in the book; I can't be sure about it till I've read to the end. What about the motivation of Virginia's prosecution of Charlie? It will be quite all right to bring that out in the course of the trial, but so far it isn't plain. She is a New Woman, living for the public, donating parks and voting, etc., but still there's not quite enough specific psychological history behind her action. The night after the fornication her rehearsal of the scene could be made to prepare for her subsequent conduct, I think, if you could put a little more time in on it, and show that the psychic mechanism that drives her to have Charlie arrested is purely unconscious and below volition. As it stands, the reader must infer that the act was deliberate and conscious, though I know that is not what you want. And it is not clear. Is it too late to do anything about it? If it is I shall regret mentioning it; since if you agree with me it will be very annoying.

I will await the rest of the proof with enormous pleasure.

If you are going to the Gulf, you will want to avoid Florida. Try

Biloxi and the Riviera thereabouts. It is an old resort, and the architecture and the people are not unpleasing. You will go to New Orleans. Let me know when; there are friends there. We expect to spend Christmas in N.O.* Warren is at Baton Rouge, 90 miles away, at L.S.U.

Love to you both, and many congratulations,   Affectionately, Allen

*Unless you & Margaret will come up to our house, which we should like to open for the occasion. It's an easy two days from the Gulf. TLS

1. Tate joined the faculty of Southwestern at Memphis in the fall of 1934.   2. A character in *Act of Darkness;* Tate is reading proof of the novel.

October 26, 1934

Dear John: I am rushing the proofs back to you, and I will say at present only that I think the book is a great success. It comes off beautifully. And of course, Boyd's speech not only explains Virginia's motives for the prosecution, it convinces the reader that the explanation was implicit from the time Virginia got home after the fornication. So my chief doubt in the psychological aspect of the situation is cleared up. On the whole I do not think that the writing is as sharp after the trial begins as before; but it tightens up again when the trial is over. The last chapter is very fine. When the discussion of evil began, I got a little nervous lest you'd fall off the tightrope, and I had to put the pages down for a few minutes when I saw Othello coming: I knew it would be either a huge success or a miserable failure. You may now judge what I consider it to be. I still don't see how it was done. If our friend Edmund had done it—as he did do it with Sophocles—it would have been off the top of his mind and unrelated to what surrounded it. I venture to doubt whether you know how you did it, or whether you could establish a purely logical or structural necessity for an outburst of eloquence that would have wrecked the book had it been wrong. Only a poet does these things properly. It is one of those unnecessary and excessive statements that manage sometimes to be inevitable.

I would much rather talk about this. I thought Charlie was a perfect type even before the trial, but you lead him to heights that I did not expect. Of course all societies destroy themselves, and I think you have given for the first time the picture of the South in the process of self-destruction. Grandfather was all of a piece; the self destruction didn't begin until the next generation. That is always true. You have handled so many aspects of the situation that I can't begin to notice them all in a brief letter. And certainly Virginia would go off to a place to study marine zoology, because the women are never destroyed;

they are eternal, and wait to be mastered by some male order of the future.

Take the characters as such, apart from the meaning of their relations, I still think the boy's mother the most perfectly drawn and the grandfather's the roundest though not the most profoundly conceived—that is Charlie. How in God's name you were capable of so much sheer sensuous memory after being away from the scene more than twenty years I cannot understand. Grandfather is a great feat of imaginative memory. I can't see in him the slightest distortion due to your own exposure to a great variety of later experience and ideas. But I must quit this. It will get so that you won't believe it.

Caroline's book is out and she awaits your permanent address so that she can send a copy.[1] It seems that Perkins is going to make a valiant effort to sell it, and we hope to God he succeeds.

We have some dear friends in New Orleans—a young couple who lived with us in a cabin on our place last year: Manson and Rose Radford. You could reach Manson—I've misplaced his own address—in care of his father-in-law, Mr. Edmond Chavanne, 1666 Dufossat Street. Of course he knows all about you. He says that we were a part of his education—that will indicate his age and say quite enough about our own. Manson is a good, but still experimenting poet, and very intelligent. I am sure that you will both like both of them. Rose has done some very good pictures, one of them having Caroline for subject, another Caroline's late cook at Benfolly.

I think you must be finding New Orleans a grand place. I wish I were there with you. Love to Margaret,   Yrs. Allen   TLS

1. *Aleck Maury, Sportsman.*

3211 Prytania Street
November 2, 1934   New Orleans, Louisiana

Dear Allen: Your letter pleased me no end. You are quite right in saying that the trial scene is not up to the rest. I felt that very much in reading revised galleys. But I doubt if I could have done better. I spent about two months on it and it does contain all the points I needed to make. But I felt no ease in the courtroom. It was one of those backgrounds I had to 'get up.' And besides, I was intimidated, first, by fear of going wrong legally, and secondly by the enormous mass of evidence I had to digest and compress from the original trial. The actual court records ran to something like 900 pages.

I am glad that you feel I have carried off the social history. You will have noticed that every generation from the first settlement of the county on is briefly touched: Charles Lee, the Justice, Caroline's great-grandfather (Senator Mason): then the Civil War generation in the grandfather and Aunt Maria. The following generation was the hardest to do. They are so formless. There is no center [?] in Caroline, for instance.

But beyond setting down [as] correctly as I could the character of each generation, realized, of course, in individuals, not types, I wanted to show the world of evil slowly being revealed to the boy narrator. In the Act of Darkness I was trying to find an evil action, one not easily to be attributed to heredity, environment, or deficient glands, though for credibility's sake I suggested various elements in all these influences that might have brought Charlie to the rape, as well as an emotional sequence of which it was the culmination, not logical, but necessary.

The return of all this action into the boy's mind was the hardest to do, for I could no longer write a scene to a chapter, which is for me the simplest way to write, and the only dramatic way. And I felt the end—after the trial—had to be brief. The greater part of the Portrait of the Artist is concerned with a similar problem. But Joyce could afford a bulk that I couldn't.

The result of Charlie's crime on the boy is hypochondria and psychological blindness. I had to bring him to accept evil, which he does first in the form of death (the death theme is the first introduced, in Chapter I not only in the boy's father dying, but Charlie enters with death in his hands) then in the shape of sex. But I had also to bring in light, both physical, what Yeats calls "spontaneous joy and natural content," [and] intellectual radiance. I used Othello, I suppose, primarily because of a similar experience with that tragedy at the age of 18. It was from reading it, that I had the first clear and comparatively complete illumination of the office of poetry, which until then had meant to me mostly lyrical poetry. Perhaps, as another, I allowed the boy to understand more consciously what I then only excitedly felt. But, dangerous as the scene was to do, I hope it is psychologically sound. Under the circumstances, there are for that boy only two solutions: the religious or the poetic. And the inclusion of Othello, and consequently Iago, allowed me to say certain things about Charlie that I could not otherwise have said.

This is my justification for the use of a literary scene. They are, I agree, very dangerous, as Edmund's novel proved.[1] If they fail, they wreck the book.

We have decided to settle down here for the winter, having been converted to New Orleans after a few days. The impression on entering the city was unfortunate.

I think we've found a house. I expect to give a decision this afternoon. It is ideal except for filth. Most of that can, I suppose, be eradicated with soap, water, and paint.

It was in our first moments of discouragement that we thought of proceeding to Memphis. Later, that project began to look impossible much as we wanted to see you and Caroline. Margaret, having once stopped, was very tired, and it seemed rather excessive to undertake so long a journey for what would necessarily have been a very brief visit with you. Besides, I believe that you are spending Christmas here.

I am most anxious to see Caroline's novel. We'll stay here another ten days at least, while the house is being fixed up—if we take that one. And if not we'll still be here, as we must go on looking.   Sincerely, JPB   AL

1. *I Thought of Daisy* (1929).

1934-1939

Following Tate's assumption of an academic career and Bishop's completion of *Act of Darkness*, his only published novel, their courses ran parallel for a time, then began to diverge, as the letters of these years show. Bishop followed his novel with a book of poems, *Minute Particulars* (1935), while Tate, having thrown over his "ancestry book," began work on his first critical volume, *Reactionary Essays* (1936). Spending his summers in Clarksville, Tate laments in 1935 that "it was fatal to live in a city [Memphis] for a year; it threw me off my routine, and now my routine throws me off my work."

Bishop, on the other hand, after living for a short time in Connecticut upon his return from France, stayed in New Orleans for a year, then moved to Cape Cod, where he assumed permanent residence. During the years 1936–1939, he turned his attention to writing essays, which earned him a substantial reputation as a literary critic, while Tate resumed work on his only novel, *The Fathers* (1938), an outgrowth of the "ancestry book," after co-editing with Herbert Agar the collection of Agrarian essays, *Who Owns America?* (1936). Tate's absorption in these latter enterprises, along with the preparation of his *Selected Poems* (1937), occupied most of his time not devoted to teaching. Bishop was preoccupied during the same period with selling his home in France and building a new home, Sea Change, on Cape Cod. These various separate concerns account for the sparseness of the correspondence between the fall of 1936 and the fall of 1938.

After a year of writing and another of teaching at the Women's College in Greensboro, North Carolina, Tate accepted a position in 1939 as resident poet in the Creative Arts Program at Princeton. The move marked formal recognition of his stature among writers and scholars and brought him and Bishop geographically and spiritually closer. At the close of this section of correspondence, Bishop is again returning to serious writing after settling permanently at Sea Change and emerging from a rather severe depression. Depression was to plague him, off and on, for the rest of his life. His rejuvenation this time resulted at least partially from his participation with Tate and others in a writers' conference at Savannah, Georgia, in the spring of 1939, and partially, too, from the knowledge that he and Tate would again be within visiting distance.

November 7, 1934   2374 Forrest Ave./Memphis, Tenn.

Dear John: We were disappointed at your failure to come. A distinct wave of depression rolled over us after the news. But we shall have a pleasant two weeks in December, far pleasanter, I am sure, than we should have in this town, which is incredible. It is a collection of some 200,000 savages making a noise on a high bluff above the Father of Waters. Neither northern nor southern, but that special product that could come out of the Delta only.

Of course we are delighted that you and Margaret are spending the winter down there near us. Are the boys with you? I suppose so.

I am inclined to think that you did in your novel even better than you intended. Most writers plan a book and have to write up to the plan, but you had to write down to it; that is, your book is richer than the pattern—which is as it should be. I suppose this is to say that the best part of any piece of literature is the unconscious element. Every novelist must plan to present types, but if he is good he creates characters, without knowing that he is creating them. That is certainly true of Tolstoy, who was always better than he meant to be.

I don't think it would be tactful for me to review the novel, but I hope you will pass on to Perkins anything in my letters that may strike you as being useful. When is the book coming out?

This will be a particularly futile year for me, but if I can get some money ahead I shall perhaps feel like doing a little work after June. My debts oppressed me so that I could write nothing.

What are you planning to write this winter? I hope poetry. . . . I was again disappointed in Edmund's latest essays in the N.R. [1] Well written; well-organized; but fundamentally wrong in the assumptions. Love to Margaret,   Yrs ever, Allen

P.S. I believe I forgot to say that our definite plan is to come down for two weeks Christmas. It would be pleasant if you all drove up and met us in Natchez. We could see the town together under the guidance of friends who are natives.   TLS

1. Edmund Wilson's series under the title "Decline of the Revolutionary Tradition": "Renan," *New Republic* 80 (September 19, 1934), 150–53; "Taine," (October 3), 207–10; "Anatole France," (October 24), 302–7.

December 18, 1934

Dear John: You do sound a little doleful, and I can barely hope that I will cheer you up. Perhaps the wines and fines of New Orleans will assist us to interinanimate our souls. We are going first to Clarksville, leaving there on the morning of the 26th; we should arrive in N.O. in mid-afternoon of the 27th. We are, of course, leaving Nancy with one of her aunts, but we shall bring Andrew Lytle, our great friend and one of the most charming persons alive. I want you all to meet him. He knows your work and wants to meet you.

It is nice of you and Margaret to want to keep us. We shall doubtless move in upon you if the beds at the Radfords overflow as they are likely to when the Warrens and their cohorts arrive. Wherever we stay we shall expect to pass a good portion of every day with you.

I enclose some verses for your meditation before I arrive. They are my total output in exactly a year. They will not strain your critical faculties.

The only good news here of recent date is that Aleck Maury has been sold for English publication in the spring. That, really, makes the trip south possible. Love to Margaret.   Yrs, Allen   TLS

February 5, 1935   2105 State Street/New Orleans, La.

Dear Allen: It was nice to get your letter after so long a silence. I quite agree with you about the poems. I seem to be in a spiritual lethargy: I have been trying to remember emotions in too great a tranquility. I'll send you some more, though I don't think anything I've done here amounts to more than a means of passing the time.

Still, I think, it is better to do something than to sink despairingly into idleness. I am not yet ready to tackle another novel, though one is shaping up in my mind. And I do believe that the only way to get anything accomplished is to utilize these dead spaces in one's life, if only to the point of doing finger exercises. Before, I have found that sometimes translation is a good way to get going again.

In going over these last winter verses, my hope was that something new would spring from them, but so far nothing better than the three I sent you has arrived. It is the hell of having a job which is not under the control of the will.

I am very glad that Caroline is doing the NR review.[1] It needs a Southerner to see some of the social implications. Though I must say that curiosity makes me wonder what Cowley would have made of the book.

There is one point in the book which I only thought of yesterday, placed there by instinct, but I think sound. In the grandfather's generation, men assume the intelligent control, women have the eternal and traditional energy. Now, one of the things that is all wrong with Charlie and Virginia's generation (as well as our own) is that they reverse this. Women have assumed the intelligent guidance (cf, Shaw and all of Norah's daughters) while men represent pure energy. The whole liberal movement, passing into the hands of women has become the stupidest humanitarianism, pacifism, etc. Men have gone fascist, communist (though there is a strong feminine side to communism) anything that represents pure energy. The act without the thought. What is really new about fascism (new for the last few centuries anyhow) is that it has no theory. Of course, in a bourgeois society the men tend to turn all the 'finer things' over to women, as they formerly turned them over to the court. They must have someone to take care of these things, not themselves. And that is not women's job. I am thinking of going into this much more deeply in my next opus.

Act of Darkness is as lousy looking as all Scribner books, but I failed to find any proof errors on my one reading. And that must be pretty near a record for them. The American Book News (a trade journal for the bookstores) concludes its notice with two beautiful words—*Will sell.* I hope to God they are right.

Walsh came in about nine o'clock one night.[2] I fed him cawn and liked him until about eleven. After one he became irksome and at two I was ready for murder. He's Irish, and that's the way they affect me.

By the way, have you made any trenchant observations on the Southern jew. I am thinking of including one in my next opus.

I can't find the Humanist jigger. The other day, I by an accident of the typewriter keys coined a fine word and started one on Wilson and the Communists. All about how he was bogeyman for Louise and wily with Elinor, but now when he asks for a broad they give him a Stein. The Commonest sectatarian, when he tries to get in, calls him a Wolfsohn in sheep's clothing.

Well, courage mon vieu. I am just reading Lawrence's letters.[3] None of us has an easy time, even genius is no cure all. John

P.S. 1. I am sending some verses.

P.S. 2. I wonder if Caroline's success hasn't had something to do with your silence. I don't mean that you begrudge it to her, nor that she doesn't richly deserve it, and more. But the relation between a man & a woman is very complicated. Think this over.   Sigmund F. Jr.

P.S. 3. Also, isn't it possible that Marse Robert and his cohorts have failed you. I felt that talking to Radford. He is using them as private protective guards. You *never* have. But you probably [need] a new departure. Forgive me if I am intrusive. But I mean well. JPB   TLS

1. Caroline Gordon Tate's review of *Act of Darkness*, "The Shadow of Defeat," appeared in *New Republic* 82 (March 27, 1935), 192.   2. Thomas Walsh, an employee in the sales department of Scribners.   3. *The Letters of D. H. Lawrence*, ed. Aldous Huxley (1932).

March 9, 1935

Dear John: Your letters, as you know, have every prospect of being answered immediately. Your latest arrived at the moment I was undoing my decision not to write an article for the anniversary issue of the Va. Quart. I wrote it—in one day; revised it in one more; and got it in just at the dead-line.[1] Think as well of it as you can; it is on a subject of their choosing, not mine; it has two hundred loose ends.

I suppose you have seen the Westminster Review containing Fletcher's lucubrations on the Southern poets including you.[2] The thing as a whole seems to me bad; but he is less bad on you, [I] think, than on any of the others; his worst effort is about me. It butters no parsnips to get labelled genius. I hadn't thought that I wrote altogether about death. Of course I am grateful for the romantic image of me that he builds up—roving life, precocity and ferocity, Jesuit influence. Anyhow I wrote a little doggerel in reply which I'll send with this if I can turn up a copy.

I do think he missed everybody badly but you. His point about your religious preoccupation is sound, and he makes it in a convincing manner up to the last sentence, where he muddles his point with the phrase "heterodoxy of disbelief in progress." But he is more sensitive to your varied range than he is to the narrower range of the rest of us. This may be due to his not knowing you personally. He overrates Davidson wonderfully, and he doesn't really get Ransom, nor, I think, Warren. On the whole his section about you is the best thing on the subject I've seen.

Red tells me that you will be present at Baton Rouge in April. We shall try to get down for the occasion, though I can't imagine what it will be like. I suspect that Red just wants to amuse himself. I am willing to help him.

I had to break this off—to be resumed.   Yrs, Allen   TLS

1. "The Profession of Letters in the South," *Virginia Quarterly Review* 11 (April, 1935), 161-75.   2. John Gould Fletcher was a frequent contributor to the *Westminster Review* during and after his extended expatriation.

[March-April, 1935]

Dear Allen: I liked your essay in the Quarterly, even though it has less finish than I am accustomed to expect from your name. Particularly I am impressed by your remark about the relation of the Southerner to the soil being disturbed by the negroes. This seems to me profound in its truth and in it implications.

I have done no work for a month. The end of Carnival, with its late hours, its drinks and its balls; then Mardi Gras with my brother and sister-in-law from Connecticut here for the festivities; finally Margaret's illness which ensued on her fatigue have cut into my time and destroyed my spirit. She is now back from the hospital, where she had to spend a week, but still in bed, with the consequence that I am mother, father, housekeeper, nurse and general errand boy.

The Alcestis Press wants to bring out a small book of my poems in a limited edition.[1] I am trying to work out how I can combine this with the lot I have promised Warren. Alcestis will not object to previous publication in magazines. The real trouble is whether I have enough first or second rate poems to make up the list, which, I should say, ought not to exceed fifteen.

I just sold Cowley a little poem called Southern Pines,[2] which resulted from my depression at the devastation of the piney barrens on the coastal plain. He wrote decently about the novel; said he had decided not to review it for fear of running into theory. Does that mean a change of heart?

I have been reading the Hour of Decision.[3] Some of the Marxist boys ought to undertake a real answer to Spengler, instead of throwing up their hands in horror. Most of it seems to me unanswerable. But EW writes me he is reading Marx and Engels in the original German in order to do some articles for the NR. Holy horror!

In the next few days I'll try to make up a batch of poems for you to look at, first with a view of selecting those you want for Warren's magazine, second with the hope that you will advise me on the book.

Yes, I thought JGF did me rather well in the Westminster. Although being told I am religious leaves me about as blank as your being told you are a genius. The real trouble with this place, otherwise so charming, is that all spiritual pressure is lacking. And the heat seems to have had a most emasculating effect on me, so that I can't even write erotic poems. Or maybe that is age creeping up on me.

Fletcher himself I thought the most unmitigated bore I had encountered in years. It wasn't that what he said was without interest, but that he destroyed it in his saying it.

I hope you are coming down to Baton Rouge, as I am planning to be there. What is Caroline doing? I have made no progress on my new novel; I can't seem to get a plot sufficient to put the material in motion.   As ever, John   TLS

1. *Minute Particulars* (New York: The Alcestis Press, 1935).   2. *New Republic* 83 (July 24, 1935), 305.   3. A study by Oswald Spengler (1880-1936), translated by Charles Francis Atkinson and published in New York by A. A. Knopf in 1934.

May 4, 1935

Dear Allen: There can be no end to our vicissitudes. After measles, the whooping cough has invaded the family. And I have had a long seance with the dentist, which leaves me depressed and groggy.

This will explain why I have let your last letter go so long unanswered. I did appreciate it.

The Baton Rouge expedition did not exactly leave me light-hearted. I feel that you have done a great deal for the Southern writer (I am not here referring to your personal aid to me) in helping him define his position and consider the existing value of his heritage. All of them owe much to your courage in attack, your fearlessness in defense. But among some of the speeches and much of the conversation, I felt an intolerable complacency, a sinking back into the comfortably warm, if slimy, waters of the home pond, an incorrigible self-sufficiency, qualities all of them which will not, I think, help Southern writing, or any writing that affects to be a creation of the spirit. I am trying to work some of these reactions out in an essay, which I will let you see.

Edmund wrote me at length on my novel, presenting, I think, the debacle of the opposing point of view. He surprisingly confesses that he thinks the agrarian life of the older America superior to anything that has come since. (This is a propos of my presentation of the "late" period of this life.) He is sailing today for Russia.

Very curiously, for the American authority on symbolism, he failed to detect a single symbol in *Act of Darkness*, but took it all as straight realistic narrative. He sent me some poems in his early manner, which do not mention the proletarian revolution. I await with interest his reactions to Russia: but what I fear is that with his radical connections he will come in contact chiefly with the ruling class. And every country looks pretty good from their viewpoint.

I have been reading some books on the U.S.S.R. and am convinced that they haven't, after fifteen years, the faintest semblance of an economic system.

On the other hand, I think your Agrarian program ignores the time-factor, although I find a number of people who never heard of the Fugitives agreeing that it is the only possible solution to our present ills. The existing agricultural system is doomed. Everybody in New Orleans knows it. But to change to another and sounder one would require nothing short of a revolution, and would have to be put through ruthlessly and under menace of the machine gun. The weakness of all attempts to restore subsistence farming is that the existing farmers, with rare exception, do not know how to farm. This is true, North, West and South. The pioneer has to be liquidated before there can be any decent civilization in this country, and that my require so long a time that America will be a desert before it is accomplished.

I have given, alas, but few thoughts to literature since I saw you.   Affectionately, JPB   AL

May 5, 1935

Dear John: I've been very busy with my essays, to say nothing of teaching; so even now this won't be a letter. A few days after I got back from Baton Rouge, Red wrote me that he was running your poems in the fall number; so I decided that I would not write my critique until about mid-summer. Maybe you will have new poems to add to the group, and naturally I want the final selection before I begin.[1] And maybe you will write one of your best. You have my prayers.... I hope I have yours. We need all the praying we can get.

I will write more soon. I hope Margaret is now entirely restored. What are your plans? Cape Cod or where? I think Benfolly will see us, and I'll be damned glad to see it.

By the way I'm negotiating with Lovat Dickson in England for a book of verse, which will include the best stuff from my two previous books and about ten poems since 1931. If any general advice occurs to you I am ready to receive it, the sooner the better. I find that the earliest possible poem goes back to 1924. Ten years of versifying and about forty-five pieces that only a conscience half dormant would let pass. Do you think those ten sonnets ought to go in?[2] I think they are terrible, but I hear the opposite from persons here and there. They are so personal I can't judge them.   Yrs ever, in haste, Allen   TLS

1. Bishop was well represented in the Autumn, 1935, number of *Southern Review*. His contributions included: "The Burning Wheel," "Loss in the West," and "O Pioneers!" (published under the group title "Experience of the West"); "The Saints"; "Another Actaeon"; "Holy Nativity"; "Apparition"; "Counsel of Grief"; "Farewell to New York." The poems were printed consecutively, pp. 343–56 of that issue.   2. Tate published *The Mediterranean and Other Poems* (New York: Alcestis Press, 1936) and included two of the "Sonnets at Christmas" but none of the "Sonnets of the Blood."

June 7, 1935

Dear Allen: We leave here in a few days for the Walker Cottage, South Harwich, Massachusetts, a place we've rented sight unseen and which I therefore regard dubiously.

Anyhow, that will be the address until September 15th.

Three months of illness hasn't helped my temper much and the effect on literature and finance has been deplorable. However, I think we ought to be through with children's diseases for a while.

I have had a brief spurt of poetic energy which, if it keeps up, ought to give you a decent offering for the Southern Review. If it really keeps up, I should have a long poem; if it doesn't I'll turn what I have already done on it into a sequence.

The cheques from Columbus have continued to come so far.[1] But fingers are crossed and there's no telling what another month will bring. I think I would almost welcome a job if it would take me out of the nursery for a while. I am so fed up with living in a house where three children are continuously present (which they have been since March) that I am ready to shovel coal to escape them.

Jonathan Cape is bringing out Act of Darkness in England. I hear it has not sold here. Something was awfully wrong with the way Scribner handled it, for if the press was good, it was very small. I had more reviews on Now With His Love than on the novel.[2] That seems bad management.

[E. E.] Cummings and Marian passed through the other day and we all spent a fine evening together. He tells me that the Russian embassy first refused a passport to Bunny. Then somebody from the American Civil Liberties Union (that may have been a joke, but somebody with Troyanovsky's ear) told the cock-eyed bastard that he had pulled enough stupid tricks for one season and to let EW go to Roosia. It seems the objection was that he had signed a manifesto censuring the Soviet muckitimucks for murdering their opponents after the Kirov assassination.

Bunny told Cummings recently that the trouble with him was, his textbooks were out of date. My god! Can't the man grow up? Why should anyone his age still have to have a textbook? And as for his own—none of them are later than 1870.

I gather from EEC that the comrades are very impotently active in NYC and that there is no escaping them. Natalia Naboukoff asked Marian what was the matter. She said, Last year when I was going out in the evening, I had a bath and perfumed my body and painted my face and put on my best clothes and got some attention from men. This year I did the same thing, and all anybody ever talks to me about are methods of production.

Esther [Strachey] I hear has gone Utopian, which is a way of being communist without bothering to understand Marx. I thought John's last book very good, that is, as good as modern marxism can be.[3]

Dickie Ames is dead. I don't know whether you remember him.   Affectionately, John   TLS

---

1. Margaret Bishop was from Columbus, Ohio, and was independently wealthy. Apparently, these are returns from her investments.   2. *Act of Darkness* appeared two days after Thomas Wolfe's *Of Time and the River* was published (also by Scribner's). Maxwell Perkins explained that this coincidence would help sales of Bishop's novel, but Bishop's notices in Scribner's catalogue were much smaller than Wolfe's.   3. John Strachey, *The Nature of Capitalist Crisis* (New York: Covici, Friede, 1935).

Route 6, Clarksville, Tennessee
From July 8 to August 1st:
July 3, 1935   Olivet College, Olivet, Michigan

Dear John: Yours of the 7th ult. I have tried in vain to get around to
for all this time. We had a dreadful ordeal opening our house. We had
an impulse that had to be conquered: when your letter came we
wanted extremely to wire you and Margaret to come by here, but the
chaos was still so great that we couldn't have brought it to order in
time to receive you.

What a waste of effort it was after all! We are leaving for Olivet,
Michigan, to be around the school of writing from July 9th to August
3rd—we leave in four days. I hate to go, but the honorarium—as they
have it—is too good to miss.[1]

I've accomplished absolutely nothing since we came home. The
revision of two essays stands between me and a book, but chores
have been too distracting. It was fatal to live in a city for a year; it
threw me off my routine, and now my routine throws me off my work.

I have been annoyed by Scribner's treatment of your book.
Caroline's was special enough to confuse them, but yours is definitely
a novel, and there's no excuse. I fear the advertising department can
handle only a single book at a time. Last fall Caroline was competing
with Stark, this spring you suffered Thomas Wolfe,[2] and both of you
met reverses. Wolfe sells, and there is no answer to that argument;
but I can't quite forgive Perkins for thinking him good. I can't read
him. I have no interest in a novelist's personal philosophy at best; it is
positively boring at its worst in Wolfe. By the way, Red Warren has
written a fine essay on Wolfe, in a recent American Review.[3]

Doubtless you've seen the particularly stupid article in the N.R.
by Hamilton Basso.[4] But in case you haven't heard Stark's comment
on Basso, I'll pass it on: "I *will* say this for Basso—he understands the
New Republic's South better than any Southern writer I know."
Basso has some curious delusions. So far as I know, you and I are in
close agreement on the properties of the old tradition, and yet he puts
us on opposite sides. In what sense you are a "realist" I cannot see; in
your different way you are as far from realism as Miss Ellen was in
Barren Ground. It is strange that the sociological approach is realism
at the same time that your method is. I don't follow this. Doubtless
Cowley does. The trouble with all these people is this: they think we
object to fornication on the part of Southern ladies as a libel on Southern womanhood. As a rule I object to it as a violation of the art of the
novel when the lady's fornication is meant to prove that she is no
"better" than the cropper's wife, and that, for that reason, the sharecropper should own all the land and rule the country. If the lady's

fornication proves only the fornication I have no objection to it. We aren't trying to conceal it (in our fiction), we only insist that it be viewed for what it is worth. When Charlie seduced the poor-white girl in Act of Darkness, it proved (according to Cowley and Basso) that her pappy was more fitten to own Charlie's farm than he was. . . . On the whole they all fail to distinguish between a literary tradition and a social tradition. The literary tradition of Thomas Nelson Page was certainly a genuine tradition, but a bad one; the Liberals assume that we believe that bad literary tradition to be a genuine social tradition. For the life of me I can't see that Faulkner in any way denies the existence of the aristocratic tradition in the South. What in heaven's name do persons like Basso and John Chamberlain think that an aristocracy is? They obviously think it is made up of the people in Red Rock and Swallow Barn![5] If the men screw and the women let them, if matters get confused, if the aristocracy shows the average of human passions, then it is no aristocracy. This delusion explains Chamberlain's recent outburst in The Times.

Tell me how Act of Darkness goes in England. Aleck Maury was published there two weeks ago, but no news of its reception has come.

The first Southern Review isn't out yet, but ought to be within a week. I could never finish that article for them, but sent in an old poem, reworked, that isn't, I hope, really bad. I don't think you've seen it—written in 1928, about 90 lines—called Fragment of a Meditation.[6] I don't know if they're using it.

When you have your group ready, send it on. I suppose their second number will be in October; so I ought to have your new ms. by the middle of August. I expect to have a very good time doing the article.

I hope the salubrious breezes of the rock-bound coast have revived you. It is hot as hell here now—no physical action possible. Shall you return to New Orleans in the fall? I devoutly hope so. We expect to go down our usual number of times. Love to Margaret.   Affectionately, Allen

P.S. I got it from Laurence Dennis the other day that Esther had acquired her Utopianism by marriage.   TLS

---

1. This was the first of Tate's many appearances at writers' conferences.   2. Stark Young's *So Red the Rose* was published in the fall of 1934; Wolfe's *Of Time and the River* in the spring of 1935; Caroline Gordon's book was *Aleck Maury, Sportsman.*   3. "A Note on the Hamlet of Thomas Wolfe," *American Review* 5 (May, 1935), 191–208.   4. "Letters in the South," *New Republic* 83 (June 19, 1935), 161–63.   5. Novels by Thomas Nelson Page and John Pendleton Kennedy.   6. *Southern Review* 1 (Autumn, 1935), 339–42.

Cornsilk Plantation[1]
August 18, 1935   Guntersville, Alabama

Dear John: We have visited around so much this summer that I've neglected all correspondence. We are now with Lytle. I understand that the fall issue of the Southern Review will go to press in a couple of weeks, and I want very much to get the note on you in in time. I will be here until next Saturday, the 23rd; so if you have the new ms. ready please send it on.[2]

I've accomplished nothing this summer.

By the way, you should approach the Guggenheims as follows: Write to Henry Allen Moe, the Secretary, and ask for application blanks. There is a lot of unnecessary stuff in the blanks, but it will have to be answered. The main thing is the statement of your project, which must be put in terms that the selecting committee can understand. John Ransom's first application was turned down because the committee didn't speak the critical language. You will have to give some "references"; four will do—five at most—and they should be evenly distributed between the academic and the literary. I've lost touch up there; so I don't know whom Moe listens to. As a matter of fact he used to listen to me, and he may still to some extent; but I sassed him once and he took it ill. Nevertheless I might be a good person for your list of references. If Dean Gauss at Princeton is a friend of yours, use him by all means. There isn't the slightest doubt of your getting a fellowship. But you may as well protect your attack as much as possible.

What are your plans for the fall and winter? I wish our house had central heat, so that your boys could survive in it; it is there for any friends of ours who want it rent free from September 7th until June 10th. It would be an excellent place to work because there is nothing else to do. It does have electricity, running water, a bathroom and two toilets. But there are open fireplaces only. The rooms can be kept warm, but the halls are arctic in the manner of our boyhood; and it is necessary to wear woolen underwear. Again: send the ms. as soon as possible.   Love to Margaret, Aff. Allen   TLS

1. Andrew Lytle's home.   2. Bishop's poems to be published in *Southern Review.*

September 3, 1935   South Harwich/Massachusetts

Dear Allen: I am enclosing a large batch of poems for the Southern Review.[1] I have had quite a streak for the last two weeks. I am afraid it is now ended, what with the intrusion of domestic concerns, getting a winter house, putting Jonathan in school and all those thousand and one things that are always there to drive off the Muse, but which once in a great while we can forget.

These, almost without exception, seem to me much superior to anything you saw last winter. The Saints, which I started then, I have completely reworked. I doubt if it will have much interest for the contemporary critic, but the subject interests me. And I think I have covered it very completely. You will, I hope, be able to see the direction in which I am working. The long poem, of which I spoke to Warren, should be the climax of the series; but it's nowhere near done. They should all tend toward an affirmation of the divine in the human and a plea for the necessity of its recognition, even in order to survive on the human level.

I am also trying to simplify my style, to make it tend toward the statement; at the same time without losing all the ground we have covered since Rimbaud. You will, I know, give me excellent criticism on my practise here. I may have slipped up now and again, badly. If I have, tell me so. I have no one here to whom I can show anything, verse or prose, and I miss the immediate advice. It's a shame we can't live somewhere within hailing distance.

This brings me to your last letter. Thanks for the Guggenheim information and the accompanying advice. Thanks, too, for the invitation to visit you. It is only within the wildest range of possibility that I may get South this winter, but if I do it will be alone, and not with the innumerable offspring. It is generous of you to offer the house; but we are staying on here, that seeming the most economical thing to do. We have found a house rent cheap, as the fancy prices end with the summer. So, too, I am afraid, do the agrements.

I am sorry to hear that you have done nothing this summer. Have you ever tried the purely mechanical writing of verse to get started? I see by his last book that Yeats recently used it to get out of sterility; the immediate results in his case were not much good, not as EP told him Putrid! but still not so good. Then, after his visit to Pound, the Muse suddenly returned and he has some of his really fine things in this last, all too thin, book. He started out, first with riming extracts from his previous prose, then by composing a play for the sake of the lyrics it would excite. The play is inferior, but the final lyric is superb.[2]

I have found that revision of old pieces and occasionally translation is often helpful. It takes some time to get into the swing, then you find yourself waking up with a poem every morning, some good, some not so good, but still something to get down and work on.

Are you going back to Memphis this winter? I presume so from your addresses given in your letter. I hardly know where to send this communication, but will try Clarkesville. My best to Caroline, John

I had a long, double postcard communication from our old Moscow friend EW. I presume there is no paper in the USSR for intimate purposes. I smell a change in our comrade. We shall have to be gentle with him. I have a feeling that the Earthly Paradise—Electrification + Soviets = Which—was pretty drab, even for a late editor of the N.R. I was delighted at the recent American slap, though I could not sympathize with the motive behind it.[3] But I am in favor of slapping the underbred whenever they stick their faces out, motive be what it may. JPB   TLS

1. See above, Tate to Bishop, May 5, 1935, note 1.   2. Bishop is probably referring to Yeats's play, *The King of the Great Clock Tower*, which appeared in 1935.   3. In late August, the U.S. State Department had formally protested to the Soviet government, charging that activities of the Communist International violated the anti-propaganda pledges of the 1933 recognition agreement.

                                              Southwestern College
September 30, 1935   Memphis, Tennessee

Dear John: I got the note off to the Southern Review last night.[1] I enclose a copy here. It seems to me very bad; it had to be hurriedly written over the weekend and it is all out of proportion. I reached the limit of the allotted space and had not discussed in detail the poems which are the excuse for the article. But there was no time to add that discussion and to cut down the general argument in the first six pages. Perhaps, however, it may be better so. The exhibit of poems will speak for itself, and my note, because it sets forth a general problem, will sound less like personal support.

I should like to say here that *Apparition* is one of your best. *Holy Nativity*, as you predicted, I found unsatisfactory, but it is finely done, and perhaps the only way we can approach the Christian myth.

More later.   Yrs. ever, Allen   AL

1. "A Note on Bishop's Poetry," *Southern Review* 1 (Autumn, 1935), 357–64.

October 15, 1935   1531 Forrest Avenue/Memphis, Tenn.

Dear John: Warren couldn't send me a proof of the note, but I wired him a good many changes that I hope he has made. I agree with you about Spenser. I asked Warren to cut the middle paragraph on page two; it was a useless digression. But even with it gone, the piece is badly proportioned. I am now working on it again. I expect to put it in my book of essays—which Perkins definitely sets for March publication.[1] Please give me the title of your Alcestis book.[2] I want to refer to that instead of to the Southern Review.

I hope you will send me the proof of the poems. I assure you that I will return the favor. Besides your general comment I shall want some specific advice; but I'll wait till the occasion. And I hope you will read the proof of the essays. It will be labor, but I depend on your advice in these matters. I expect to send the ms. to Perkins by November 1st.

I am glad that you thought my comment on Edmund sound.[3] I may elaborate that passage for the book version. Of course, since like other heretics of the didactic, he finds the message of art sufficient, and has no use for the art of the message which is form, he misses the difference between tragedy and the novel. It is curious that the best minds of that school always use the word tragedy in the newspaper sense.

If I can locate an extra copy of the preface to the essays I will enclose it. I should like your remarks from all points of view.

Love to Margaret,   Yrs. Allen   TLS

1. *Reactionary Essays on Poetry and Ideas* (New York: Charles Scribner's Sons, 1936).   2. *Minute Particulars* (1935).   3. "A Traditionalist Looks at Liberalism," *Southern Review* 1 (Spring, 1936), 731–34.

October 23, 1935

Dear John: A hurried scrawl between lectures to tell you that the new poems are very fine. There ought to be a place for them in the book, especially since you're cutting from 40 to 30.

A suggestion: get Scribner's to let you reprint *The Return* with *Collapse of Time*. You might even run them under a single title.

I don't mean to say that *Collapse of Time* is as good as *The Return*. It isn't, but it is very nearly; and the two pieces together would be vastly interesting. The material of the new poem apparently doesn't offer you the chance for such a magnificent statement as that at the end of *The Return*. There lies the difference chiefly.

If you're going to answer my *Note*, do so soon, because I've decided to put it in the book, ms. of which must go to Perkins soon. Again: *What is the title of the Alcestis volume?*   Yrs. aff., Allen

P.S. Reconsider *mawkish* in *Death of the Sideboards*. Only flaw I can find.   AL

October 25, 1935

Dear John: You did exactly the job on the Preface that I wanted done.[1] I knew it ought either to be elaborated and made explicit, or cut down and sharpened. The latter is what I will do. Elaboration would do what the book is supposed to do. You have anticipated, of course, all the leading points of discussion.

As to the tone, I'm not sure you're right. It's all very well to tell the Colonel to up and at 'em, but fortunately the Colonel, who has a fair notion of the force he is about to exhibit, isn't so confident that he will defeat the enemy. He is confident that he has the right plan of attack, but his tactics may be bad. He feels genuine timidity, and if it weren't arrogant to say so, humility.

I'm going to incorporate many of your suggestions, as you will see when you read the proof. Do the same job on the proofs if you have time, but of course you will remember that the opportunity for improvement at the late date will be limited.

I've just read F. O. Mathiessen's book on Eliot.[2] I quarrel on some details, but as a whole it is the best study we have of a contemporary by a contemporary. As a matter of fact, it is the preliminary work to a criticism of Eliot but that preliminary had to be done. The book is certainly evidence of the salutary effect of Eliot on younger men, for Mathiessen sticks like a leech to the work under examination. He is unanswerable in his reply to our straw-man Edmund and that whole school. (Is Edmund really straw? Perhaps.) But I see that he agrees with you on E.'s great talents—"the most valuable critic in America." The phrase reminds me of some of E.'s when he doesn't quite know what he is saying. I do think that E. has great curiosity—indispensable in a real critic; but to say that he has fidelity to the work before him is wrong. He goes from one thing to another out of curiosity, and he pauses long enough in between to be credulous. Powers of exposition, but no analytical powers (read again his essay on Valery—juvenile, absolutely). But, Governor, you're a gallant friend.

I'm awaiting the new Southern Review and its cheque. If they don't learn how to get their journal out, it will never get a public. But Red can't be on time with anything. If his wife ever bears a child it will take twelve months.   Yrs ever, Allen

P.S. I disagree with only one statement in your fine notes. I don't believe that we must have the experience before we can understand the poet's illumination of it. Ash Wednesday, for example. For me it was the experience plus the illumination. That is, I could *understand* the illumination without first having had the experience—which doesn't mean that Eliot gave me a religious experience of my own.

TLS

---

1. Bishop had read and criticized a draft of the "Preface" to *Reactionary Essays*.   2. *The Achievement of T. S. Eliot: An Essay on the Nature of Poetry* (1935).

November 13, 1935

Dear Allen: The flesh is weary—I have been correcting proof all day on an article on Williamsburg restored—but I don't want to let more time go by without saying how fine your poem is.[1] As far as style goes, you have never done anything better, not even the "Ode to the Confederate Dead." It has all your best qualities. How have you happened to keep it up your sleeve all these years?

I liked the essay even better than on first reading: it is very sound and, I believe, profits by the omission of Edmund Spenser.

Caroline's story is one of her best.[2] I should say the best, were it not for the pioneer tale which I read in the Hound and Horn,[3] and which is superior largely because of its greater length and those less tangible qualities that only come through length. Bu I don't believe Caroline has ever touched this story for charm and tenderness. And in any other hands, it would have had neither! Nor are they forced. I think it closes just a little quickly, but otherwise is quite perfect. I should like to have had the close delayed for one paragraph, perhaps two, just time to contemplate the end when you begin to see it and have not been told what it is.

In fact, the Tates do themselves proud in this number of the Southern Review.

I liked the appearance of my poems. *The Saints* seems to me to require cutting. I think all the material I added last summer (after showing you a draft at Baton Rouge) in the interests of clarity is a mistake. It's probably no great jakes as a work of art: but I wanted to do two things, write a two-foot verse that would not be fast and dismiss the problem of asceticism. I think in view of Eliot's personal predilection it may again become identified with religion.

I thought the whole number of the Review good, though I could have done without Herbert Read and some of the political guys. All this politico-economical journalism of today is like the fourth day of turkey, when finally the carcass and feet and neck are boiled up into a thin, very thin soup. There is not enough political imagination in the country to fill a soup-bowl, probably not enough for a soup-spoon. It's all comment on the commentators. It reminds me of the rhyme we used to say in school for the letters of the word PREFACE: Peter Rice eats fish, alligators catch eels, eels catch alligators, fish eat raw potatoes. We have reached the eels catch alligators phase. What is this I hear about a new book of poems from you?[4]   Affectionately, John
                                                                        AL

1. The article was "Onward and Upward with the Arts: Mr. Rockefeller's Other City," *New Yorker* 11 (November 30, 1935), 26–28, 30, 33. The poem was "Fragment of a Meditation."   2. "A Morning's Favor," *Southern Review* 1 (Autumn, 1935), 271–80.   3. "The Capitve."   4. *The Mediterranean and Other Poems* (1936).

November 25, 1935

Dear Allen: I think your suggestion for turning my note on your note into an essay a good one. You may therefore send it back to me with, if you have them, any suggestions whereby unity may be secured. As a matter of fact when preparing my comment on your commentary—how we do take in each other's washing!—I wrote out at some length a statement of principles, detached sentences, a la Nietzsche, Mm Coeur Mes a Me[?], Marriage of Heaven and Hell. I have long wanted to use the apothegm as a form of composition. Do you think Warren would be interested? Financially, such a method is wasteful. But otherwise there is much to be said for it. In our time Cocteau and Valery have employed it with some success.

As to the purpose of a Critical Review, you have stated it precisely.[1] But we can't tell the public that in so many words. Why don't you develop the patron parallel? The editor has assumed the place of the patron in this respect at least: we get our checks from him.

My typewriter is busted and I have been idle some days. But it doesn't make much difference. I seem momentarily dry. I have been trying to finish up the long poem I started in New Orleans. It has a decided tendency to turn into a third-rate Waste Land. However, I'd like to put it behind me. It has some good passages which I hate to lose.

Your own letter sounds very gay. Keep up the good work. ever,
JPB   AL

1. "The Function of a Critical Quarterly," *Southern Review* 1 (Winter, 1936), 551-59.

January 12, 1936

Dear John: I've been trying to get down to your proofs, but three things have stood in my way. First, doing half of the editing of a new symposium to be published this spring.[1] Second, writing an article for same.[2] Third, correcting my own proofs, the book of essays.[3] The article is written, but the proofs and the editing remain.

I've gone through the proofs twice (yours) and I find no fundamental objections. Indeed I find very fine things to applaud. I know you aren't waiting for my word before you return the proofs.[4]

I don't think you have anything as good as Ode, The Return, or Perspectives; but on the whole the exhibit is much better than Now With His Love.

Flint's review—which you've doubtless seen—seems to me to get the matter of our taking in each other's washing quite reversed.[5] I thought I took in more of yours—whatever it should be to indicate that I borrow from you. But if you've done any borrowing from me, you are welcome to it. I still maintain that we are anonymous, and it doesn't make any difference under what name the results appear.

The trouble with Flint, good as he is, is his passion for the intellectual background—a passion that misleads him. It misleads him because he tries to reduce everything to historical fact. The obscure family tragedy that I am supposed to adumbrate does not, so far as I know, exist. It is a possible view of any one's experience; but with almost the researcher's passion he tries to factualize it. The blunder about your ancestry was the result of inference, an attempt to locate historically your Beyond Connecticut, Beyond the Sea; the location had to be pure and simple, without the real complication, part N.E. and part Va. Nevertheless, Flint is no fool, and I think on the whole he did very well by us. I was particularly glad to see Warren get some attention.

My Alcestis proofs have not arrived—though the "book" has been reviewed.[6] I want you to look them over when they come.

By the way, don't you think the winter Southern Review very fine? I've never seen a better issue of an American magazine.   Aff. Allen

TLS

1. *Who Owns America?: A New Declaration of Independence,* ed. Herbert Agar and Allen Tate (Boston: Houghton Mifflin Co., 1936).   2. "Notes on Liberty and Property."   3. *Reactionary Essays* (1936).   4. Tate read proofs of *Minute Particulars.*   5. F. Cudworth Flint, "Five Poets," *Southern Review* 1 (Winter, 1936), 660–70.   6. *The Mediterranean and Other Poems* (1936).

March 6, 1936

Dear Allen: I have been a frightfully long time thanking you for going over my proofs. When your letter came, I was deep in work and didn't really get out of it until I left for New York. We were both there last week. It does have the air of a capital—which no other city in America that I have ever seen has. But it also seems a city that has passed its heydey and is now on the decline, a very grimy and nervous decline. I left it with no desire to live there, though I do feel one shouldn't go too long without revisiting the glimpses of its towers.

I didn't like Flint's review much, though it was honest and painstaking. Nor did I feel your enthusiasm for that number of the Southern Review. I can't help but think Hilaire Belloc a mistake for Warren's magazine. What he says is all right, but he's said it so often, that it sounds flat. And I thought Wade's article on Erskine Caldwell exhibited that weak-mindedness which I have always deplored in Southerners.[1] Whether the Jeeters are typical Georgians seems to me irrelevant. And the attempt to shift all the blame toward Wall Street for the sharecropper's condition wrong-headed. In fact, it seems to me that the fault of most of the agrarians (you are the exception) is to identify the agrarian life with the Southern life. The two are by no means coincident. I think you and I are in agreement as to what in the Southern way of living should be defended—not because it is Southern, but because it is, or was, good. But there is much that existed, and exists, in that region which is indefensible. Of course, I feel that attacks on these positions by the N.Y. Jews are annoying, as they are also ineffective. I think they should be attacked by Southerners. I didn't see Edmund in N.Y. Comrade Cowley was gracious. Write me. I need a good word from you. John.

P.S. I have meant to explain to you the change in dedication of *Minute Particulars*.[2] Last spring, when I was writing a good portion of the poems in that book, my old and dear friend Dickie Ames died. In my grief, I said at the moment to Margaret that I would dedicate my next book to him. But as time went on, the necessity seemed less. He was dead. And there was no living person, I thought, to whom the dedication could mean much. So I put your name on the mss. when it went off. But when I thought there was no one to whom Dickie's dedication would be important I had counted without Margaret. I found she felt very deeply on the subject: that we both owed Dickie a long and immense recollection of pleasures shared with him, and that there was no other way I could signify this than by appending his name to these poems. Then, too, after your article in the Southern Review, I thought it perhaps not too politic to let your name appear on the book. I was afraid it might to others seem that your praise had been prompted by personal considerations. No doubt, they have entered somewhat into your opinion of my work. But I trust your integrity too much to think they could consciously influence you. But you know what our friends and enemies in N.Y. are.

I only go over this long explanation lest you think there was shift in my affection and admiration for you, which in the interim between mailing the mss. and correcting the [proofs] might have prompted the change. I think I should have let it stand, even though impolitic, had Margaret not felt so deeply that I owed nothing less to Ames. That, of course, implies no lack of consideration for you on her part, but merely the feeling that it was now or never that I could dedicate a book to Dickie. JPB.   AL

---

1. "Sweet Are the Uses of Degeneracy" *Southern Review* 1 (Winter, 1936), 449–466.   2. *Minute Particulars* appeared in bookstores early in 1936, though its official publication date was 1935. The book had originally been dedicated to Tate, but Bishop changed the dedication to Dickie Ames on the galley proofs he sent Tate to read.

March 25, 1936

Dear Allen: Your reactionary essays seem to me completely admirable.[1] It is certainly one of the best books of criticism of our time, quite comparable to the Sacred Wood,[2] and I can give it no higher praise.

The various essays hold together extremely well; for the center is very well established. And for that reason it is possible for you to include the Humanistic attack and the two Southern defenses. And yet, in a way, I rather wish you had left those essays out and kept the apparent subject matter to poetry. I can see how they fit in; that they are buttresses to your main position. And if I say that the essay on the Humanists is to me the least agreeable one in the book, that is in part to say that you have gained in force and clarity since it was written. It is too argumentative. I know how skillful you are at argument; it is nevertheless inferior to clear statement; it is the last place the writer has reached in his processes of thought that should be given the reader, not the minute steps of his progress.

I was particularly pleased with the opening essay.[3] For you show there that you can deal as ably with New England as with the South. In fact, your very [thorough] knowledge of one particular region of this country probably gives you a better understanding of others than those who are unable to see that there are regions. I am delighted that you took a crack at Charles Beard, surely the dullest writer ever to study American history, unless it is Frederick Turner whose Frontier I am just reading.

There are one or two minor flaws. You say that Conquistador was MacLeish's first attempt at the long flight. But, as a matter of fact, he had written a play, Nobadaddy, and the two longish poems Hamlet and Pot of Earth. And after (or in the book before) giving Millay high praise, you cite her as an example of rubbish, along with Masefield.

You do as well with me as can possibly be done, and I am duly grateful. I have been much depressed of late, but your essay cheers me no little. That I should not by this time have got rid of the influences of Eliot and Yeats is not only deplorable, but it suggests some serious moral flaw, as well as a literary one.   Affectionately, John
TLS

1. *Reactionary Essays on Poetry and Ideas* (1936).   2. T. S. Eliot, *The Sacred Wood: Essays on Poetry and Criticism* (1921).   3. "Four American Poets (Emily Dickinson, Hart Crane, Ezra Pound, John Peale Bishop)."

March 31, 1936

Dear John: Your fine letter, with all the fine things said about my book, gives me immense pleasure. I am willing for the book to be overpraised—so long as I don't think it's all true! I do agree with you emphatically about the piece on Humanism. I should have substituted for it the essay on the *Function of a Critical Quarterly* (S.R., Jan.) and a new piece just coming out in the S.R. on the nature of traditional societies—the best essay I've ever done, I think, in the field of general ideas.[1] But these pieces would have got in to Perkins late, and the expense of setting up the Humanism would have been lost. The book is pure charity on the part of Scribner's anyhow, and I desisted. I regret it now.

So far as I know I shall get exactly one *fair* review—Mark Van Doren's, which will be in *Books*. I will catch it from the two leading factions in N.Y.—communists and liberals alike.

When I saw in your proofs the dedication to Ames I understood precisely what had happened, and applauded the change. No explanation was necessary, but it is fine to have it. We have many years before us (I hope) in which to dedicate our works to each other. Apart from the death of Dickie Ames, other considerations—chiefly our enemies—would have made a dedication to me the subject of attack, at least of a whispering campaign, at the present time.

I am sending you a reprint of some of Herbert Agar's articles from the *Courier-Journal*. It's the best political journalism of its kind in America today.

I will try to write a better letter in a few days. I've been so harassed since Christmas that letter-writing has been impossible. For one thing I've written a play! (Of this more later.)[2] Love to Margaret—

Aff. yrs., Allen   AL

1. This essay, "What Is a Traditional Society?" appeared in the *American Review* 7 (September, 1936), 376-87.   2. With Anne Goodwin Winslow, Tate wrote a drama based on Henry James's *The Turn of the Screw,* entitled "The Governess."

March 31, 1936

Dear John: After I mailed this morning's letter I thought of something I wanted to ask you about—My Alcestis volume is not yet in print. I read the proofs more than two months ago. Latimer promises to do something—but it's always the printer—drunk, absent, ornery in general.

I want to ask if your book is out, or if it isn't, have you found Latimer unsatisfactory?

About two weeks ago I learned that Latimer is Latimer by grace of some legislature, that his real name (or original name) is Leippert of the erstwhile *Lion & Crown* who got us to make the holographs and then disappeared without an address. I shall not hold that against him if he fulfils his contract for this book. But I'm getting very restive. What is your view of Leippert-Latimer? Yr. in haste, Allen   AL

April 14, 1936

Dear Allen: I'm sorry not to have answered your letters sooner. In part, I have waited till I could find my last letter from Latimer (né Leippert) which I had misplaced and had to look for.

Your intelligence on his secret identity disconcerts me a good deal. I distrust anyone who changes his name. It costs $50 and I agree with E. K. C. that anybody who wants to change the name he was born to ought to be shot. Then, too, there was the disappearance act.

I recall now that my first communication from Alcestis was signed in typescript *The Editors* and initialled AF. Latimer's name did not appear for some months in the correspondence and then there was a good deal of hesitation on his part as to how he meant to sign it. The Christian (?) names varied. It's all very suspect.

However, to be fair, my relations with him as a publisher have been as satisfactory as I could hope from a little one such as he obviously was. Of course, I wonder a lot about whether he has any means of getting the books on the market. But that is something I foresaw. My book came through within a reasonable time and is printed on very fine paper. The type was old and showed it. But that you probably know. The trouble with the printer is probably a fact. At all events, Latimer has a new one. The address of the Alcestis Press is now Peru, Vermont; Latimer's own, 77 Columbia Heights, Brooklyn.

I tried to see him in New York, and was a good deal alarmed when I couldn't trace him through 551 Fifth Avenue. He seemed to be quite unknown there, and, as far as I, or the Western Union, could find out, had left no forwarding address. Once back here, I found his apartment and street number and wrote him there.

In his reply he says: "No, nothing serious has happened to me or the press. Both have to go on because I arranged for bks (with both authors and a new and better printer) up to spring '37 publication."

To sum up: only your revelation on the change of identity disturbs me. The delay in getting out your books can be explained by the change of printer. This must be a fact. He'd have no reason to lie to me about it.

It's my laziness that has kept me from sending you a copy of my book, which I want you to have. You'll get it, if I can pull myself out of my lethargy which I have suffered since the year began. It is probably neurotic.

Thanks for the Agar. I read it with interest, and for the most part with approval. I'll talk about his book later.

Edmund has a good piece on Russia in the latest New Yorker.[1] It's quite sane and sound.   My best to you both, John   AL

1. "London to Leningrad," *New Yorker* 12 (April 4, 1936), 36, 38, 40, 42, 47, 48.

June 19, 1936

Dear Allen: You must think me an ungrateful reprobate. I have let your letter go so long unanswered. It arrived when I was in the midst of an essay for the New Republic on our friend Hemingway,[1] and at the moment, the problem it brought up seemed more than I could deal with without distracting my mind. Even now, I don't quite see what to do about it.

I can't very well take over the books from Latimer, ne Leippert without paying him for them, and this I am in no position to do just now. I don't think he is selling any. I went around in New York and saw no signs of any of his editions, including that of Stevens. And it is not, as the bookstores showed, so very difficult to place the products of the small press on sale if one knows how to go about it. Though how it is done, I for one do not know.

I suppose we were all fools to commit ourselves to a publisher about whom we knew so little. Latimer played one of us against the other so that his group of names inspired a confidence which should not have been placed in him.

We have moved into another house, on a year's lease, one less conveniently near the beach, but very well arranged for our purposes. There is almost unlimited space for taking people in, or rather there is a sleeping porch and a barn, to which the children can be transferred when their rooms are wanted for guests. So that, if your plans are still to come north for a lecture tour at Columbia, I shall hope to have you, and Caroline too, if she accompanies you, here.

The best way to come up is to drive. But if you haven't your car with you, there are two other fairly comfortable means of transportation. Come to Providence by train, where we'll meet you; or take the Fall River boat at night, in which case we meet you at Hyannis, to which point a small boat train brings you.

I have done no writing since we moved. I have been waiting for things to settle down and in the meanwhile attempting to start a vegetable garden, a labor which has left these old bones aching, until at night I had the appearance and the feeling of one of Caldwell's crackers.

And I feel as ignorant as they of the proper processes in this plague ridden country. It really is much simpler in France. There, you put on rotted horse manure and that takes care of the nourishment. You kill off the slugs and snails, and that takes care of the pests. But here, there are only chemical fertilizers procurable, and the pests are beyond number. By the time I have learned (it may be too late) to spray for one insect, another, more devastating has arrived. I suspect that the killing off of game birds has a lot to do with it.

By the way, have you seen my essay in the Virginia Quarterly?[2] I should be glad to have your frank comment. It provides the intellectual background for the poems you did not like in last year's production. At least it is an attempt to resolve the unbelieving belief of which you complained.

I greatly disliked Bunny's book on his travels.[3] And I have still to write him about it. This is hard to do, because the book reveals his incredible ignorance of himself. The story of Lieutenant Franklin is immensely revealing, the naivete of the approach to the war is beyond my comprehension. And he is just as naif in his approach to Russia, if it is true that he thought, as he says, that Russia would be just like the USA with the added advantage of socialism. And the conclusions, have been arrived at before he started on his travels, are therefore valueless.

Give me the news on yourself. Is your symposium selling? I noticed that it was on the best seller list, but that in actual numbers may not mean much.   As ever, John   TLS

1. "Homage to Hemingway," *New Republic* 84 (November 11, 1936), 39-42.   2. "The Golden Bough," *Virginia Quarterly Review* 12 (July, 1936), 430-47.   3. Edmund Wilson, *Travels in Two Democracies* (1936).

July 21, 1936

Dear Allen: I want very much to urge you to reconsider your decision to speed away from New York after your lectures. That it will give me great pleasure to have you here goes without saying; I also think you owe it to yourself to see the Cape. It is the New Englander's best attempt to reach a relation with the land he lives on. It is like nothing else in America. Thoreau gives a very bad account of it, which may have been accurate in his day, though I doubt it was so desolate even then.

I probably made the journey sound more difficult than it is. And you'll certainly need to cool off after New York (if present temperatures there are a sign of what you'll find) before starting toward your own warm climate. Do think it over. I'd like so much to have you both and can at least offer such a quiet pleasant time as we had together on the Riviera.

I'm glad you liked the essay in the Quarterly. It was originally much longer. In fact, the greater part of the labor was getting it down to publishable length. The last section is, for that reason, very choppy. I just choked in paragraphs, which in the first version were parts of something more substantial. You know our friends the editors. I have just done Cowley a very good piece on Hemingway which he has cut all to bits in order to get it down to a preconceived length.[1]

I have just finished a long poem for Warren, the expansion of one I started in New Orleans.[2] It is on the same subject as the essay. The verse is good. How good a poem it is I don't know. I suspect it is pretty silly in places.   As ever, John   TLS

1. "Homage to Hemingway."   2. This poem was never published in *Southern Review*.

October 18, 1936

Dear Allen: Zabel of *Poetry* has written me that he gave John Crowe Ransom my book of poems to review, but that nothing has happened about it although he has written Ransom three letters, all of them remaining without response. I presume there is some quarrel going on here, into which I don't want to enter. But I should like to have Ransom review it. You may know whether his relations with *Poetry* forbid this, in which case I should think he would want to return the book. I don't want to drag you in on this, but I know of no one else who can elucidate the situation for me.[1]

I have just done an essay on Fitzgerald, Hemingway, & O'Hara for the Va. Quarterly, which relies not a little on your essay on Emily Dickinson, a piece which I have read and reread, always with increasing admiration.[2]

Lytle's novel is superb,[3] absolutely one of the best books ever written by an American. He is that now very rare thing, a real storyteller and he happens also to be a rarely intelligent man, a combination almost unknown these days. I was continually reminded of both Hardy and Fielding. He has the weight and density of the one, with the easy narrative flow of the other. He is certainly to be congratulated.

I am doing my scrappy things, in the meanwhile enjoying the autumn weather.   As ever, JPB   AL

1. Ransom did not review Bishop's *Minute Particulars*.   2. Bishop's essay is "The Missing All," *Virginia Quarterly Review* 13 (Winter, 1937), 106–21.   3. *The Long Night* (1936).

November 3, 1936

Dear Allen: I am glad to hear that there is nothing between John Ransom and Poetry. I suspected all along that he was probably suffering from my complaint of procrastination.

I didn't know until your letter that you had quit teaching.[1] I can understand your depression at having to undertake a job of writing at which you have grown cold. Nothing is harder. I have never had it to do with a whole book, but I have with shorter pieces, and my experience is that it is imperative to add a new element in order to take hold again. Something fresh must be put in to revive what has gone stale. Sometimes the very incongruity of this element adds a complexity to the subject matter it did not originally have. But you can't possibly go back to The Fathers and take it up where you left off four years ago. At least not, if you are at all like me.

Don't let it get you down. One can live with a good deal of depression. But it is harder to write when depressed. I know. You are indeed lucky if this is your first real fit of it.

I wish I thought I could meet you in New Orleans. I find myself, as winter comes on, remembering that charming city with regret. I wish I could arrange to spend about two months there every year; but now with the three children in school we are pretty well tied down. I dislike it. It fills me with envy the way the Dos Passoses, officially in residence on the Cape, flit about forever; but they have only cats and poodles.

The Va. Quarterly has taken my article on Hemingway Fitzgerald O'Hara for the next number.[2] It is not too good; but the one on Hemingway alone in the next New Republic I think is quite good. There was originally much more of it, but you know the N.R. I suppose you saw that the Nation had printed Collapse of Time along with the Prize Poem of Wallace Stevens.[3] Much as I admire Stevens, I think in this particular case that mine is the better poem.

I have loaned The Long Night around and it is having great success on the Cape. My regards to the Lytles and to Caroline.   As ever,
John   TLS

1. Tate resigned his academic position at Southwestern at Memphis at the end of the 1935–36 academic year.   2. "The Missing All."   3. "The Collapse of Time" appeared in *Nation* 143 (October 24, 1936), 479. Stevens' poem, which was the *Nation* Prize Poem for 1936, was "The Men That are Falling"; it appeared on the same page as Bishop's.

March 20, 1937   Chateau de Tressancourt/Orgeval (S & O)

Dear Allen: Your letter reaches me in Paris, where I have been trying to clear up all my affairs.[1] I believe that when I sail on the Bremen the 26th I shall have succeeded. At any rate, I have sold Tressancourt, and not so bad a price, all things considered, and trust to leave with no unpaid debts behind or before me. It has been a miserable business, but I won't expatiate on my troubles during the last three weeks. It is enough that within that short time I have been able to more or less get things through.

The conference in Nashville sounds interesting and I should love to come. But it doesn't look too possible. My sister is having a baby in April and I had promised to go to Hagerstown for the event. If I could find some means of cheap transportation, I might make it. But it is a long way, and I am not sure I can afford it. But thank Ransom for thinking of me and let me know more of it at S. Harwich.[2]

I am glad the book goes forward.[3] The problem of the personal narrator, a survivor of the fifties, is, I think, largely one of rhythm. If you get that right at the start—and I presume that you have from what you say of the first sentence,—everything follows naturally. At least I found that to be true of the aged narrator in *The Cellar*.[4] His diction could be improved—could in other words be a little more nearly authentic—as Lytle's superbly is in *The Long Night*—but the rhythm of his speech carried me right along. As to *Act of Darkness*, don't introduce, as I did, scenes not seen by the narrator without more justification than I gave. Of course, I had in my adolescent a special problem, which will not be yours if you use a mature, not to say old, man. I will read what you send with pleasure. I expect to be on Cape Cod sometime in the first week in April.

You are quite right about *The Missing All*. It is nowhere near as good as *The Golden Bough*. But I had said all or nearly all I had to say about Ernest for the New Republic (the cut portions are being restored in book form when they collect the revaluations) and Scott is interesting only as an example of the deplorable thinking of the period in which he rose to fame.

I saw Ernest here a week ago. He liked both articles and that was for me a source of gratitude. I was fearful of offending him. He has another novel now in proof.[5] I think he is in good shape.

I want to start another novel myself as soon as I get back, if I can work out a plot. I have no invention that way. But I do want to get a long book underway soon.

France is in a deplorable state, morally much worse off than the papers would lead one to expect. My first impression was that I had arrived the day after the funeral. There was the same sense of emptiness, of something gone never to return. Everything smells of death, in spite of a premature spring. There will be a reaction against Blum's social legislation, which is bringing everything to a standstill, and it will be bloody, and the end will be a hatred between classes, of which we will not live to see the end.[6] Already that hatred exists, indeed is the striking thing, and its sterility spreads over everything. Yours,

[JPB]   AL

1. Bishop had returned to France briefly to sell his home there, ending his extended expatriation.   2. Ransom was attempting to organize a Southern Writers' Confer-

ence at Vanderbilt, and at Tate's suggestion had invited Bishop as one of the speakers. When Ransom could not get the speakers he wanted, he decided to delay the conference for a year. The conference was never held because Ransom left Vanderbilt for Kenyon College in August, 1937. 3. Tate has resumed work on *The Fathers* (New York: G. P. Putnam's Sons, 1938). 4. A story in *Many Thousands Gone* (1931). 5. *To Have and Have Not* (1937). 6. French socialist Leon Blum (1872–1950) led the Popular Front to an election victory in 1936; Blum's program focused on the nationalization of key industries.

[June 1937] South Harwich

Dear Allen   I am sending a not very inspired tribute to Ransom.[1] We are preparing to move, which puts my mind in a turmoil and destroys any continuity it might otherwise have.

We have to get out of this house on the 19th. The three boys are due at camp July 1st for two months, and Margaret & I are planning to more or less camp out in a small cabin here for the summer. My address will remain the same.

We are building at South Chatham, a house that promises to be both livable and hospitable. The exterior is to be the grey shingle to fit into the Cape Cod landscape. But the plan includes many Virginian features, not a few from Monticello (the non-visible staircase, for instance) and there will be two guest rooms.

The foundations are not yet finished, but we hope to get into it in September. Alas, literature suffers.

Do keep me in touch with what you are doing.   As ever, JPB

AL

1. Tate collected a number of tributes to Ransom from well-known literary figures in an abortive attempt to convince James H. Kirkland, Chancellor of Vanderbilt University, that he could not afford to lose a figure with an international literary reputation to "a small college in Ohio."

October 22, 1937

Dear Allen: I can't wait any longer to write you about your *Collected Poems*.[1] I have waited already much too long, since receiving a copy from Scribner's. But I have been frightfully distracted: we are building a house at South Chatham and the responsibility of trying to get things the way we want them without going bankrupt has entirely destroyed my capacity for concentration. I have been hoping constantly for an interlude in which I could accurately sum up my impressions. But it has not come. And now I can only say that I approve completely of the collection. There is not a poem whose presence is not justified. And none of the omitted ones are seriously missed. My books all being packed, I cannot compare the present with previous versions. But all, as I read it, seems to be finely wrought and nowhere do I find a word to cavil at.

The effect as a whole is much more impressive than any one of your earlier books has been. An authentic poet, of course, always gains by adding one poem to another. His whole is certainly far more than the sum of his parts.

That must be all for the moment. I wish I could give you more generous and accurate praise. But however long I wrote of your poems, it would still be all praise and gratitude.   As ever, John AL

1. Bishop is referring to Tate's *Selected Poems* (New York: Charles Scribner's Sons, 1937).

December 27, 1937   Benfolly/Clarksville, Tennessee

Dear John: Your Christmas card reminded me that we never send any but think it pleasant to get them. I observe your new address, and the name of the new house which I am sure you & Margaret suffered to achieve; but I hope you are rich. Do not, I pray you, become strange.

I take my carpet-bag in hand towards mid-February for Cambridge where I must be on the 17th. I expect to be there about two days, and I hope that you can come up or over, or whatever it is, to see me. I will be in N.Y. two days going and returning, and we might connect there.

We shall return not to Benfolly but to Greensboro, North Carolina, where we have one of those jobs that writers are always looking for but never expect to get: we shall each "instruct" in writing three hours a week at the Woman's College of the Univ. of N.C., and receive a joint salary that I consider fabulous.[1] I still can't believe it. We go February first. I don't know how long we can stand it, but we can stand a good deal for the money. It is expressly stipulated by the officials that we coordinate the work as we please, ignoring the academic pattern.

I am trying to finish my novel before we go,[2] because once there I shall want to begin a long critical book, not essays, but on one subject. I haven't had the glimmer of a poem for three years.

Love to Margaret and our best wishes for the coming year.   Yrs. aff., Allen   AL

1. Both Allen Tate and Caroline Gordon accepted positions, beginning February 1, 1938, in the English department of the Woman's College of North Carolina and almost persuaded John Crowe Ransom, who had just moved to Kenyon, to join them as chairman of the department.   2. Tate completed *The Fathers* on July 21, 1938, at Scoville Cottage, West Cornwall, Connecticut.

[January 1938]

Dear Allen: I shall carefully keep the days around the seventeenth of February clear, so that we can meet either in Cambridge or here. I do wish you could arrange your schedule so as to include a stay, even though a brief one, on the Cape. We have room for you and your carpet-bag and it would be the simplest thing in the world to meet you in Boston and drive you down here.

I would like you to see the house, which has indeed cost us great pain, not only to get it built, but even more to pay up the immediate bills. Still, I can't but think it is a sort of miracle that we have it at all.

There are two guest rooms, both of which are provided with beds of comfort and curtains to keep out the morning sun. I mention those, because as yet the rest of the house is very scantily provided. It would certainly make us both very happy to have you here.

I am glad to hear about the job. It is not the worst of this craft which we both off and on practise that it adds nothing to a solution of the problem of how to keep alive and going. But I cannot but envy those whose work and means of subsistence coincide.

I have done almost no work for the last six months, but am now trying to do something and at least succeeding in spending the mornings before the typewriter. There was not only the building of the house to distract one, but I contracted a loathsome disease from the children, who brought impetigo back from camp. I have had the devil's own time getting rid of it. I think it must have been something akin to it that the Lord visited Job with when He was annoyed with him.

Curiously, your letter found me reading your poems, which impress me more with each perusal. In fact, I varied them with readings in the Fleurs du Mal (which I had not seen for some time) and I could not but be struck with the many qualities you share with Baudelaire.

I also have had time to go over a lot of your old letters. I believe that correspondence was very valuable to both of us and certainly in my case led to an unwonted output of what I should like to call poetry. It is always so much easier to get people to take prose seriously that when we are surrounded by the usual run of our kind we get turned from poetry. I am trying again to woo the Muse, but as yet she is shy. However, I think it is by paying her addresses, in other words versifying as best one can deliberately, that one gets the lady back into speaking distance.   My best to you both, John   TLS

January 11, 1938

Dear John: It was good yesterday to have some real news of you. I write this on the fifth day of confinement to my room, mostly in bed, with flu. Don't expect anything bright. (It feels like that especially *ornery* kind of flu I had in Paris.)

I'd like to promise to stop at Sea Change,[1] but I'd better not just yet, until I learn more about distances and train connections, and what is expected of me in Cambridge besides the lecture. But I'll look for you in Cambridge where I expect to arrive on the 17th, morning; I can be found at Eliot House.

I hope you *will* get back to poetry. I fear more and more I may never. Of course there's no reason why we should, except to make bearable the rest of life, or rather I suppose to justify it. We are all sufficiently Protestant to need justification; I am, at any rate. Unless I am writing verse, or am about to write it, or have just written some, that I can more or less believe in, everything else turns flat, and a good deal of it turns sour. I suppose that is nothing to complain of, when friends of ours turn sour of conscience because their incomes are derived from capitalism. The only income that distresses me is the income I am not getting. I am fastidious only in privation.—Of course I've never credited with much final integrity the conscience-about-capitalism: I don't doubt its motives; I merely think there's something else to explain the scruple—maybe a personal emptiness. I feel that too, but with such intensity that I can't do anything about it. I suppose one difference between a poet and a reformer is that the latter thinks he can fill up his void with any sort of odds and ends; the poet must take the punishment.—That, by the way, may be a quality that I share with Baudelaire: he took his punishment and didn't pretend it was Society. I would agree with him that somebody is to blame, and his name is Satan, or Evil. It is so simple that few of our contemporaries can believe it.

I have felt in recent years that our correspondence, beginning, I believe, just ten years ago, was the most valuable intercourse of my life. As you remember, it came of a chance acquaintance boiling up upon the disordered surface of the twenties. I apologize for the reminiscent tone, yet we *are* getting on, and it is easier all the time to look back to the time when it was possible only to look forward.

I am trying to work at my lecture, which will really be an essay. Its subject is: "Tension in Poetic Imagery."[2] You recall Francesca's description of her birthplace: those lines are the text.

Love to Margaret.   Yrs., Allen   AL

1. Bishop's new home.   2. Tate wrote his best-known critical essay, "Tension in Poetry," in the early winter, 1938, and gave it as a lecture at Harvard on February 19, 1938, before it appeared in print in *Southern Review* 4 (Summer, 1938), 101–15.

                                               West Cornwall, Conn.
July 24, 1938   Telephone: Cornwall 74 ring 1–2

Dear John: We have been hiding here for three weeks in a cottage on a back road, until I finish my book—which I did only Friday.[1] I hope you will be coming this way. We are hampered in our movements by the children—Nancy and a little girl we borrowed and brought along as company for her. We shall probably be here until early in September; though I may go to England with my brother around August 8th, for a month. We are going down to Stamford to see Edmund on Friday. When I talked to him yesterday, he said how nice it would be if we could all get together. Why don't you get in touch with him, and come down?

I finished the novel the night of the 21st: the last incident was on July 21st 1861. Nancy became a woman on the 21st. The book will appear on Sept. 23, her birthday. The moon seems to favor it. . . . I wanted to show you the ms. but there was no time. It was already being set as I wrote the last word. Love to Margaret.   Yrs. Aff.,
Allen   AL

1. *The Fathers.*

August 2, 1938

Dear John: Your plans ought to work out nicely as far as we are concerned. We leave today for a brief visit with Colonel [Phelps] Putnam at Pomfret Center, and return Thursday to go to New York for the week end. So any time next week that you can come will suit us perfectly. I had to call off my visit to Doctor Wilson on account of page proofs. Now I will probably wait until [you] get here so that you can go with us. It would be easy for us to come to Georgetown and pick you up, go to Stamford for an afternoon and evening, and then bring you back here. We can work this out in detail after you are at Georgetown. It would be nice to see Ed Donahoe. (I liked his book in spots very much but thought it didn't get anywhere.)

I thought your essay in the current Va. Quarterly one of your very best,[1] better in fact than your Cummings piece in the SR,[2] though it has some very fine observations. I suppose I felt that Cummings wasn't quite worth the formidable critical apparatus you get up for him. As the years pass and we get bald and our hair grows gray, I see a little less all the time in his verse.—I see you are down as official critic of the Writers' Project number of POETRY. I am glad I don't have the job. What will you do with A. MacLeish's puddle?[3] If I were doing the job, I'd get out the old Confutterate wunderbusser and pee on it. It is bad with that special kind of badness that only a gifted person can occasionally produce. I reckon he knows he rewrote Shelley's Defense, but it's Shelley without balls, though I daresay Shelley's balls warn't anything to write home about. I am, governor, as always,   ever Yrs. Allen   TLS

1. "The Discipline of Poetry," *Virginia Quarterly Review* 14 (Summer, 1938), 343–56.   2. "The Poems and Prose of E. E. Cummings," *Southern Review* 4 (Summer, 1938), 173–86.   3. The July, 1938, issue of *Poetry* was devoted to selections by Federal Writers' Project grantees, and included an essay by MacLeish, "In Challenge Not Defense." Bishop was commissioned to write a critique of this issue, and his essay, "The Federal Poets' Number," appeared in the August, 1938 issue, pp. 276–83.

Aug 10 [1938]

Dear Allen: Various troubles—my sister in law and her husband arrived some days later than expected and to make their week are staying later, in fact over this week-end. Then, when they leave, they are not returning to Connecticut, but progressing north, toward Maine. So that they offer no ride down. I shall have to make other arrangements. I will let you know as soon as possible what they are and will hope that I can fit my movements with your convenience.

The Cape is so difficult of access or egress, except with a car of one's own, as was shown by old Dr. Wilson's contretemps yesterday, when after coming down with Mary from Provincetown, at great expense, by taxi, he tried to take a non-existent train from Hyannis for Boston. He wound up, hours later on another train for New Haven, with the prospect of sitting up until 3/20 AM or thereabouts, then changing to a milk train for Stamford.

I have been in an alternating state of pleasure and dejection through conceiving lots of poems and having them when brought to light prove mostly miscarriages. One or two are in the incubator and may develop.

Suggestion for a poem (after a phrase by Allen Tate)

The question, lords and ladies, is
With what did Percy Shelley piss?
Was light dissolved in star showers thrown
When Percy Shelley had a bone?

Transcendental love we know
Is packed, but has no place to go.
And Percy's love, as he has said
Resembled roses when they're dead.

And rose-leaves when the rose is dead
Are out of place, like crumbs in bed.
No letter yet has come to light
To say if Percy rose at night.

No lady for whom Percy pined
Has left a diary behind;
And so there still remains a doubt
What Percy's love was all about.

Though scholars search, no letters come
Written in a flurry home;
We ask and ask, till silence palls,
Did Percy Bysshe have any balls?

John   TLS

August 31, 1938   West Cornwall

Dear John: I am just back from a week of exhausting relaxation at a
swank fishing club on Lake Ontario. Very little may be expected of me
this morning.

I enclose a copy of your meditation on P. B. S.

On the way to the fishing club I spent a week-end with Edmund
& Mary. I shall expect to hear from him tomorrow about a plan for
which he had great enthusiasm, being: Edmund and Mary will come
here by train, and we shall all go for a night at Pomfret. Then we
should drive by to see you and Margaret on the way to Provincetown
We aren't quite certain that we can go, but we shall know by the time
we hear from Edmund. By the time we reached South Chatham we
should be a mob (Putnams being included); so our stop would necessarily be a brief call. I'll let you know by Friday. Love to Margaret.   Yrs. aff., Allen   AL

September 6, 1938

Dear Allen: I have read *The Fathers* with great satisfaction and
though you have said you want me not to write anything about it, I
have composed a paragraph, not of praise, but, I hope, of elucidation,
which you may send to your publishers if you care to. I include it with
this letter.

The novel shows the same intensity and concentration that I am
accustomed to associate with whatever you have previously written,
and besides it shows complete competence in what is for you a new
form. I think you did well to have a narrator, despite Henry James's
strictures against using one. Because for the writer who is used to
seeking extreme concentration of expression, as a poet must, some
device is necessary to enable him to "loosen up the language" as
Ernest put it. He, of course, was aware of that necessity when he, as
short story writer, came first to the novel. James's practise is another
matter; for James was not only a born novelist, he was so much the
novelist that no existence apart from the novel was possible to him.
The poet attempting a novel is in another case entirely.

I cannot but think however that you did not allow your narrator enough distance from the scene he describes. I see the practical problem. But he seems to me to fall between Maisie and the Je of Proust's ponderous work. By allowing him to write long after, you remove him from the scene, but you do not allow him enough in the way of powers of analysis to get everything out of the material that I feel was there. Your characters are perfectly real, as far as they go, but I had expected from you a more profound penetration. But then [it] may be that you, by virtue of being a poet are really too removed from the society you describe to know all its workings. I know that is true in my case, and I have of course been most interested in the parallels between your novel and my own Act of Darkness. In a way, the same characters repeat themselves, as they were bound to do in any account of the Virginia scene. Your interpretation is certainly more finished than mine, it adds up in the end more completely to a whole, partly because you deal with them at a time when their society had far more life in it than it did when I came to describe them. You lead them to the crisis and then to the edge of the abyss. Mine were living on the edge of the abyss, like people who return to live on the sides of a volcano, after an eruption, and go on quietly tending their vineyards as though they could ignore, which they can't, the smoke from the living crater. Yet some of them had looked down into [the] crater and some I think had dangerously gone down the sides. But even when you bring your characters to the abyss in that scene where it is physically presented as the cliff above the river into which bodies can disappear, not to be found again, or found dead, their very death concealed, they show only a partial awareness. That is all right, in the dramatic sense. But someone, I feel, should be aware, possibly not your narrator, but someone, of all that is happening, of the full implications of what is, after all, the *clou* of your novel. That scene, I found hurried. It is not the violence of it that disturbs me, but the fact that I don't completely understand the motives of that violence.

That is, of course, because I don't, deep down, understand the Virginians. I don't really know what it was that maintained my mother, who was so essentially Virginian, through all her vicissitudes. I know, as you do, that they acted thus and so, that those who accepted the code acted thus and so, and that those [who,] like your George and my Charlie, refused to accept the code rebelled against it in such and such a manner. But ultimately there is a place where I do not understand them, where I do not know them at all.

Now I feel that you should have provided the reader with somewhat more help by the way. If the narrator had been willing, or made able, to explain the small events leading up to the scene by the cliff, I should perhaps know more. I am, as I say, asking of you something I could not do myself.

To return to 1938. I did not answer your letter, which I did not see, having been out on a deep sea fishing trip all day, until after your telegram came. The later message seemed to make the former out of date. I couldn't possibly come to West Cornwall as matters stood, and even had I been free, I doubt if there would have been time enough to make the trip before you all parted. It is some eight hours from here by motor.

I hope we meet again, somewhere, before too long. Give my best to Caroline and tell her not to starve Nancy. I should guess, by the way, having seen similar instances of that sort of thing, that she is undergoing some sort of glandular disturbance, connected, no doubt, with puberty. At the same time, if I were you and Caroline, I'd have her looked over by a gland man in New York, on your way south. No one seems to know any too much about such things, but I have seen girls thinned out by supplying them with thyroid, which apparently is apt to be insufficient in girls at a young age. I hope you'll forgive me, if I seem to be giving advice where it is not called for, but I think I should do wrong if I did not, out of some experience of these things, speak out.   Yours, John   TLS

October 11, 1938

Dear Allen: I have written the review of *The Fathers* for the N.R.[1] I hope you will have no occasion to repent having given me permission to do so. It is not what I should have written had I had more words at my disposal—but you know the N.R. My mind—being a this way and that sort of mind—needs space.

We had a visit from old Dr. Wilson & his youthful bride last week end. Margaret went on with them to the Dos Passoses at Provincetown, while I went to bed with a cold, from which I am only now recovering. Bunny has written a parody of A. MacLeish, extremely cruel, which is to appear in the N.Yr. He is not really fair to Archie, who is scarcely more dependent on other people than others, whom EW finds occasion to praise.

J. C. Ransom has written me about his new Review and I am to contribute an article on T. Wolfe. Not having read *Time & the River* I don't know what it will be like, but somehow suspect the greatness of that late genius.[2]

I am very stupid this Sunday morning & will not pursue you further.   Affectionately, John   AL

---

1. "The Death of an Order," *New Republic* 97 (November 9, 1938), 25–26.   2. "The Sorrows of Thomas Wolfe," *Kenyon Review* 1 (Winter, 1939), 7–17.

The Woman's College
Greensboro, N.C.

November 19, 1938

Dear John: When your review appeared we were just setting out for another trip to Tennessee. The review, of course, is the best I've seen.[1] I suppose there *is* some emotional confusion in my attitude towards the subject, or at any rate I do see the subject in terms of an unresolvable conflict. But here I would say that, looked at closely enough, all human situations have that aspect; hence, the necessity of literature. You are right about my disappointment in the quality of the men the South produced—or rather their capacity; but if we look at them in the limited perspective of comparison with the men of New England, I think they stand in a less favorable [sic] light. At the moment of their success they were easily the superiors of the modern American, who has only a harassed sort of success to give him any interest at all. A review in *Partisan Review* asks the question:[2] Why has Tate constantly urged the Old South as a good society when at the same time he has never spared its limitations? Well, I see the limitations beside the great cultures of the past; its virtues in the limited perspective I've mentioned. For some reason Northern critics always assume that a Southerner's awareness of the South's historic defects means his acknowledgement of the superiority of the North. It doesn't follow!—The fellow in *Partisan Review* (my best reviewer except you) commits himself to one of the standard Marxist, naive revelations of the soft spot in that point of view. He discerns the ostrichlike code that refuses to acknowledge violence and evil below the surface, as if that were special to the Old South and as if the Marxist state could miraculously eliminate the evil! I would say that all highly developed societies arrive at that contradiction, and the fact that the South reached it is one reason why it offers one of the fundamental subjects for literature. I shouldn't care to live in a world from which the contradiction is eliminated. I know that I won't; neither will the Marxist. At present we live in a world where the disorder is at the surface. So all honor to Major Buchan. Yrs. aff., Allen   AL

1. Bishop's extremely perceptive review of *The Fathers* focuses on Tate's ambivalent attitude in the novel, "his dispassionate approval of a society which he believes to be as good as any ever known on this continent and his passionate disappointment in the limitations of the sort of men it produced." 2. Lional Trilling, "Allen Tate as Novelist," *Partisan Review* 6 (Fall, 1938), 111–13.

November 20, 1938

Dear Allen: My word confusion was not as well chosen as your word conflict. My own belief is that where there is no conflict and no confusion there is no consequent poetry.

The Marxists don't understand this, hence the appallingly primary quality of their writing. It makes it impossible for them to understand any of the really great writers. And as far as that goes the list of those who do not understand that Dante's poetry comes of a conflict between his intellectual judgement, portrayed as divine justice, and his heart, portrayed as human love and pity, is by no means confined to those of the Marxist persuasion.

As to the reservations that you make in your judgement—which I take it is in your poetry of an absolute quality—in your letter I am too much in agreement with you to make argument possible, and comment seems superfluous. That's a badly made sentence, but it's the day's end, so forgive me.

I had a great deal more to say on your novel than it was possible to say in the small number of words allotted me. I hope sometime to have an opportunity to return to it and to discuss more fully what, as shown by you and others perhaps, it meant to live in an orderly society. That is another word that no one understands now, since law and order mean only the policemen beating up a striker. Still, I can't see much other order abroad today.   Affectionately, John   TLS

January 13, 1939

Dear John: After an exhausting Christmas in Tennessee, we pause for breath.

The Savannah people write me that you've accepted the invitation to their conference; so have we. It would be fun if we were the invitations committee, but alas I am getting too old to be polite to bad poets, who more and more affect me like Jews, and I find myself getting committed to something. But it will be fine to see you.

I thought your Sorrows of T. W. one of your best essays—by far the best thing in the Kenyon Review. But I hear that Ransom is going to be a bad editor—said, for example, that Marianne Moore was not good enough for the magazine!

I wish you would tell me if there have been any developments concerning the editorship of the Virginia Quarterly. Unless something is done, inertia will keep Lee in the job the rest of his life. I want to do something, but I'd rather act with knowledge of what has happened in the past few months. Lee has improved the make-up of the magazine, but he will otherwise not be as good as Davis, who at least was humble.[1] Lee is dull and aggressive about it; being a "poet" he will make the magazine safe for his order of talent. And that will mean a loss for everybody. Our sort of journal is rare enough as it is.   Aff., Allen   AL

1. Lawrence Lee succeeded Lipscomb Davis as editor of the *Virginia Quarterly Review* in 1937–38, and served in that post through 1940.

March 7, 1939

Dear Allen: I want at once to thank you for your invitation, which is attractive and cheering. I had thought of going down by boat, but that is slow—four days, and it might be better to come back that way.

But will you give me another day or two to think it over—it's only the practical end that I must think of. It will be good to see you. The winter has gotten me down. Even the dogs have suffered a decline. Both have been given a chance to breed—and failed lamentably. Yesterday Judah passed a tape worm.

I have been working on—of all things—a long essay on Matthew Arnold.[1] I got started with Trilling's book—which stinks—for which I did a review. I am now doing a long thing of my own, whose real title should be The Poet and the Middle Class. It has good things in it. If only I don't bog down before weaving all my threads and knitting them at the end. Remember me to Caroline. John   AL

1. This essay never appeared separately, but was included in Bishop's *Collected Essays*, published posthumously. Bishop also wrote a review of Trilling's *Matthew Arnold* (1939) for *Partisan Review*, but the editors declined to print it.

March 11, 1939

Dear John: There's no hurry. You don't need to let me know until the end of the month; then you need only to wire what I am to expect.

Mr. Axley asked me to suggest some "features" for the conference.[1] I suggested that books by the staff should be exhibited and sold; so I've written to Scribner's that your, Caroline's, and my books ought to be there.

I hope you finish the Arnold before we meet. I liked Trilling's review of my novel as well as I could like any Marxist view; and I thought his piece on Ernest (in the current *Partisan*) had a good general point, though it was foully* written.[2] But when you get the English Department mentality combined with the Marxian dialectic, the result is a Y.M.C.A. Secretary.

Dogs down here do very well the year round. How about your own self, Sir?   Yrs. Allen

*This word reminds me of Edmund's poem beginning:

"The next on my list is Malcolm Cowley
Who edits the New Republic so foully."

I suppose you've seen it. Middle age does not sweeten him, nor even the solace of a young wife.   AL

1. Axley, not otherwise identified, was coordinator of the writers' conference to be held in Savannah.   2. "Hemingway and His Critics," *Partisan Review* 6 (Winter, 1939), 52–60.

[March 1939]

Dear Allen: You ask me, sir, how I be. I think I am like the psychologist's rat who in a maze finds every turn changed and every exit closed. I am not so happy. This winter—not the winter as a cold season, but as a passage of time has brought me very low—lower I think than I have ever been since the winter after the war. And I am less young by twenty years. Depression has brought on a blood prssure some fifteen points higher than the starving Gandhi when his became a matter of comment in the House of Commons and a matter of grave concern to the British Empire. No one from Washington has spoken of mine.

Well, enough of that. I am sure nothing will so cheer me up as seeing you. If you have no cheer to impart, you can always make me feel I am sane, which in this world as it goes I sometimes doubt.

To come to practical matters. I think I'll have to decline your invitation to journey down with you and Caroline from Greensboro. I can't get away earlier than the 3rd. And I believe it best to get on the train and go straight through to Savannah. I am sure the trip will do me good. But at this moment I am tired in a ridiculous way after small effort.   My best to you both. John   AL

                                                   The University of North Carolina Press
April 17, 1939   Chapel Hill, N.C.

Dear John: This Press is planning to get out under my editorship a series of modern poets, to be called the Chapel Hill Poets. We should expect to publish three books in the fall and three in the spring for a number of years. Each series of six books will be bound uniformly, but each volume in a different color; we should probably sell the books at $1.50 the single copy, the whole series of six for $6.00 to subscribers in advance.[1]

Before we definitely decide to go ahead we are asking the more prominent young poets of America and England whether we might in the near future be permitted to publish books by them. An expression of interest on your part would not in any sense commit you to giving us a book, although we do hope that you may be willing to do so. We should like the privilege of using your name in stimulating interest among possible subscribers to our first and second series.   Sincerely yours, Allen Tate   TLS
John Peale Bishop, Esq.
South Chatham, Massachusetts

1. This project was never undertaken.

April 21, 1939

Dear Allen: If my name will stimulate any of your potential readers
of your series of poets, I shall be only too happy to have you use it.

Now as to my giving you a book I should like both your friendly
and your editorial advice. I have been trying to pull myself together
for some time to get out another book, largely made up of the poems
in Minute Particulars, with certain omissions, and some additions of
more recent works. I meant to send it to Scribner's and shall probably
do so.

But it is just possible that I might be able to put together two
volumes. I think one of the things that has bothered reviewers of my
previous poetic volumes has been the too wide range of subject matter. The reviewers like a unity to hold them through the pages of a
book. Now I might put all my American poems into one book—for
Scribner's—and give you all my pseudo-Roman poems: The Return,
No More the Senator, An Interlude (which needs another title) and
perhaps two or three others which you have not seen which use
mythological subjects for psychological situations. It would make a
small book, but I don't see any objection to that.

It did me lots of good just to see you all in Savannah and I have
come back in a more or less normal state of nerves. But I still labor
under a sense of abnormal fatigue, both mental and physical, which is
making work hard.

Two of my poems have just come from Mesures,[1] very well translated into French. It has been fun going over them.   Sincerely yours,
John   TLS

1. "Speaking of Poetry" and "The Truth About the Dew," with translations by Marc Le
Templier, appeared in *Mesures* 5 (July 15, 1939), 191-95.

May 4, 1939

Dear John: The letter I wrote you about the poetry series was
dictated—the same letter to about a dozen people; hence, the un-
natural tone. Your idea about a book of Roman poems is excellent. I
see no reason why it wouldn't go very well indeed. So, if the series
goes through, as I think it will, let's put it down as one of the first six
books. If the plans work out, this would mean publication just a year
from now at latest; possibly next November.

It was fine to see you in Savannah. Since then, I have been much
distraught making a decision; now that it's made, depression has

succeeded distraction. I've consented to go to Princeton for one year, with possible renewal for a second year, to take charge of the literary part of the Creative Arts Experiment.[1] You will know what it is— music, painting, sculpture already operating; now literature. The money and the release of Caroline from teaching were the decisive features. I am depressed because Princeton, pleasant though it may be at 20, seems stuffy to a man of 40. But as jobs for men of letters go, it's a good one, and doubtless it will not be too onerous for a man credited with being a "good teacher" which means a certain facility of the tongue that the pen lacks.—Part of my duty will be the exposure of the boys to other writers in the flesh. Maybe you'll come down.

I wish I could turn the job here over to a man of my choice. It seems probable they will not get anybody to succeed us. Which shows that they never believed in our work, but simply wanted some travelling salesmen.

You must keep in mind the visit to Tennessee after Olivet. We're expecting you.   Affectionately, Allen   AL

1. Tate remained at Princeton until 1942, when he returned to Monteagle, Tennessee, because teaching was interfering with his writing. He apparently made a wise decision, because the early 1940s were one of his most productive periods.

May 16, 1939

Dear Allen: Your letter arrived just as I was leaving for New York a week ago and so has remained unanswered until now, when I am rather limp from the trip. But I don't want to let more time go by without saying that I am glad you are going to Princeton. I am glad for Princeton and while I am not sure how happy you will be there, I am glad for you. I rather hope a season among the enemies will provoke you to poetry.

It isn't that Princeton isn't a pleasant place—it is, but sleepily so, unless it has changed plenty and the lotus-eaters have no longer their old diet. But in one year, you won't drowse too deep. I suspect, on the contrary, you will have some fights to face, and that is why I think it will bring you back to poetry.

I went to New York at the behest of Br'er Ransom to cover the World's Fair for his Review.[1] It's a sight not to be missed. Coming back, I stopped to see Edmund, his new wife, whom I like, his new baby, who is buxom and bouncing.[2] He spent a good deal of time cursing out our Alma Mater, while consuming a perfectly incredible amount of whisky. He goes to Chicago in a few weeks to teach for the summer and possibly longer. I think he hopes to get R. M. Lovetts's job—he now having gone as administrator, or whatever the title is, to the Virgin Islands.

I heard E. W.'s piece on M. Cowley, which is even wickeder than the Omelet of A. MacLeish.

My two trips have greatly rejuvenated me, except for my hair which is now about like the Prisoner of Chillon's.

I am doing Ransom's article for him, then tackling *Finnegan's Wake* for the S. R.[3] It is hard going, but great poetry in spots.

My love and congratulations on the Princeton appointment. Before you go I'll give you the names of some people whom you might like there. John   AL

1. "World's Fair Notes," *Kenyon Review* 1 (Summer, 1939), 239–50.   2. Edmund Wilson married Mary McCarthy in April, 1938. Their son, Reuel Kimball Wilson, was born Christmas day, 1938.   3. "Finnegan's Wake," *Southern Review* 5 (Winter, 1940), 439–52.

May 24, 1939

Dear John: As to Princeton, I am glad to have the good wishes of all good men and true, because it is not going to be easy up there. But I am no longer like Browning, who was ever a fighter; I am now a man of peace; so I look for no wars at Princeton. I don't see why you didn't make it a duet with Edmund in cussin' Princeton. You or Edmund should have been asked to take the job. Instead, they got a Southerner who had not been at Princeton, nor is he even an alumnus of the University of Virginia; whom the Alumni Weekly describes as "the most promising of the younger poets, who is perhaps best known to the general public for his collaboration with Herbert Agar in *Who Owns America?*" I should think they could have got somebody better than that. As a matter of fact, if I am going to be in a university, I ought to be at Vanderbilt, which wouldn't have me for the same reason that Princeton overlooked you and Edmund: they know me too well. I am sure that Edmund's politics and the cracks that he took at his Alma Mater in his piece on More made them fear him. For similar reasons my name has been dropped from the rolls of the Vanderbilt alumni; I am cast out.

I am trying to do an article, before June 6th, on Ransom and Wilson, Critics—a tough assignment that I've been dallying with for ten months; but I am determined to finish it this time.[1]

I look forward to your piece on the World's Fair: it will be the nearest I'll get to that graveyard of an era.   Yrs. aff. Allen   TLS

1. "The Present Function of Criticism," *Southern Review* 6 (Autumn, 1940), 236–46.

May 28, 1939

Dear John: I'm sorry I can't help you about the Alcestis Press. They've done another disappearing act. About a year and a half ago

Latimer wrote me that I could buy the remainders of *The Med.*, but I didn't want them. I forgot the address he gave, if any, but I think it was a number on Charles Street. It seems that Stevens is the only poet he treated decently.

After June 6th our address will be "Westwood," Monteagle, Tennessee. You must come down from Olivet.[1]   Yrs., Allen   AL

1. Bishop was scheduled to participate in the annual writers' conference at Olivet College (Michigan).

[Summer, 1939]   Olivet, Saturday

Dear Allen: I wish I could accept your invitation and it would be possible to do so, since Sherwood Anderson wants me to drive with him—which is on the way—but I have promised to deliver a series of lectures on Cape Cod, which means that I must hurry back as soon as the Conference is over. The worst is that they won't amount to much when I do. Ralph Lawton, a musician friend of Paris days, is trying to found a school of the arts on the Cape and I am supposed to help out with more or less a repetition of my lectures here. I shall probably have an audience of five. But it was one of those things I couldn't well get out of. I find Olivet much easier than Boulder, though at the moment I'm fairly weary. The reason undoubtedly is that Sunday a representative of the League of American Writers turned up and argued their case in an hour devoted to Propaganda vs Literature. The very existence of such people tires me, and I was suddenly thrust into the position of chairman of the military.

You are generous to say the World's Fair article was excellent. But I will say it was better before JCR edited it. Why does he feel *that* is the essential job of the editor?

Thanks for the invitation. I wish I could accept it. John   AL

1939-1944

After Tate's accession to the resident poet's chair in the Princeton Creative Arts Program, and after Bishop's appointment as the chief poetry reviewer for *The Nation*, the frequency of their contact increased markedly, as this last section of the correspondence shows. When Tate invited Bishop to appear as a guest in a lecture series at Princeton early in 1940, he urged him to bring along his current and past poetry manuscripts, and the two men spent much of Bishop's visit planning an edition of his selected poetry, which Tate successfully urged Maxwell Perkins to publish.

Early in 1941 Bishop took up temporary residence in New York City when he accepted the post of publications director of the Office of the Coordinator of Inter-American Affairs, under the Office for Emergency Management. He and Tate saw each other frequently for the next eighteen months, and the letters of this period document fairly closely the editorial collaboration of the two men on *American Harvest*, a United States anthology to be translated into Spanish for a Latin American audience. Already fluent in French, Bishop in his new post studied Spanish and translated some Spanish poems as he planned and supervised several South American anthologies. Tate served while at Princeton as a permanent panelist for nine months on the CBS series "Invitation to Learning," broadcast from New York. Bishop was an occasional guest on this program during his tenure with the Coordinator's Office and afterwards.

With the publication of *American Harvest* and *Reason in Madness*, Tate resigned his Princeton post in 1942 and returned to Monteagle, Tennessee, where he began once again to write verse. The letters of the last three years or so exhibit a resumption of the detailed and careful criticism the two gave each other's work in the early years of their correspondence. Bishop's specific recommendations improved one of Tate's finest works, "Seasons of the Soul," and Tate dedicated the poem to Bishop in gratitude and affection. Similarly, Tate's close scrutiny proved invaluable in revising "The Hours," Bishop's elegy on the death of F. Scott Fitzgerald, and surely one of his finest poems.

Fitzgerald's death affected Bishop profoundly, manifesting itself in a pervasive sense of his own mortality. This event, coupled with the fall of France and the advent of World War II, dispirited Bishop greatly. His wife's involvement in the Women's Army Corps left mundane household duties to him, and he sank into a depression as severe as any he had known. Tate, who had in 1943 accepted a post as consultant in poetry in the Library of Congress, persuaded Archibald MacLeish, the librarian, to offer Bishop a post in comparative litera-ture. After serving only a few days as a resident fellow at the Library, Bishop suffered a heart attack from which he never recovered. He died four months later at Cape Cod Hospital in Hyannis, Mas-sachusetts.

September 28, 1939   16 Linden Lane/Princeton, New Jersey

Dear John: Two weeks of Princeton today. If the sample is represen-tative, I shall hate to leave it. Nobody knows what ought to be done, nobody seems to care. Like the grave, a fine and private place; and if there are no embraces,* then that too makes it easy to work. I had heard that the pace is fast; if it is, we are out of it, and pray not to get into it.—You must come down in November (you choose the date), and talk to my boys. It is my impression—to be confirmed in a few days—that I am to bring friends here at the expense of the University. I hope this will please my friends as much as it does me.—If by chance you will be in N.Y. the week end of October 7th, let me know: I will be there.

What are you doing? And how are Margaret and the boys?   Aff., Allen

*don't misunderstand me.   AL

October 3, 1939

Dear John: It is fine to know that you've had a spurt of poesy. I hope I will see the results soon. I had a brief one this summer, but if you've seen the results in the new *Kenyon*, [1] you will agree with me that it was not attended by much fire. But it may be leading to something. We grow more and more like childless women, who hope that this month they will become pregnant.

The whole question of paying people to come here to talk to my group will have to be settled very soon. I know that Gauss favors it, if he can get access to a fund. Occasional expenses, I gather, can be charged to some general account, but fees for speakers seem to be a separate problem. He will very likely ask me for a memorandum on the subject, expecting me to say that we can't ask people to work for nothing; then he will present the case to the committee.

I have been told that a certain clique here, Humanist disciples of More and the research scholars, have decided to ignore the ignorant writer—which is splendid; it means that I will see very few people, and having already met those few and like them, I am happy. Gauss is a very remarkable man, whose elevation to the deanery is a mystery to me. He is the only academic official I've ever known who is intelligent enough to be something else, and something else extremely good. Aff., Allen AL

1. "The Trout Map," *Kenyon Review* 1 (Autumn, 1939), 404–5.

October 23, 1939

Dear John: I doubt if it will be necessary for me to exploit you. Gauss said the other day that if his present plan went through there would certainly be a fee. His plan is this: He wants to have a series of lectures on the interrelations of the arts—an effort to make the Creative Arts Program work as a unit. I suggested you for the relation between poetry and painting. How does that strike you? You could certainly sell the lectures to the Southern Review, and add to the fee here. I don't know yet just when Gauss would want you to come. I'll ask him this week.

I am glad you like the poem. It is the only one I finished of several that got off to a poor start. But I may do some more. It seems I will have a good deal of leisure here.

Caroline has done about 50,000 words on a pioneer-Indian novel.[1]—If you come to N.Y. suddenly, let me know. Have you seen Dr. Wilson? I hear he's on the Cape. Yrs., Allen AL

1. *Green Centuries* (New York: Charles Scribner's Sons, 1941). This title comes from Bishop's 1936 poem "Experience in the West," and was one of many phrases from his poetry which Caroline Gordon and Scribner's had considered. In an undated letter to Bishop in 1939, she reported Scribner's had narrowed the choice down to "The Burning Wheel" (also from "Experience in the West") and "Green Centuries," and had decided finally "that Green Centuries is best after all. Max has decided that with the world in the condition it now is we need not action but rest in a title."

Sea Change
South Chatham, Massachusetts

October 25, 1939

Dear Allen: I think your suggestion a good one—that I do a lecture on the relation of poetry and painting. Your letter has just come and I have not had much chance to think its contents over. But off-hand I should say that the thing for me to do would be to begin with the breakup of sensibility that occurred somewhere between 1908 and 1914 and show how this had worked out in painting and in poetry. I proposed an essay on the subject to S[tringfellow] Barr some years ago, when I was still in Paris, where I was always in contact with what was happening in painting. And it would be harder to do it now in proportion as I have lost touch with painting. Not that anything significant has happened in painting since I left there, and I think that it was only in Paris that anything significant did happen in painting. The poets on the other hand with whom I should deal would be mostly Americans, though I think I should have to consider Joyce as a poet in Ulysses and Finnegan's Wake. I don't take much stock in American painting. All that has happened so far is that the market has moved to America and also, I think, though I may be wrong, some of the awareness that was once only in Paris.

But do you think that I should treat the subject only historically? Or, since it is one of the ideas with which you have concerned your-self, would you like me to do a Lessing and go into the essential difference of the two arts.[1] That could be done, incidentally, in the course of covering the happenings since the Cubists and the Imagists.

I should need at least two weeks to turn out an essay-lecture, so let me know as soon as you can when you want me at Princeton. There is, as a matter of fact, no reason why I shouldn't get to work on it at once, though it will need some days' contemplation and the hunting up of old notes. The thing is, of course, to show that the same fundamental changes were taking place simultaneously in both the arts, as both reflected the changing times.

I am glad to hear that Caroline has been so prolific. And also that you, too, are having time for poetry. If I get one poem out of seven I start, I think I am doing well.   Yours ever, John   TLS

1. Bishop is referring to Gotthold Ephraim Lessing (1729-1781), a German man of letters whose theoretical criticism provided a model for many twentieth-century critics.

November 8, 1939

Dear John: The wheels of the Academe are not wheels of fire. After elaborate conferences with Gauss on the subject of conflicting dates, we have found that the first free date for the purpose will be Tuesday, January 23rd. That will give you plenty of time to develop your sub-ject. And I hope you can come. The lecture, mainly for the Creative Arts groups, will be thrown open to the public. And there will be a fee—somewhere between fifty and a hundred dollars, probably nearer the latter. Gauss still has to fix the price of my lecturers with the University Lecture Committee. It is wonderfully complicated.

I should prefer to hear you do a Lessing, rather than a strictly historical account of poetry and painting. A little background of course will be necessary, so that the audience will understand the illustrations that you will use. In my group, I talk constantly from an un-historical (not anti-) point of view, largely to offset what they hear from the professors, who teach literature as history only.

Of course you will stay with us, and I hope you will stay several days and let my boys see you and ask questions.   Yrs. in haste,
Allen   AL

November 28, 1939

Dear John: I hope I didn't send my last to a fantastic address; I don't see how I could; but then anything can happen.—We've put you down for January 23rd; in order to secure that date on the University Calendar we had to seize it before we heard from you.—I spent yesterday in New York—have been depressed all day as a result.   Yrs.
[Allen]   AL

December 7, 1939

Dear John: It's fine that you can come; we had gone ahead and put you down for January 23rd, so the delay of your consent caused no confusion whatever.

I didn't mean at all when I suggested that you "do a Lessing" that he need come into the discussion. I only meant that for our group here a theoretical discussion, as opposed to an historical, would probably be more effective. But that was only a suggestion. What we want is what you are most interested in and can do best.

When you come I wish you would plan to stay on for at least a week or ten days. We have an extra room of moderate size which we seldom use. I would like for you to bring all your poetry down here and go to work on organizing it for a Collected Poems. I believe it is easier to do that sort of thing if you are with somebody who will prod you (if you wouldn't mind my prodding) and who wishes to talk it over as you go along. Please consider this seriously.

Of course, Dr. Wilson has never been quite human, and I am not surprised to hear that he has become a metabolic machine for the transformation of alcohol. The remarkable thing about him is the way in which he emerges from one of his heresies, all ready to start over again—rather like those women who after bearing six children look, act, and feel like virgins. (What will his next heresy be?) I too have taken a melancholy pleasure in the gyrations of the comrades. But it has all had a very bad effect on my character; it does one no good to be in a position to say several times a day, "I told you so."   Yrs aff.
Allen   TLS

December 29, 1939

Dear Allen: I'm sorry to hear that the appendix is making trouble, but the delay suits me very well. Margaret has been through a siege of grippe, which first attacked one ear, with intense pain, then developed into pneumonia. She is pretty well now and will probably return from the hospital tomorrow. But I have been and still am under a considerable strain. I have done no work for two weeks and am now so nervously exhausted that I wouldn't work if leisure were restored to me. That is the way middle age affects me—I simply can't take it any longer. I am all too easily depleted. Yours, John   AL

[January 1940]

Dear Allen: I am going to accept your offer of help to collect my privately published and unpublished poems—with gratitude and alacrity. Your offer is indeed just what I need to make me put them in shape. I will get them copied before arriving in Princeton and we can go over them selecting and arranging.[1] My trouble is that I have so little interest in a work that is finished and when I try to deal with poems in that state I at once start on something new. An endless process_____.

I get no satisfaction from saying "I told you so" to our Marxist friends, but only silently and villainously smile. But I do find it possible—and satisfactory—at last to talk freely to Edmund. I haven't done that for years. He has consumed those years laboriously arriving at conclusions which we reached by intuition long ago. At the same time, he is now able to discuss Marx with an authority which I don't possess, lacking his learning. However, I am quite happy in my own simple condemnation which has sufficed me all along. I read the news about Finland, I think of Thermopylae and I say to myself, if they are defeated, Thermopylae remains. Not even Stalin can take away the three hundred that died.

Give my best to Caroline. Yours, John   AL

1. Bishop's *Selected Poems* (New York: Charles Scribner's Sons, 1941) appeared the following year.

January 3, 1940

Dear John: Just before your letter came Paul Rosenfeld told me in N.Y. about Margaret's illness; and it is good to hear that she is well enough to leave the hospital. I get alarmed when I hear anything about ears. Eleanor Agar had a strep germ in the ear for six months; but I gather that Margaret escaped that.—It is well, then, that we put off your lecture. I go to the hospital on the 15th, and unless curiosities are found in the peritoneum, I shall expect to be out by the 25th, and easily on my feet, but not running marathons, by the time you arrive. I look forward to going over your ms., and I hope you will be able to stay on the ten days or two weeks, as we planned.

At Paul Rosenfeld's I saw Cummings (plus beauteous young wife: the two E's[1] wives miraculously keep the same age year after year), and greatly enjoyed him. I felt that we were both a little smug about our aloofness from Father Marx. I observed a great change in Estlin;[2] for example, he had all the politeness of a Southern gentleman towards Jean Untermeyer—which the Southern gentleman present achieved only with great difficulty. He was actually sweet-tempered.

I was a little surprised to see you liking Kenneth Patchen. I can see nothing in him but insolence—not youthful spirits, as you seem to feel.—Your piece on Joyce is, as I expected it to be, the best yet published.[3] But I remain unconvinced by *Finnegan's Wake*.

Give Margaret my greetings. Let us, at our age, wish ourselves a New Year no worse than the last.   Aff. Allen   AL

1. Edmund Wilson and E. E. Cummings.   2. E. E. Cummings.   3. "Finnegan's Wake," *Southern Review* 5 (Winter, 1940), 439-52.

[January 1940]

Dear Allen: This is to wish you all good luck with the peritoneum and any other parts the surgeon's knife is about to lay bare.

I am looking forward mightily to seeing you. Margaret's illness—and the consequent falling of her household care on my incompetent head—have rather held up all work. But she is now pretty well recovered—though she is still confined to the house—the boys are all back at school—and life is snowy, but otherwise ordinary. I have been revising poems and hope to have a large batch to show you.

I thought [Delmore] Schwartz did a pretty good job on you.[1] Someday, I hope to attempt the same task, which I shall approach in another way.

I understand your reservations on *Finnegan's Wake*. Just the same, you can't shake it off, once you have gone through the book.   See you soon—John   AL

1. "The Poetry of Allen Tate," *Southern Review* 5 (Winter, 1940), 419-38.

February 10, 1940

Dear Caroline: My visit to Princeton gave me great pleasure—not the least part of which was seeing that you and Allen were content with your choice to accept the post there. I greatly appreciate all you both did in going over my manuscripts and I feel sure I derived profit from discussing the future—and now less definite—novel.

I saw Max Perkins in New York and he asked, perhaps not without impatience, how your novel was coming on. I put in a good word for it and swore you were working hard. He accepted the poems unseen, delaying decision on the essays until he had seen them. Which is fair enough.

I got an outraged cry from MacLeish on my return, objecting to my review of *America Was Promises*. I have heard a little more of his position in Washington and will write Allen shortly on that subject.[1]

I met [Arthur] Mizener at Yale and delivered your messages.[2] He is certainly impressed—I might say awe-struck—by you two. He seemed to regard you as little short of the super human.

I was wonderfully treated at Yale myself and Finnegan's Wake went on after an hour's formal lecture for another two hours, first in the hall where I had spoken, then in the living room of the master of Pierson College.

With much love and many thanks for your excellent care of me—
John   AL

1. Bishop's review appeared in *Nation* 150 (February 3, 1940), 132-33.   2. Bishop delivered a lecture on *Finnegan's Wake* at Yale on his return from Princeton to Cape Cod.

1940 Feb 11 AM9:14 [rec'd]   WESTERN UNION
Allen Tate/16 Linden Lane   I heard of you at Yale quote at last Princeton has got a man who will not tolerate mediocrity.

Bishop

February 11, 1940

Dear Ole Br'er Bishop: Your telegram bearing the news from Yale contains like all compliments at least an unintended irony. The question here at Princeton is not whether I will tolerate mediocrity; it is whether mediocrity will tolerate me.

You know I felt that you were in better shape than I had ever seen you. The old man evidently has a lot of ergs in him yet. It all gave me great satisfaction—which I regret that I was too listless to communicate to you.

After New York we went to the wedding on Saturday in Philadelphia—all of which, as to the viscera, I survived beautifully; but Sunday I came down with the flu, and am just up. And I must lecture in Brooklyn Tuesday.

What were the results with Max and Colston Leigh?

You will be amused to hear what is being said about your lecture. All my boys were enthusiastic about it. The profs said *no*. That's all Gauss will need to know to make up his mind in your favor.

Old Dr. Wilson, in a letter the other day, was still trying to put over on me as *his* subject the Boyhood of Lenin, and so rigged his request as to make my refusal seem to be skittishness about Communism here. I had to read him a pretty stiff lecture on that bit of casuistry.

I see you are back on the Cape. How is it? Love to Margaret.   Aff.
Allen   AL

February 12, 1940

Dear Allen: I am enclosing the Cordon Bleu recipe for *Moules a la Mariniere,* which I forgot to put in Caroline's letter. This seems to be the classic recipe. I haven't been able to locate my parsnip wine directions. When I do, I'll forward them. By the way, I've quantities of French cookbooks and can probably supply any recipe Caroline wants, at any time.

My trip did me lots of good, even though the cold that was starting when I left you did develop into uncomfortable proportions by Sunday. I went out to stay with Edward Donahoe who, his wife, whom he now abhors, being in his own house, entertained me at Lifford Cochrane's,[1] in a style to which I have been too long unaccustomed. Cochrane's house is a pretentious, very late classical mansion built about 1840, and has been furnished at great expense and with New York interior decorator accuracy in early Victorian fashion. The servants were three and trained: the food good and the liquor unfailing and of the best quality. I sank into the great mindlessness and stayed there with the morning aid of wine, the evening assistance of whisky, until leaving for Yale.

No, that is not quite accurate. I pulled myself together on Monday, saw Perkins (who accepted the poetical arrangements we had worked out, but reserved a decision on the essays) and Colston Leigh (who was willing to take me on, but held out little promise of making much money).[2]

My lecture at Yale was such a success as I have dreamed but never known waking. I am afraid it went (temporarily) to my head. At the end of an hour, I came to a close by reading the last page or so of Finnegan's Wake. I think some four or five boys then left. The rest of the audience stayed on asking questions for another hour. Then a selected lot moved on to the Master's House at Pierson College, where we ate, drank, and talked more Joyce.

I got back here to find a pained letter from A. MacLeish. He did not like my review in The Nation.[3] As a matter of fact, rereading it, it seems fairly sharp to me. I intended to make it as mild as I could and not myself lose countenance.

My family are all in good shape and were very glad to see me. Nothing like a separation to improve familial relations. Jonathan has picked up wonderfully at school. Margaret seems quite herself again. So that there was nothing to mar my homecoming but Mac-Leish's letter and the Massachusetts Income Tax, which I have spent today preparing to pay.

I am sorry about your flu, especially since it was probably I who dropped the germs about you. I am still a little sniffling, but expect to get to work as soon as I have disposed of a few accumulated chores, like preparing tax returns.

By the way, I found I had your brother's letter secreted in my manuscripts. I return it with apologies.

I can never thank you and Caroline enough for what you did for me at Princeton. I was so well-fed, both as regards the material and the metaphysical man.   Affectionately, John   AL

1. A wealthy New York social and cultural figure.   2. A collection of Bishop's essays was published posthumously in 1948, edited by Edmund Wilson. Bishop's *Selected Poems* appeared from Scribner's in 1941.   3. Bishop reviewed MacLeish's *Air Raid* and *American Was Promises* in "The Muse at the Microphone," *Nation* 150 (February 3, 1940), 132–33.

March 8, 1940

Dear John: I've been working a little, and sinking back into depression a little; and now MacLeish's latest diplomacy irritates me a little. I send you the specimen. It is competent in its way, but far from masterly; even I could have suggested a better way to dispose of the offer he made me.—Of course, I hadn't set March 15th as a deadline; I had merely said that March 15th would be convenient for me, but for him to take his time. So he has set up a nice dilemma: either before March 15th (which is impossible) or a year from now (which would be never). He could have disposed of me much better by saying that he couldn't hold the job for me a year; I had given him the opportunity. But instead he lamely refers to the difficulties of getting the money for the job—which casts suspicion upon his original offer. I had assumed he had the money. And why shouldn't I? You don't offer jobs if you can't pay.—I am considering the question closed.[1] But I couldn't resist writing MacLeish a letter (of the most polite sort), which will make him very uneasy.

There's something a little sinister in this, or there is when you think of it in connection with similar actions on his part. It would define the kind of insanity he would have if he ever went off.

I've done one article since you were here, not a good one, but an article at any rate; for The English Journal, the teachers' magazine in Chicago, a foul sheet but it pays well. And I tried to write it for the teachers; you can imagine how well I succeeded.[2]

Have you begun to send mss to Perkins?[3] I had a long letter from him the other day, in which he said he was delighted to publish the poems. That's the way I like to hear 'em talk. I hear it so seldom.— Love to Margaret.   Aff. Allen   TLS

1. MacLeish had offered Tate a position in the Library of Congress and Tate had replied that he would have to give Princeton ample notice and requested postponement of the appointment for a year. MacLeish responded that he had planned to request money for the position only after Tate accepted it. Tate eventually became consultant in poetry at the Library of Congress in September, 1943.   2. Apparently this essay was not published.   3. *Selected Poems* (1941).

May 10, 1940

Dear Allen: I just saw Dr. Wilson and he tells me that you are expected *chez lui* sometime within the month. I shall hope that you and Caroline will arrange to stay here some days, as long as you can.

The weather, after an interminable winter, is now fine. I have spring fever, but have succeeded in turning out the enclosed poem—which may be a product of spring fever.[1]

I have my collected poems at the typist's—at last. Due no little to your aid, it is a good book. I have done no end of work on it, though the revisions are so few and so slight that they will not show how much labor went into them.

Margaret and Robert are in New York, having a holiday which both deserve. Jonathan is in the school infirmary with pneumonia, but we hope to bring him home in another three or four days. It was apparently a slight attack, but pneumonia is nothing to be foolish about. Margaret is still not entirely *remise* from her show at Christmas.

The poem is very new and there are still some lines I am not sure about. I wish I would stop writing on this theme, but it must be exorcizing my unconscious in some odd way, for whatever I do write on J. C. simply pops into my mind with no preliminary meditation.

Give my best to Caroline. How are the explorers and scouts and Cherokees and things?

Now do come to stay with us. I want you.   Yours, John.   TLS

1. Not identified.

May 24, 1940

Dear John: Yes, we expect to come up to the Cape but because we've decided to stay in Princeton all summer we shall not come before August 1st. I fear that will miss you, if I remember the dates of the Olivet affair, but we shall see.[1] We have fixed the date at that time because I have a lecture at Bread Loaf, which will pay for the excursion.

I am delighted that the poetry ms is in shape: I hope you will let me read the proofs. The new poem is a good one, but not your best, except in the two last stanzas. I would certainly put it in the book.

The war has me hanging on to the radio all day and half the night. I still don't believe the Germans will win, but the Allies will take so long to fight them off that we shall get into it, and I will go to gaol as an Isolationist, or worse. As you know, I have strong sympathy for the Germans politically & economically, but not "culturally"; the result is a perfect neutrality.

If we miss you on the Cape, stop here when you go to Olivet.

I am trying to start the new novel, but as usual I can't get the rhythm for the first page.   Aff. Allen   AL

1. Bishop was scheduled to attend the annual Writers' Conference at Olivet College.

May 30, 1940

Dear John: The remotest smell of gunpowder puts Max into a state, and I know he is unmanned now. (As who isn't?) I think he would not object to the change to another publisher if he felt that his delay was hampering you. Max likes to publish us, but we don't make him any money; and he would not contest our wishes.

I am afraid now you are right: the Germans will win. I incline to the belief that the Nazis will ignore England for a while after the clean-up in Flanders, and attack France, not only along the Somme-Oise line, but from the rear through Spain, with or without Italy. A dash to England would be heroics only: the British are already defeated in so far as effective combat is concerned. For several years I've thought that Nazism had us in the position of heads-I-win, tails-you-lose. In order to fight them, we shall have to be like them; even if we won a war against them, they would still be the victors. It seems to me that the sooner we accept this probability, the easier we shall feel. It is curious that Hitler has not yet made a mistake, while Russia no less than Britain has made nothing else. There may be a moral in it. If we see Communism as an extension of capitalism (as I've always seen it), the failures of Britain, France and Russia indicate the proper way for a civilization to collapse, in terms of war; and in this picture belong the withdrawal of Belgium and the disaffection in the French army.—The French Revolution was a mere cloak-and-sword romance.

Well, here we are with our nerves exposed, and no protection—which is also as it should be at such a time.   Yrs. aff. Allen

P.S. Why don't you just write Max about the other publisher? I shouldn't do it until I had the other man's definite offer.   A. T.

AL

July 8, 1940

Dear John: I am sending this to South Chatham although I suspect that by "leaving Sunday" you meant yesterday and that you are already with Anderson. (Your note of the 5th just got here today—the 8th). But if you meant next Sunday, please start a few days early and stop here. Or by all means stop between the 27th and the 1st. That might be our only chance to see you this summer; the trip to the Cape is not so distinct as it was. It now depends upon the collection of some cash in the next two weeks. (No salary in the summer.)

My second performance on CBS I felt better about than I did about the first.[1] The great trouble is that they won't let you talk long enough at one time to make a point: it must sound like "conversation." I'm on again on the 21st—Cicero's dull *De Officiis.*

The first shock of the war is over for me, and I cease to hang upon the news.—I'd like very much to talk about it with you. I imagine we'd agree. If it comes to an issue between our sort of fascism *vs.* the German, I'm willing to fight; but for democracy, no. I have a quite credible report (from the man who heard it) that Lord Lothian recently said privately that democracy (i.e. laissez-faire capitalism) is done for even in England, and that they don't even want it back.—I don't either.

Remember us to Sherwood and to all friends at Olivet.   Aff. Allen

AL

1. Along with Mark Van Doren, Katherine Anne Porter, and other guests, Tate appeared as a panelist on the CBS radio show "Invitation to Learning" for a period of nine months in 1940–41.

August 6, 1940

Dear John: The enclosure got buried under papers, has just emerged; and I sent it so that you may file under Dictated but not Read.

We still plan to come up, if the Wilsons can find us a house.

Edmund showed me your poetry ms. which I intended to borrow, but at the last minute forgot. I want to read it closely.—Did you say that Max had put it off indefinitely? Edmund's notion is that the postponement is for a season only. I expect to see Max next week, and should like to discuss it with him. Love to Margaret.   Aff. Allen

AL

August 8, 1940

Dear Allen: I was more sorry than I can say that I missed your visit to the Cape. But I am glad that it found sufficient favor in your eyes to make you want to return. You will, I think, like it even better after Labor Day, when the great majority of tourists and summer people move out.

I haven't seen any of the Wellfleet-Truro contingent since I returned. We have had domestic difficulties and guests, cooks that walked off in the middle of the night and guests that arrived at unholy hours in the morning. But we now have our old cook back—I hope to stay—and things are a bit calmer, though more guests are arriving tonight.

The latest I have heard on the poems is that they are postponed until February. The whole publishing world seems shot. I saw Allen Churchill of McBride's in New York on my way out to Olivet and he tells me how their income has sunk since May. And as we all know, Max can always be counted on for the worst jitters in New York. I had a long talk with Mary Colum on her troubles with him, or rather her suffering as a Scribner author from Max's private troubles.

Thanks for the MacLeishiana. Whatever he may be doing in the political world, he has certainly got himself in wrong with the writers. There wasn't a person at Olivet who wasn't eager to take a crack at him. I thought Edmund did him up rather well in the N.R.[1]

I came back from Olivet in much better shape than I went out. I still have a lot of French furniture to move about in my mind, and some, no doubt, to cast out, but both Glenway Westcott and Katherine Anne [Porter], who had suffered no less than I over the French collapse, were something of a help in making the readjustments I must make. I care greatly about France and not at all about England. Unless the British navy can defend the little island, I can't see that it will be of much use in defending our immense Atlantic coast-line. What has happened, of course, is that a lot of people are just waking up to the lessons of Jutland—that the British navy was a greatly overrated fighting force, that in fact it is not much good when it comes to fighting. If the British can convince me other wise, I shall gladly change my mind.   Yours, John   TLS

1. "Archibald MacLeish and 'The Word,'" *New Republic* 103 (July 1, 1940), 30–32.

November 26, 1940

Dear John: As you probably know, Edmund gave me your complete poetry ms. at the end of the summer. Off and on I have been reading it, and I want to tell you (what you already know) that it is a very impressive book. And I am not moved to that opinion by the dedication; but by the dedication I am greatly moved and pleased, all the more because I think I do not deserve the honor.[1]

The honor disqualifies me as a reviewer, but Dr. Wilson and I are conspiring to get you a somewhat better one; namely T. S. Eliot, if he can spare the time from his duties as air-raid warden, which I hear he performs with great celerity and skill.[2] (I am told further that he has invented a new fire-extinguisher—perhaps a confutterate wunderbusser—which he wears in his trousers leg.)

Are you coming to New York soon? I hear rumors about a magazine with you as editor—something hemispheric north-by-south; and I hope to hear shortly that the deal is closed.—I am in New York every Tuesday evening; so come down.

I will not be here next year, and I am a little relieved, even though at present I see no job.[3] I do not know who my successor will be; I have not been consulted, contrary to my expectations. I hope he is you. Affectionately, Allen AL

1. *Selected Poems* (1941). 2. T. S. Eliot never reviewed Bishop's volume. 3. Tate returned briefly to Monteagle, Tennessee.

[Autumn 1940—after Thanksgiving]

Dear Allen: We have had four boys in the house for the past three days—over the N.E. Thanksgiving holidays. And I know what the old New England houses were like with a maniac caged upstairs. Except that these aren't caged.

So don't expect much of a letter. But I don't want to let your own very good letter go longer unanswered.

Of course you deserve the dedication of the book of poems, since there is no one who did so much to get them written in the first place and none who, once they were written, has done more to promote them. As witness your latest endeavor—to get T. S. Eliot to read them between bombings and the invention of fire-extinguishers. Perhaps that is what he has been doing all along—pondering the perfect fire-extinguisher. (See The Waste Land & the passage about St. Augustine & Carthage.) But seriously I hope the conspiracy works toward the desired result. I should like nothing better than Uncle Tom's approval. In the meantime I am sustained by yours.

I have heard nothing about the magazine of which you write and so far as I am concerned am afraid it is only a rumor.

It has meant a lot being able to hear your voice once a week, as I have followed the Invitation to Learning program since its inception. I am more or less planning to come to New York just after the New Year (d.t. [?] and money being available) and if I do will make a point of being there on a Tuesday to see you.   Affectionately, JPB   AL

December 8, 1940

Dear John: This note, in case you don't get back to the hotel in time to get my telephone call.

It's fine you're in N.Y. Let's settle definitely on 4–6 (at the Chatham bar). The evening will be complicated. We are dining with Stark [Young]. At 8:45 I will take K. A. P. [Katherine Anne Porter] to CBS, along with Edmund, who is getting his voice tested for the air. We shall be through at 10:45, and can then come up to Glenway's [Westcott]. Why doesn't the dinner party come down to CBS for the broadcast? You are all hereby invited.

Till Tuesday, then.   Yrs. Allen   AL

December 20, 1940

Dear John: It's a little late to be telling you how sorry we were not to get up to Glenway's. What happened was that Slater Brown, who was staying with us, came to the studio completely boiled, and there was nothing to do but to take him back to Princeton as soon as possible.—We were extremely sorry to miss seeing Margaret.

I am sending you a still further revised version of my new poem.[1] You will immediately perceive that your fears for the decline of the Confutterate Wunderbusser were groundless. It fires as heavy a charge as ever, though I cannot vouch for the accuracy of its aim.

It's a little hard to create a date for you on the radio, but I see a place for you in February, and when the time comes to fill it I will bring you forward: the others will not have anybody to suggest. Your voice was excellent.

We hope that you all will have a cheerful Christmas. You know what mine will be like: CBS.   Aff. Allen   AL

1. "False Nightmare," New Republic 104 (March 24, 1941), 399.

January 8, 1941

Dear Allen: I am greatly disappointed that the radio appointment has been postponed. I understood, of course, that it was rather a possibility than an appointment, but I had nevertheless set my heart on Dante.

Now, if it is the matter of expenses that stands in the way, they can be dismissed. I did not, after talking to you, suppose that there was an allowance for expenses. I understood that there was a fee for visitors of seventy-five dollars and that if they happened to live out of New York, that was their hard luck. In any event I am quite ready to be responsible for my own expenses. I do not—between the two of us—greatly care whether I make anything out of this or not. It would please Margaret so much to have me on the program that her plea-sure would be a considerable recompense. And while I don't take the postponement too hard, I have no zeal to talk about Lessing.

What worries me about your poem is the *Who now reads Herrick?* I don't see its appropriateness. I should think there are other possible rhymes on which the line could be constructed. *Hysteric,* at once occurs to me.

The lack of precise observation in my own poem was intentional.[1] You may be right in thinking that I recoiled unconsciously from the subject, but as far as I was aware what I was trying to do was to give the occupation of Paris the quality of an anguished dream. Which is what it is to me; I have twice dreamed of being in the occupied city, of wandering through known streets for hours, and finding them almost deserted and altogether silent; at last, after traversing a great part of the city, I come on small groups of German soldiers, around the Arc de Triomphe. Both the dreams and the poem were influenced by a photograph, which I saw reproduced a number of times, of the con-quering troops entering the Place de la Concorde, and whatever is precise in the poem comes from that photograph, especially the ex-pressions on the faces of the soldiers.

Bunny doesn't like the poem and it may be I overrate it. But it still seems to me quite good.

I was delighted with what Katherine Anne has to say in New Directions on the subject of technical difficulties.[2] Otherwise, I can't say much for the new number, though I shall probably review the Surrealist portion, laying out the Surrealists as I was unable to do in my note on them in the volume itself.[3] Yours, John

[*marginal notes*] Thanks for Rose Radford's address. I shall hope to make good use of it.   TLS

1. "Occupation of a City," *Decision* 1 (March, 1941), 18.   2. "Notes on Writing," *New Directions in Poetry and Prose* (1940), 195–204.   3. "Chainpoems and Surrealism," *New Directions in Poetry and Prose* (1940), 363–68.

January 12, 1941

Dear John: I should have found out long ago your attitude about your expenses for your trip through the air. When CBS said they would pay expenses for the guests, they added firmly that we must get them from the immediate New York area; so, until I saw you in New York, it didn't occur to me to bring up the question of your being with us.—I fear now that Dante is out of the question; when Gauss couldn't come on for the Florentine, we took Auden for him, and switched Gauss to Lessing. BUT we are now planning a series of thirteen broadcasts on the novel, to begin April 9th (a sad day for persons of your history), and you will be my sole nomination for that series. (I have selected more than half of the guests for the present series.) So you may consider yourself engaged. The list of novels is not yet fixed: we do that next week; but as soon as we know the titles and the dates, I can give you something like a free choice. So tell Margaret that she will hear you in the spring; and tell her to be sure to remember where you are. One day Caroline forgot where I was, and shouted downstairs for me to stop talking so loud. I was disturbing her at work.

Alas, what can we hope for from our friends? Edmund doesn't like your new poem. You don't like mine. You think "Herrick" pointless; Edmund thought it a brilliant touch. Whom shall I believe? However, I don't see how you could have missed the point of Herrick. Isn't it plain that the barbaric yawp will try to supplant the art of the Herricks and their kind?

This letter may run on for a while; so I take time for an aside about [Randall] Jarrell. I hope you won't be too hard on him. He has a lot of poetry much better than his selection for the anthology. There are three poems scheduled for Edmund's special literary issue of the N.R., and they are the finest work by any new man in ten years. And on any relative scale isn't he immeasurably better than Patchen, whom you liked last year?

I like very much your piece on the chain-poems, and I await your onslaught upon the more general problem of surrealism.[1] I believe your critical style in this piece is the best you've ever done—very direct and sharp.—I don't quite follow you in your judgment of Katherine Anne's revelations. I believe if you will look at them more closely you will see that she really says nothing of any interest about the problems of the craft; she merely adjusts something quite commonplace to a certain tone which puts before the reader her own personality. That is growing on Katherine Anne all the time, and I fear for its results. There has been a wonderful change in her since I first knew her, even since about 1932, and I don't think it means anything good. She has become a Great Personage, and my experience of this sort of transformation convinces me that it signals, in her as in others, a weakening of the creative powers. It is easy to see how she has drifted into this state of mind: she has few of the ordinary human satisfactions—she can't live in the world, she can't have a deep emotional relationship with anybody, she is always moving: in fact, she is trapped in a cycle of romantic emotions that repeat themselves about every five years. I have watched her through three marriages and divorces, and the pattern in all three is identical. When the human personality suffers repeated failures in a fundamental objective experience, it recoils into self-worship, or at best a refined egoism; and women usually achieve only the former. She has got so that she can't distinguish between admiration of her work and admiration of herself; and the one feeds the other—which I need not say is a very dangerous situation. Look at the end of Old Mortality: all the rich life of those people is swept away with a callow judgment by MIRANDA (significant name); look at Pale Horse, Pale Rider, whose heroine's emotions are commonplace but whose personality is handled with a solemnity that comes very near being sentimentality. This is a distinct defect in K. A.'s work, and I don't think we are doing her any kindness at all in pretending that it has no defects. She is the kind of person, of course, who every one feels should be spared criticism; and I think we are right in sparing her. But I don't think we ought to praise her limitations. I have gone into all this just to make that one point. And, finally, I think some of her friends of the epicene order are very bad for her; they do nothing but flatter her, and while the flattery seems to be coming from men, it lacks the necessary element which would keep it in the right perspective—sex.—Look again at her notes in N[ew] D[irections], I beseech you. She owes, she says, nothing to observation: by putting the observation so far back into her childhood she virtually claims to have invented it. She owes nothing to experience—just as Ernest used to owe nothing to any other writer. This is the last vanity of the artist; and I have never known a woman writer who has survived it. Ernest survives it by getting a new war and a new girl.

I hope you will let me know when you expect to go through N.Y., going or returning from Gambier.[2]   Yrs. aff. Allen   TLS

1. "Chainpoems and Surrealism."   2. Ransom had invited Bishop to lecture at Kenyon.

January 18, 1941

Dear Allen: I had trailed the Florentine deep into Hell when your letter came, postponing my appointment with Invitation to Burning. However, I think it's just as well. There is never any harm in reading Dante. But as things have turned out April will be better for me than February. I have got myself too messed up in a muddle of things.

As you probably know, I have read only about a half dozen novelists in my life, so don't put me down for someone like George Eliot, which would entail, on my part, a lot of unprofitable work. If you are going to do Joyce, I speak for him; if not, I would prefer Stendhal to any of the classics.

I am going to be in New York next Tuesday night, arriving probably in good time for dinner, and going straight from the train to the Little Hotel. I would like to see you, but don't want to get into anything like a party that night, or stay up late, as I shall need a clear head the next day.

I am rather tired, having worked furiously all day on an elegy on Scott Fitzgerald for Bunny's memorial issue of the N.R.[1] So I shall say no more except that I do like your poem with the exception of one or two words. It was foolish of me to give the impression that, because of those words, I failed to understand or appreciate the poem as a whole. The end is strong and fine. I still don't like Herrick, and don't like rune. It isn't a question of meaning, but of tone. But I'll write more on this and the other topics of your letter when I am rested. Yours, John   TLS

1. "The Hours," *New Republic* 104 (March 3, 1941), 312–13.

January 18, 1941

Dear John: The *Selected Poems* arrived yesterday and were greeted as they deserved, with great satisfaction. It is a very fine book, and it will be here long after the noisy reputations of our time are forgotten. That is both an expression of feeling and a prediction. Wait and see. To see my name honorifically on the dedicatory page gives me the most intense pleasure.

At first I thought that Max's fit of economy, which ran all the poems together, had injured the appearance of the book; but I don't think the effect is bad. It is, in fact, a handsome book.

Will the new smell of new print stimulate the muse? It often affects me that way.   Affectionately, Allen   AL

January 22, 1941

Dear John: The poem gets better with every reading.[1] It is very, very fine—one of your best; and I am sorry it isn't in the new book. I have questioned rather narrowly a good many words and lines, thinking it better to err on the side of pedantry in my gloss than to miss anything. I believe the only serious criticism is the Ash-Wednesday tone in two passages; but I see no reason why you can't fix them up without sacrificing anything essential. The main problem is the repetitions. I think sections III and IV ought to be transposed, though this would lose the carried-over rhyme, *hid-did*.

I hope you will write me that the New York plans have been completed. It will be good for you to be there, good for your "employers," and it will mean a great deal to me to have you there. Aff. Allen   AL

1. "The Hours."

January 24, 1941

Dear Allen: Your eagerly awaited letter has just come and I am more grateful than I can say for your comment on the elegy. Your objections are made almost always at the same points that Bunny made his; but at the risk of pedantry, you have been precise as he was not; so that your notes will be much more useful to me in correcting the poem.

If there is only time enough I feel confident I can eradicate the weak passages and those recalling Ash Wednesday. The passages of which you approve are those which have been thoroughly written. The last two sections I had not been able to go over until I was at all satisfied with them. In fact, they were little more than drafts. For they had been gone over but twice, which in my case is not enough.

The whole question is time. I must get this damn lecture done for Ransom, though I have stolen time out today to work on the poem. But I am going to start in tomorrow and rush the lecture through. I have already worked out the 'thoughts' involved in the prospectus for the proposed review which I had made for Wheeler and MacLeish.[1]

I have agreed to work in New York for three months on the project along with another which will pay me a living wage.[2] Beyond that I have not implicated myself, remembering your experience with a certain person, as well as my own.[3] However, I might say here that the trouble is not, as far as I can make out, that he means to let people down. His enthusiasm runs away with him. He considers matters settled, when the wherewithal has not been found. That applies in the present instance, though there is some indication, through other sources, that it may be found. So far as my temporary position is concerned, I don't anticipate any trouble, though I wait until Monday to know definitely that Washington has agreed to New York's proposals. So until then, I had best say no more.

Again, thanks for the careful going over you have given the poem.

I hope Caroline gets back to see the Indians in less of a crush than

IV

Now you have outlived the nocturnal terror
The head hanging in the hanging mirror
And the hour haunted by the haggard face.

Now you are drunk at last. And that disgrace
You sought in oblivious dives you have
At last, in the dissolution of the grave.

V

(redo out line)
Concealing of sad self-loathing, nothing?

I have lived with you the hours of your humiliation,
I have seen you turn upon the others in the night
Concealing nothing
Of sad self-loathing *lost*
And heard you cry, I am low. But you are lower!
And you had that right.
The damned do not so own to their damnation.

I have lived with you some hours of the night,
The late hour
When the lights lower,
The later hour
When the lights go out.
The dissipation of the night is past,
Hour of the outcast and the outworn whore.

Hour when no other sorrow helps our own,
Hour when another's sorrow haunts but does not help
        our own.
Hour of the dejected and rejected,
That is past three and not yet four,
When the old blackmailer waits beyond the door
and from the gutter with unpitying hands
Demands, the old payment of-remorse.

Hour of utter destitution,
When the soul knows the horror of its loss
And knows the world too poor
For restitution.

Hour when not pity, pride,
Or being brave,
Fortune, friendship, Fforgetfulness of drudgery

A page of Bishop's poem "The Hours" (an elegy for F. Scott Fitzgerald), with Tate's comments.

IV

Now you have outlived the nocturnal terror
The head hanging in the hanging mirror
And the hour haunted by the haggard face.

Now you are drunk at last. And that disgrace
You sought in oblivious dives you have
At last, in the dissolution of the grave.

V

I have lived with you the hours of your humiliation,
I have seen you turn upon the others in the night
Concealing nothing
Of sad self-loathing
And heard you cry, I am low. But you are lower!
And you had that right.
The damned do not so own to their damnation.

I have lived with you some hours of the night,
The late hour
When the lights lower,
The later hour
When the lights go out.
The dissipation of the night is past,
Hour of the outcast and the outworn whore.

Hour when no other sorrow helps our own,
Hour when another's sorrow haunts but does not help
          our own.
Hour of the dejected and rejected,
That is past three and not yet four,
When the old blackmailer waits beyond the door
and from the gutter with unpitying hands
Demands, the old payment of remorse.

Hour of utter destitution,
When the soul knows the horror of its loss
And knows the world too poor
For restitution.

Hour when not pity, pride,
Or being brave,
Fortune, friendship, forgetfulness of drudgery

Another copy of the same page, with notes by Edmund Wilson. Wilson's note on the opening page reads: "Mary has just read this, and we have gone over it together carefully."

we went through the other night. Tell her I want, in addition to the buffalo robe, a necklace of bear claws. I think they would help my morale.   Yours, John   TLS

1. This project was never completed. Wheeler has not been identified.   2. Bishop spent the next several months in New York while his family remained at Cape Cod.   3. Bishop is referring to Archibald MacLeish.

February 10, 1941

Dear John: I'm in a dither—last touches on the ms. of my book of essays which goes to the printer tomorrow.[1]

So this is just to say that the revision of your poem is excellent.[2] All the *Ashes* are shaken down. I still feel that the last line of the poem is not clear, and I feel that it ought to be clear beyond doubt, for the impact. It's a fine poem. When do you come to N.Y.?   Aff. Allen AL

1. *Reason in Madness: Critical Essays* (New York: G. P. Putnam Sons, 1941).   2. "The Hours."

                                          33 West Fifty-first Street/New York
March 2, 1941   Telephone VOlunteer 5-2000

Dear Allen: This is to say that I have arrived in New York and shall hope to see you and Caroline here before long. I thoughtlessly made a dinner date with Janet Flanner for Tuesday 7:30. But we might have a drink somewhere before that hour.   Yours, John   AL

March 19, 1941

Dear John: I have a plan which would put you, Katherine Anne, and myself on the air together with a program something like, but I think better than Invitation to Learning.[1]

The situation at CBS is getting more difficult all the time. The backstairs intrigue is now so complex that I don't intend to unravel it; and the interference from higher up is getting worse constantly. I don't pretend to understand all this; and it is not pertinent here.

After K. A. was on Invitation to Learning we discussed a program which we thought of trying to sell to NBC. At that time we could not think of a third person. Now you are in New York, and you are made to order. I am convinced from my experience at CBS that three is the ideal group: two offers very little variety, and four makes for confusion unless a group of four is led by an interlocutor; but this is not the kind of thing I have in mind.

Now I don't know whom to see at NBC. If you are interested in this, can you make discreet enquiries? We could work out a definite plan.

My tentative plan is something like this: or rather two alternative plans. Each of them emphasizes the idea of a "course" in a field of literature, instead of the eclectically scrambled series of books that we give at CBS. Our chief selling point would be the value of our program as a systematic survey. 1. A course in English lyric poetry (13 broadcasts) from the 16th century to the present. 2. A course in the American novel, 13 broadcasts. Either of these programs would stress indirectly the Anglo-American tradition, and would fit into the defense policy of NBC.

I believe we have something here. Of course, like Invitation to Learning, it would go sour too after a while; but we should not have to put up with a Cairns.[2] Our group would be made up of the same kind of people. Our present trouble at CBS is largely due to Cairns' restlessness and resentment. He is trying to eliminate both Mark [Van Doren] and me, and to get two men whom he can control. I predict that Mark will fight him (I won't) and that it will end up with Cairns and me out; Mark will form a new team. He would want me to remain with him, but the long period of uncertainty makes it desirable for me to try something else. And I think my experience ought to be useful at NBC or somewhere else: I've had nine months of it.

I think I know how to put on a program, with you and K. A., that would be practically perfect. In saying this I don't mean that I would expect to "lead"; that has been one of the main faults at CBS—the leader who gets the discussion keyed wrong with an "idea" that the rest of us must correct before the discussion can begin. No leader is necessary; or rather each time a different member of the team should be responsible for the direction of the discussion. In that way we should approximate a natural conversation; and this method would bring out, in turn, the capacities of each member of the team. Our method at CBS is a constant frustration. Cairns has nothing to offer; and he keeps Mark and me from offering our best.

Shall we talk this over? I believe that K. A. will add a new feature to this idea—a Woman; and she will attract the female audience. If you want to dine over this next Tuesday, drop me a card. It might be worthwhile to wire K. A. to come down and join the discussion.

Of course all this must be kept to ourselves for the present. It would be fatal to let it get around. Yrs. Allen TLS

1. This program did not materialize.   2. Huntington Cairns was a permanent member of the "Invitation to Learning" series.

March 21, 1941

Dear Allen: I got back from Washington last night to find your letter, containing your plan involving Katherine Anne and the two of us. There are so many things in this to discuss that I think you had better try to see me when you are next in New York. In the meantime, I shall try to make inquires about NBC.

I am enormously interested in the possibilities of your proposal and I should only hesitate in joining you if it involves a great deal of reading, which the work here would prevent my doing.

At any rate, let's get together next Tuesday. Jonathan is going to be with me, and possibly Margaret, so I cannot invite you to stay overnight with me. On second thought, perhaps I can, because I do not think there will be any difficulty about getting a room for you at the hotel. So far as dinner is concerned, I can dispose of Jonathan by sending him to the movies or something, and if Margaret is still around, I shall be glad to have her hear about this if you don't mind. I think, as a matter of fact, that she is going back on Monday.

I should say, offhand, that we ought to work out things a little more definitely ourselves before inviting Katherine Anne to come down, particularly since she writes me that she is very busy on her writing.

Until Tuesday then,   Yours, John   TLS

May 22, 1941

Dear Allen: I agree with you entirely about the list of names proposed for poets' academy.[1] I've been having a bad attack of grippe and the day the Membership Committee met, I was not able to bring much vigor to bear against the Irish forces.

Real trouble is beginning, not from the clear start, but with the ragtag and bobtail of the poetry Guild which existed some years ago, and at least three of the people on the Membership Committee were the worst sort of weaklings.

Margaret Widdemer has not yet appeared. I think she alone is enough to disgrace the whole affair. I gave myself credit when we were at Olivet for having been able to be in the same place with her and completely ignored her existence.

Peter Munro Jack's presence on the list does make some sense, for it is only through Jack that any pressure can be brought to bear on the poetry situation in the New York Times' book review section. Although the book review is beneath contempt from any serious critical standpoint, it is, as you know, very important from the standpoint of sales to libraries.

I am going down to Princeton for the weekend and will stay with the Raymond Harpers at a place called "Mansgrove."[2] I hope that we can get together down there.   Sincerely, John   TLS

1. Tate's letter listing the poets for membership in the academy does not survive. Some are mentioned below. The idea never progressed beyond the conceptual stage.   2. Harper has not been identified.

August 7, 1941

Dear Allen: I received a few days ago a call from Levine asking me to speak on the Invitation to Learning program on Bleak House, August 24th.[1] He told me that the others would be Mark Van Doren & Cairns. I suspected nothing untoward and accepted. This morning I received a letter from Katherine Anne telling me that you had resigned from the program, giving me your reasons of which she approved.

Now Levine spoke informally of my becoming a permanent member of the program. When I talked to him I blithely supposed that it was Cairns who was dropping out and signified my willingness to accept. Your absence changes the whole complexion of the affair.

I shall go on Aug. 24th but reserve any other decision until I have seen you. My office affairs are also going through a crisis and I may shortly resign. If I don't, I shall find myself in Washington, under the dome of the Capitol wondering what we built it for.[2]   Yours ever, John   AL

1. Levine, not otherwise identified, was an executive with the Columbia Broadcasting System.   2. A reference to Tate's "Aeneas at Washington."

August 9, 1941   First Colony Inn/Nags Head, N.C.

Dear John: Yours of the 7th caught me here. I hope you accept the job. I didn't resign: I was fired. Just that. I don't mind in any sense but the financial. This was evidently planned as early as May, and if I had been notified then, I could have taken a teaching job for the summer. The result is a net loss of about $400.00. So I now have an added interest in the editorial job on the anthology.[1]

I think Cairns got me fired, as a way of eliminating not only me but Mark, who wrote Levine a letter, after he heard I was fired, saying that he would not stay on with Cairns if he and Cairns alone were the permanent team. Levine prefers a team of two, with a guest each time. But if there is to be a team of three your presence might make it possible for Mark to stay on. It is probable, however, that you will find yourself with Cairns and a guest week after weary week. I imagine you will want to compel Levine to be frank about his plans.

The only reason given for letting me go was that I "interrupted too much." Of course I did interrupt Cairns constantly: I couldn't bear to let him finish a sentence, every remark he made having a degree, usually high, of fundamental misconception.

I have no doubt that Cairns would prefer colleagues of his own sort. He feared to attack Mark directly since CBS values the "van Doren name." But he knew that Mark would not remain with him alone.

Mark told Levine that he would continue with me and without Cairns; whereupon Levine assured Mark that "Cairns is not indispensable." Levine simply doesn't know what it's all about.

My feeling is that you ought to accept if Mark continues. Your rejection of the job would not benefit me in the least. I can come back only if Cairns is eliminated.

I ought to say that if Cairns is back of this intrigue, I don't blame him. He could hardly remain unaware of our lack of respect for him. We will be back in Princeton in two weeks. Address me here until the 12th; after that, until the 24th, at Monteagle, Tennessee.   Affectionately, Allen   AL

1. Tate is referring to *American Harvest: Twenty Years of Creative Writing in the United States* (New York: L. B. Fischer, 1942), an anthology he was to edit with Bishop, at this time publications director for the Coordinator of Inter-American Affairs.

February 3, 1942   Coordinator of Inter-American Affairs

Dear Allen: Because of a cold, I stayed home for two days and hence did not receive your letter in time to call you on Friday.

Before deciding on the Princeton University Press, I think I had better see Dodd, Mead again. I shall do this today.[1]

I spent the weekend going over Erskine Caldwell's stories, only to discover that I agree with you that almost none of his stories completely comes off. I have so far found one that I think possible, "Priming the Well." At all events, I believe that is the vein in which he should be represented.

I received the copy of Putnam's poems. I want to read "Hasbrouck and the Rose" over again. At first reading, I must say it seems to be definitely below the standard of the other poems we have selected. In fact, the whole volume, as I glance at it for the first time after a good many years, seems to me amateur.

I believe we can have "Christine" copied here if you will send it to me.

I should be glad to hear from Mr. Wells of Columbia, and should very much like to make a phonograph record, a copy of which I could own myself.[2] Are you, by any chance, going on the WQXR program?

I am lunching next week with Eve Merriam, who is running it. If you want, I will speak to her about your being put on.   Yours, John TLS

1. Bishop is attempting to place *American Harvest* with a publisher. It was eventually published by L. B. Fischer.   2. Tate and Bishop were contemplating recording the sort of discussions held on the "Invitation to Learning" series, but the project never materialized.

February 27, 1942

Dear John: I'm sending this to your hotel in the hope that you will be able to add your revisions and get it typed up by Monday noon. It is, of course, a prospectus for the U.S. broadcast.[1]

I would like to be able to take to Mr. Trammel a first copy of this and also of the list of books. I believe we ought to show him a copy of your South American prospectus at the same time. Although Levine has expressed interest, I am sure he would see the wisdom of having both broadcasts at one place.

I will come to your office shortly after twelve on Monday. I may have Willard Thorp (the American Lit prof) with me. We could hear his ideas on the pictorial history, if you are prepared to discuss them. He will not have heard about it when we arrive.

Love to Margaret.   Yrs. Allen   TLS

1. Tate and Bishop were proposing a radio series, along the lines of "Invitation to Learning," to discuss the writers they included in *American Harvest* (1942).

April 27, 1942

Dear John: Here's a preface for the anthology. If you want to add anything to it or change phrases, please do so at once, so that I can get it to Pereyra, who has consented to translate it.[1]

I wrote it with translation definitely in mind. You will see what I mean.

We'll be leaving the East early in June, so I hope you'll be in N.Y. before then. We may come back to N.Y. for the winter, but this isn't certain.

What are you doing? Love to Margaret.   Yrs. Allen   TLS

1. Tate is referring to *American Harvest* (1942).

April 28, 1942   Sea Change/South Chatham, Massachusetts

Dear Allen: The preface seems to me just right. I cannot suggest further additions or improvements.

I will be in New York June 1st to act as ΦBK poet at Columbia, a

dubious honor, but one which will force me to write a long poem.[1]
We should certainly meet then. I may come a day or two earlier,
rather than linger, as the boys' school closes June 4th, for which
occasion I must be in Concord.

It seems as though I'd never left the Cape. For two weeks I didn't
try to do anything but restore the garden—which needed it—and to
sort my papers. Neither task is done, but I am beginning to be able to
catch my breath from time to time. I have translated two poems, one
by Iran Gall [?] on the Jews and another by Enrique Gonzalez Martinez on expressive form.[2]

I have an 'idea' for my own poem. That is all.

I have heard nothing from Diomedes.[3]   Affectionately, John AL

1. "A Subject of Sea Change," *American Scholar* 12 (April, 1943), 216–19.   2. "Then
Twist the Neck of This Delusive Swan," a translation of Martinez' "Tuercele el Cuello al
Cisne." This poem and two other translations by Bishop, "Hymn to the Volunteers of
the Republic" (from Vallejo's "Himno a los Voluntarios de la Republica"), and "The
Peasant Declares His Love" (from Roumer's "Declaration Paysanne") appeared in Dud-
ley Fitts's *Anthology of Contemporary Latin-American Poetry* (New York: New Directions,
1942).   3. Bishop may be referring to Archibald MacLeish.

May 20, 1942

Dear John: I used to tell Donald Davidson that he not only wanted
us to feel like Confederates, but insisted that we write like Confederates too. Content yourself with feeling like a Phi Beta Kappa on June
1st.

I see that it is a Monday, and what could be better than that you
should spend the week end here? We leave for Tennessee the next
week for an indefinite time. I have turned down two jobs because
together Caroline and I have raised between us enough publishers'
advances to live on for a year.

There are two troubles about my living in the East. First, I can't
write here. Second, I forget who I am. I had a nightmare recently in
which I couldn't remember my name. Of course, that may be only a
political prophecy, but at the present phase of the national life I can
still interpret the dream personally.

How about coming down Saturday and staying till Monday
morning? Or come Sunday. As you choose. You will need a retreat in
which to polish off and up the poem.

I am glad to know that the anthology is definitely through. I await
the money. Just last week Nannine Joseph began negotiations which
will probably lead to U.S. publication. I have taken the liberty of
adding and subtracting a few things without consulting you, because
there is a rush. The firm is a refugee Dutch (Jewish) firm called Fischer

Publications, which salted down its cash before the war began. They want to publish American books, and ours looks like the best way to start such a program. I will let you know the results.

Love to Margaret. We're sorry not to get to the Cape. Another time. Aff. Allen   TLS

May 24, 1942

Dear Allen: I would like nothing better than to accept your invitation, but so much remains to be done on the poem that I don't think I shall be able to. I would give a great deal to have you go over the poem before it is read. But I am not sure that it will be worthy of your eyes until I have been able to make a much more drastic revision than I can make in the time that remains. It has good things in it, but is terribly shapeless, a statue of putty. Maybe I can later carve something out of more durable material.

Things haven't been helped by the servants leaving on three hours notice, with a dinner party of eight planned for last night. I didn't mind cooking the dinner. But I made a great deal of very *mauvais sang* over the departure. I still want to kill them by some slow and protracted method of torture.

Well, I am glad the anthology went through. I would like to think it was my last letter to Charles Thomson that did the trick.

I am so relieved that I no longer have to take the South Americans seriously. They are a tiresome lot. The only good things the year brought me were Dr. Wolf,[1] whom I owe to you, and the frequent occasions when I saw you in New York.

The thought of your successor appalls me.[2] He was the dullest man in my class. But I am glad you are to be free for a year. Maybe the mountains are the place to go. We are living here under military direction, which is not arbitrary, but rather a nuisance. I can't work up any zest for the war. It's just something like the depression, which I shall try to survive.

My most affectionate regards to Caroline, and a salutation to Nancy. Yours, John   TLS

1. A New York physician who was so successful in treating Bishop's high blood pressure that Tate recommended him to Robb Ransom.   2. Tate is leaving the Creative Arts Program at Princeton.

June 14, 1942

Dear Allen: Nannine Joseph has written me, first, enclosing her letter to you in regard to our friends who, she thinks, are holding her up in regard to the royalties offered the editors and other things which will be familiar to you; second, in regard to collecting the contents so that the prospective publishers can see them, not merely a table of contents. This she asks me to do.

I can arrange to get the books for her which contain selected material in all cases where we planned to send books to Nascimento.[1] In regard to the material which we had typed, I have written to Miss Flack to learn whether there are extra copies in her files which I can have. In the meantime, you might let me know what you have in the way of copies of the typed material, both prose and poetry.

I had hoped to send you a copy of my PBK poem with this letter. But I am undertaking a rather elaborate rewriting of the last half of it, which I did very hastily in order to read it at Columbia. Dr. Wilson and spouse spent the week end here and both pronounced favorably upon it, though the Doctor thought fit to lecture me on departing about the necessity of writing in poetry the way people talk. This was followed by a second lecture, equally familiar, on the decline of verse as a technique. However, he was in very good shape and I enjoyed the visit throughout. He is on the wagon except for week-ends and even then has come to a moderation surprising to me who saw him down seven martinis practically in one gulp that day we met at the Chatham.

I am feeling so good myself I can't believe it. The Coordinator's Office seems far away. Did you see Heptisax attack on Wallace's War of the Common Man?[2] Thank god, somebody has called the VP asinine. Unfortunately I am the only cynic around here and have no one to talk to on these and kindred subjects, now that you have taken to the mountains.   Yours, John   TLS

1. The publisher of the South American edition of *American Harvest*.   2. Heptisax was the pseudonym of Rodney Yonkers Gilbert (1889–1968), an editorial writer and columnist for the New York *Herald Tribune*. Henry Wallace was vice president during Roosevelt's third term.

June 21, 1942   Monteagle, Tennessee

Dear John: This is the first letter I've written in two weeks. We had a very hectic trip down, and we had to see dozens of people in Nashville and Clarksville before we could even begin to settle for the summer. But order is beginning to appear.

I am sending you all the typed copies of the poems that I have. It will not be the complete poetry section because we subsequently made changes and additions. I have no way of making it complete without going to Nashville. I am sorry to pass the buck to you.

I will see that the additional biographical sketches are done and sent to Nannine.

Of course I am in a bad state of nerves as I begin my book,[1] but as soon as I get some bottom under me, say 15,000 words, I will feel better. It is a little absurd for us to feel as good as we do. I feel uneasy only because I am so far from 79th Street.

I didn't see Heptisax on Wallace, but I'm glad to hear about it. The feeling in the South is very reassuring. War sentiment is very high but there's great scepticism in that realm in which the South has always been famous for it: moral idealism. Nobody knows what the four freedoms mean, and those who have heard of them resent them pretty severely because of the effect they will have on the negro situation.

Let me know if I can do anything more about the anthology. You go ahead and sign up when the time comes. I will write more shortly. I can't answer the letters before me, but I will have to acknowledge twenty-one today somehow.   Aff. Allen   TLS

1. During this period, Tate edited *The Language of Poetry* (Princeton, N.J.: Princeton University Press, 1942) and *Princeton Verse between Two Wars* (Princeton, N.J.: Princeton University Press, 1942). But the book referred to here is apparently the novel, never finished, mentioned below on July 16 and 22.

[Early July, 1942]

Dear Allen: You have doubtless received Nannine's scolding letter addressed to both of us.[1] It was dictated partly by a bad conscience. She was unable—because of the death of a friend—to give me the necessary time. I left N.Y. in as great a state of confusion as when I arrived.

I have arranged the material for Nascimento and presume that in general the same arrangement will do for the Fischer publication. As soon as I have a copy, I will send it to you for your approval.

I will do the introductory essay. Will you at once send in a complete and revised table of contents, giving the books in which the selections are to be found. I attempted to do this from memory in the Fischer office—all of my files on the subject being in Washington, as I had given up hope in April of an American edition—and made a number of mistakes. Hence Fischer's.

I think the best of D[elmore] Schwartz for our purpose is *In the Naked Bed in Plato's Cave*. *Scyros* is the best of [Karl] Shapiro, but not very good. I don't know the Bogan & L[eonie] Adams selections. I am in favor of dropping *Gerontion*, which has a fairly high fee attached, since T.S.E. is well represented by two contributions. Gerontion is one of his best poems, but almost too well known now.

Please send me a list of the new material you have sent in. Sorry to be a nuisance. I will do all I can, but some information I lack and have no means of reference here.   Yours in frantic haste, John

Nannine's office closes August 1st for two weeks.   AL

1. Bishop and Tate are trying to assemble all the material for *American Harvest* in both editions.

July 16, 1942

Dear John: I've just sent off some mss to Fischer which ought to complete the copy for the printer.

Don't you think there ought to be a brief note or preface for the U.S. edition? Won't you write it? I should think a couple of pages would do. I am well started on my novel and I am afraid to put it aside even for a brief essay.[1] Without such a note we are going to be vulnerable at several points, particularly the poetry and the criticism. It can be said that we have made a very few changes and additions for the U.S. edition, but that on the whole the anthology represents what would both translate and communicate to a foreign reader.

I feel that all this work is wasted, because only after an astronomical number of copies will we make any money.

What are you doing?   Aff. Allen   TLS

1. This novel was never finished.

July 17, 1942

Dear Allen: I have sent Nannine copies of the Cummings sonnets 94 & 95; Scyros by Karl Shapiro; 90 North by Randall Jarrell. I was just about to copy the Millay sonnet when something broke or jammed on my typewriter and I had to stop.

I have given her the selections from The Long Night and Time & the River as follows.

The Long Night, p. 107 (top) through section 5, middle of p. 115.

Time and the River, beginning with section II p. 25 through section V p. 77.

Do you approve?

The Brooks selection I began p. 55 "If whatever land was idyllic..." and continued to end of chapter p. 65.

I loaned some thief *The Adventures of a Young Man.* Can you cite pages in American edition for the selection in *Mesures.* I do not know the selection from Stark Young. Can you supply Nannine with necessary information?

I have reread the Blackmur essay on Emily Dickinson and find it far inferior to yours. Do we have to keep it?

I think it is a pity to use Leonie Adams & Louise Bogan and not Elinor Wylie. I get no thrill out of either of the first mentioned ladies. Bogan seems to me absolutely [illegible]. I suppose you put in Shapiro and Schwartz to give proper representation to the young. Of Shapiro *Scyros* is the best; of Schwartz, probably the Bear poem is the best. I doubt if it is possible for a Jew to write poetry. The whole younger generation seems to me strangely without eloquence. Jarrell by comparison is good—though only by comparison.

The contract with Fischer demands that we supply material. I told them to go ahead and buy the necessary books and bill them to us.   Yours, John   AL

July 22, 1942

Dear John: I enclose my only copy of the contents of the U.S. edition. My additions were hasty; so I hope it isn't too late for you to send in a poem by Elinor Wylie if you still want to.

When I left the East I had no suspicion that we should have to furnish mss. and that this work would fall to you. I hoped that you would write the preface to make our collaboration equal.

I had already written Nannine to drop *Gerontion*, but I'm not sure she attended to it. I thought her reprimand rather silly, but I wasn't annoyed by it.

Schwartz's *In the Naked Bed* I have already sent it.

You were wrong about the Wolfe. Your selection runs to about 50 pages; mine, the original one, to 9, making it about 5½ times as good as yours. Zero would be perfect. I wired the pages to Nannine.

I wish I could have helped more effectively. I am already well into my novel. I wish I could show you the opening pages. I like them better than anything I've ever done.

I assume that since you didn't mention it there is no ground for the rumor I heard here the other day that Dos is dead—suicide, in fact.[1] Or is it true?   Aff. Allen   AL

1. John Dos Passos had had a severe attack of rheumatic fever, but was not dead.

July 28, 1942

Dear John: I think your arrangement of the material is excellent, and I look forward to your Preface. As I understood it, my S.A. preface was to follow yours in order to emphasize the fact that we did the book for a foreign public.

In your table of contents I notice one omission: Wallace Stevens. Doubtless we shall catch it in proof. After talking to Andrew, I changed his selection to a complete short story called *Jericho, Jericho, Jericho*. I sent the ms. of this to Fischer (and also to Benjamin).[1]

Nannine is a little hard on us, I think. Before I left the East I was not told that in case of acceptance we should have to get a complete ms. together. Had we known this, we could have got together when you came down to read at Columbia and accomplished more in two days than in a month of letters. I suppose you must be as thoroughly tired of this business as I am. I don't know what good this book will do. It will certainly do no good to our finances. We shall suffer a small net loss in the long run.

The war news makes a daily inroad on my work, slowing me up and lowering the intensity of the writing. But what else can I do? I can't give it up. What are you doing?   Aff. Allen   AL

1. Robert Benjamin was Bishop's successor in the coordinator's office.

August 5, 1942

Dear John: Last week Nannine wrote me that you had to go to Washington and couldn't do the Preface for two weeks. I did a single page to supplement my South American Preface and sent it to Fischer on Monday (Aug. 3rd). I took the liberty of putting your initials to it along with mine. I had no carbon paper, so I couldn't save you a copy. Why not wait for proofs before you edit my Preface? What I say in my new short piece may cover the ground to suit you. We should have proofs in a few days.

I am thoroughly tired of this anthology, and I imagine you are. And I am a little tired of Nannine.

Let me have some news of you.   Aff. Allen   AL

August 10, 1942

Dear Allen: I am feeling quite ashamed of myself at not having done the Introduction to the Fischer Anthology and having, after much delay, come back to depending on your own. Before I went to Washington, I did not seem to be able to get two days completely free of interruptions, annoyances and other duties. And once I had gone to Washington and had another look at your introduction for the Nascimento Anthology, there seemed no great point in trying to do what you had already done.

While waiting for your reply to my request to edit and use it, I went through with the editing. I send you a copy of the results. Most of the cuts were so obvious, that I think you will agree to them. The only one on which you may stick is the one toward the end, where I omitted the quotation from J. J. Chapman. Despite the fact that the remark on New York is from another man, I felt that it introduced a personal note at a point where the reader's mind was being asked to go out over all America. Besides, the thrust at New York needs a little more elaboration to tell, a little more behind it to really go home. It seems unsupported as it is and hence a gesture of irritation. Perhaps I am unfair, but I have been thinking quite a bit lately on this, comparing Boston as a port in the heyday of New England with New York as a port between the Civil War and the advent of the New Deal, with all the consequences to our culture. The trouble with NYC is not that it is a railroad station—that is all to the good—but that when you arrive it is—and never has been—anything but a trading center.

I have done almost nothing useful or ornamental lately. Even with the loss of gasoline, the outsiders throng to the Cape at this season and as much as I like guests they are invariably in an idle mood and expect you to be idle with them. We have just had the [John] Biggs, whom I like immensely. But days passed and nothing done.

I spent a week in Washington and cleaned up everything as far as I can tell. Unfortunately, in that city, the swept litter keeps blowing back in your face. But I did do all that was left to be done on the Nascimento anthology and am told it has gone off. It was just as well I went down, for it had been reposing in Pereyra's drawer all ready to go for weeks, but timidity had kept Benjamin from sending it off.

Like you, I am sick and tired of the whole business. Which has made it hard to do what Nannine and Fischer demanded. I believe they are both now satisfied. And I shall turn to other things. John

TLS

August 28, 1942

Dear John: Nannine asked me to pass this clipping on to you. She says it is evidence that Fischer is making great efforts to sell the book.

Have I written you that I thought you did an extremely good job of editing the preface? Your edited version should have been used in the South American edition too.

I'm having—after a couple of calm months—another attack of the jitters. It all looks worse from day to day. And I fully expect to be drafted in about six months. We shall be like some of Tiberius' legions on the German frontier—toothless, our hair long and gray, and so decrepit that we shall be scarcely able to march; yet we shall still be in the army. At the age of 67 I expect to be assigned, as a private, to the inspection of whore-houses in Sumatra.   Aff. yrs. Allen   AL

September 4, 1942

Dear Allen: You are kind to approve of my editing. I did it in fear and trembling, not wanting to alter your tightly written Preface.

However, it seemed to me pretty obvious what, written for the South American edition, had to go out in the North American. I made some further changes at Fischer's request, which you have not seen and may not approve of. But he wanted to end on a more enthusiastic note; to lure the reader into the book. By that time I was frantically bored with the whole thing and probably did a poor job.

Your mental state seems to rival my own. I started the summer well. I was so cheered at getting away from the suzerainty of Washington that I launched into a long poem, which I finished for the Phi Beta Kappa doings at Columbia and have since revised.[1] It is not as good as the Fitzgerald elegy, which in style it resembles, but it is not disgraceful and has some very good lines. Since then I have not been able to concentrate on anything. The various anthologies have been a constant interruption. But more to the point is my state of mind.

Margaret thinks I am very defeatist and resents my expressing my doubt and contempt for our allies before the children.[2] She herself is pained by my misprision of both the English and the Russians. So I try to keep my mouth shut and do, except for occasional outbursts of rage and fury, which do me little credit, being uncontrolled and often unjust. Even before I left New York, I found you almost the only person to whom I could talk freely and honestly. Here, practically everybody adheres to the party line, which I could never follow.

John Biggs was here recently and told a funny story. He and Anne were staying with the Wilsons. John and Bunny sat up late and did a good deal of drinking. After he got to bed—around 1:30—John heard Bunny fall down the cellar stairs. He sat up in bed. "Is that Edmund Wilson, the critic?" he asked himself, preparing to rush to his rescue. "No," he said, "that's that lousy communist to whom I have just been talking," and went promptly to sleep. Communist or critic, Bunny was knocked out by the fall and didn't revive for some time.

By the way Dos is not dead. He has been ill with his old rheumatic fever, but is better now and on the telephone sounds cheerful enough.   Yours, John   AL

1. "A Subject of Sea Change."   2. Bishop's wife had taken a commission in the Womens' Army Corps.

October 18, 1942

Dear Allen: I thought with publication of *American Harvest*, our cares would be over. But you, like me, have received Nannine's communication.

I have gone over the biographical notes very carefully and made the enclosed notations. Inasmuch as Caroline made them up, I don't want to do more than make my suggestions.

I have rather unsuccessfully tried to bring them up to date. If you are unable to check on the dubious items, I am going down to New York for Invitation to Learning on October 25th and can do so then, though that will mean a considerable delay. You are probably no nearer a reference library than I am. But you seem to hold on to periodicals better than I do, and may be able to check through them.

How's your morale? I haven't the jitters, as you say you have, but something probably worse, a complete absence of any thought or emotion.

Je plains le temps de ma jeunesse,
Ouquel j'ay plus qu'aure galle
Jusques a l'entree de viellesse,
Qui son partement m'a celé.[1]

And that's about all. One needs to be young to take a war.   Yours ever, John   TLS

1. Bishop is quoting an excerpt from *Le Testament* by Francois Villon (1431-c.1465): "I mourn the days of my youth / When more than most I had my fling / Until age came upon me / It gave no warning it would leave." *The Poems of Francois Villon,* trans. Galway Kinnell (Boston: Houghton Mifflin Co., 1977), 37.

October 20, 1942

Dear John: I was glad to get your notes on the biographical sketches. I have already used them as the basis of the revisions which I have just completed today. In going into this matter I found that Caroline's *first draft* had been sent to Fischer. The mistake came about because I didn't even know she had made a second draft, and supposed that the carbon copy which I found after great difficulty was the same as had gone to South America.

But I do think that Fischer on his own initiative might have put the names in alphabetical order. I will get the revisions off tomorrow.

Have I written you that Andrew Lytle has become managing-editor of the *Sewanee Review?* The president of the college couldn't get an outsider to come in (Andrew was already teaching there) because he couldn't be persuaded that contributors should be paid. He tried half a dozen people, including me indirectly. Andrew is wholly unfit for the job: he doesn't know whom to approach and he doesn't know any writers outside this region well enough to beg for mss. I can't beg for him with much conviction, but I have promised to ask some of my friends for mss. that they can't sell. Have you been able to sell your

Phi Beta Kappa poem? If you see no prospect of selling it, won't you send it to me for Andrew? Caroline, very reluctantly, has given him a story.¹ I have nothing to give.

We are settled here for the winter in a large cottage equipped with two bathrooms and a furnace, not to mention the nine double beds. If the Anglophiles get too trying, come down. I have never had such leisure in my life. The difficulty is to know how to use it after three years in a university. Love to Margaret.   Aff. Allen

Mary Wilson writes me that Dr. Wilson is teaching at Smith. La, La!
AL

1. This story did not appear.

[Late October, 1942]

Dear Allen: I was in New York for Invitation to Learning (Mark Van Doren's last session) on Sunday and made the enclosed notations at the Public Library. I hope they will be of some use in revising the bibliographies.

I saw Cummings, who is much better physically and I don't doubt psychically, since the pain in his back was undoubtedly a reflection of some more intangible pain. He was able to walk to Marta's, where we dined, and back to Patchin Place, where I drank and he maintained his sobriety. He is still against the world and all its works and wars. It did me good to see him.

I spent the night with Dr. Wilson at Wellfleet a week ago. He also looks very well, all roses in the cheeks and less bloated in his chins. He was working out a lecture for the Smith girls on various poetic devices. He is beginning to read his texts for their own sake and is perfectly delighted with his discoveries. He goes up to Northampton for two days each week, a most difficult feat of commuting, since it is harder to get from one corner of Massachusetts to the other by train than to go half across the country.

I have the Phi Beta Kappa poem out. When it comes back, if it does, I'll think of the Sewanee Review.

I am trying to get together a book of essays for publication, if that can be arranged for anything not having to do with the war.¹ So many of them were originally compressed at the behest of editors more than they should have been. And the problem arises, Is it worth while to expand them to those dimensions they would have had had there been no limits placed on them. You must have faced this yourself with both your volumes of essays.

If I were to respond to your kind invitation to come to Tennessee, I would rather come next spring. That's the poor season here and should be nice in the mountains. I'll have to see if I can't work some racket to pay my way down, a lecture or something of that sort. My best to Caroline, John TLS

1. This book of essays was not published.

November 2, 1942

Dear John: I was so rushed when I sent you the carbon of my reply to Jones,[1] that I couldn't write you a note.—I wrote the reply for one reason only, that the rumor had already reached me that Jones' review was the public front of an effort to get our anthology withdrawn from S. A. by the Coordinator's Office; and I thought that a strong counter-statement was necessary. So I made a special point of saying that the South Americans are tired of North American noise.

I don't know whether this rumor has reached you. I am perfectly ready to fight the issue. If these people (the old N.Y. and Sat. Review gang) have their way, critical standards here will receive a knock-out blow. More is involved than an anthology. There is already going a strong movement in favor of bigness, Americanism, and "democracy," and a hatred of the subtle and the intelligent—which is the way our totalitarianism will develop on the literary front. (See Alfred Kazin in the New Republic, Oct. 19th).

I am sending you some of the reviews that Nannine sent me. Cowley touched a new low, I believe, in taking us to task for omitting Pearl Buck. This is a new low in taste; he reached a new low in dishonesty in suggesting Cabell, whom he despises.[2]

Well, I thought we'd get it strong from all the N.Y. gang. It only goes to show that our anthology was needed.—We could have improved the U.S. edition, but there simply was not enough time; and we had to leave N.Y. We should, for example, have had a story by Scott.

The invitation to come down is a standing one. Act upon it whenever you can.

Mark wrote me that CBS had turned him out. Apparently it was just *that*. It seems that Louis Untermeyer will succeed him. I feel a little relieved at this, because it confirms my judgment that CBS was acting out of character in having people like us.—This will be good for Mark because the program was bad for him. It developed in him the small fraction of Van Dorenism which he shares with Carl.

I had a long letter recently from Mary Wilson asking me to recommend her for a Guggenheim. I can do this in the highest rhetorical style because I have not yet read her book.[3]—I am glad that Dr. Wilson is learning again that poetry exists. But you know what happens to him when he reads poetry with young women. If it were Latin poetry the case would look very discouraging. I shall exhort him to read only English.

Love to Margaret.   Aff. Allen   AL

1. Howard Munford Jones's review of *American Harvest* appeared in *Saturday Review* 25 (October 24, 1942), 16.   2. Cowley's review appeared in *New Republic* 107 (October 19, 1942), 505.   3. Mary T. McCarthy, *The Company She Keeps* (1942).

November 9, 1942

Dear Allen: I am glad you wrote your reply to Mumford Jones though he is one of the unreachable ones. I remember hearing him at Boulder proclaim that what people really liked to read was the Saturday Evening Post and that anyone who denied that preference was a hypocrite or a liar. What I can't understand, is his reputation, which is not large, but still allows him to appear in print. God! all that parade of erudition only to prove that he couldn't read a clear piece of prose like the Introduction. I know and you know that Americans read foreign writers before we were born. But something happened in our generation which did not happen before about that reading. As I thought your essay made very clear.

I don't think that he is part of a conspiracy to drop the Nascimento anthology. That seems to be going through, though there were, according to Miss Flack, doubts about the advisability of dealing with Nascimento, who is reported by the coordinator's Chilean representative to have Fascist leanings. Said representative is probably one more of Hutch Robbins' friends, who know nothing and are incapable of learning anything. It's an open scandal. Robbins is a nephew of F. D. R. and has filled South America with playboys. All of which has served to discredit the Coordinator's Office and given the advantage to the State Department in the struggle between them.

Bob Benjamin has just written me that he has lost the list of permission fees. I haven't a copy. Have you, or can you procure one from Nannine? This is typical of the way that office is run since I left it. Benjamin thought he was going to be very important. Instead, he has been ignored completely and has been able to accomplish nothing.

I was in New York—to see Dr. Wolf—last week. I telephoned Nannine to learn what was on her mind. She sounded much more genial than her letters, which, I must say, have gotten under my skin. She seems to have taken the reviews in her stride. They have been stupid and it is to their stupidity that she attributed Fischer's annoyance. Her letters turned that annoyance toward us.

Of course the attack on us is really a part of the general campaign to lower standards and to have literature compete with the headlines—the old Chicago school of book-reviewing. How much it is the thing now is indicated by Cowley's review. He can't see a band-wagon without climbing on it.

I was with Mark on the last Invitation to Learning program of that series. I thought he was very glad to get free of it. Irwin Edman[1] was perfectly terrible last Sunday. There was no discussion and no life. I think what has happened is that Levine is packing his box with people who have no prepuces. It looks that way. Forward but without a foreskin! That's the motto always.

Mary Wilson's book is well written. Don't judge it by the story which appeared in the Partisan Review.[2] It gets better after that.

I am trying to get together a book of essays. For that reason I have been rereading Finnegan's Wake, which is, just now, Bunny's particular enthusiasm. He is making his whole course at Smith lead up to it. It is much clearer to me on second reading and much more distasteful. I don't think the triumphs—and there are triumphs—quite compensate for the failures.   As ever, John   TLS

1. Professor of philosophy at Columbia.   2. "The Man in the Brooks Shirt," *Partisan Review* 8 (July-August, 1941), 279-88, 324-43.

December 4, 1942

Dear John: Your last letter has been neglected in favor of verse, which I have been writing steadily for almost a month: four more "Sonnets at Christmas," three short pieces, and a long "Ode," already 90 lines and almost finished.[1] I don't think any of it touches my best, but it is a start at any rate. If I can manage the end of the ode it will please me. It is a war poem in the stanza of Drayton's *To the Virginian Voyage*. When all this seems a little more "done" I will send it along for your advice. I hope you are likewise active. Two sorts of escape have made this outburst: the novel and the war had to be denied somehow. I write better when I am in trouble, but the trouble of the world answers the purpose.

The Saturday Review ignored my letter; at any rate it hasn't appeared and the editors have not acknowledged it. I don't like to see them get away with this; so won't you return the copy I sent you? I didn't keep one for myself.

I have been putting my correspondence in order at odd moments, and you would be amazed at the number of letters you have written to me! I suppose you don't know that you are one of the best letter-writers in the world, and it is time you knew it. We have spilt a great deal of ink towards each other, which I suspect has not been wasted, if anybody cares in the not too distant future to examine the curious record of two friends and poets who always managed to keep at least one foot on the ground.—I have been thinking of depositing my entire collection at Princeton. Why don't you?

You must come down in the spring. It is a little cold here now but not uncomfortable.

We shall spend a quiet Christmas, without a single party. Love to Margaret.   Yrs. aff. Allen

P.S. Caroline made a flying trip to N.Y. two weeks ago to see Dr. Wolf about her ailing sigmoid. The expected result has been achieved. She's cured after two weeks of Dr. Wolf's treatment. The Nashville doctors hadn't even diagnosed it.   A.T.   AL

1. "Ode: To Our Young Pro-Consuls of the Air," *Partisan Review* 10 (March-April, 1943), 129-32; "More Sonnets at Christmas," *Kenyon Review* 5 (Spring, 1943), 186-88.

December 10, 1942

Dear John: I am sending you the finished (or nearly finished) pieces from my late revival.[1] Please tell me what you think of them.—As to the Ode, I had always felt that Drayton's stanza in the *Virginia Voyage* could be used for satire, and I think my poem fairly confirms me. Of the sonnets I will say nothing except that the first seems to have some good things in it.

Caroline has just finished an article on the South and the War for *Mademoiselle*.[2] I am amazed at how good it is without seeming to be. At first reading it sounds like *Mademoiselle*. She is exhausted, but continues well.—Love to M.   Yrs. aff. Allen   AL

1. "Ode: To Our Young Pro-Consuls of the Air" and "More Sonnets at Christmas."   2. "All Lovers Love the Spring," *Mademoiselle* 9 (February, 1944), 102-3, 164-65.

December 23, 1942

Dear Allen: I congratulate you on the reappearance of the Muse. The *Sonnets at Christmas* are a worthy addition to the ones you have already written on the season. But it is the *Ode* that interests me most. It is the richest working in this vein you have yet made. You have I know put your pick in it before, but I haven't felt in the past that you had developed it. The satiric pieces you did while teaching at Princeton had in them something new—even for you, something new. They were not like your early ventures in satire. At the same time, they all seemed to be fragmentary. You appeared to tire of the subject before you had exhausted it. The new *Ode* is worked to a finish. I am not sure that it will be clear in its conclusion to those who have not had, as I have, the benefit of your conversation. I know why the grand Lama is brought on at the end. But will most of your readers know, or even guess, why he dies. There is a confusion in your emotional attitude toward the war—which God knows I share—but I am not sure you have poetically resolved the conflict, or, for that matter made clear the issues that clash. I don't want to be harsh: for I feel that when you go back to the poem you will give it the ironic sharpening it needs.

We have been snowbound for a week, but yesterday a light rain, today the sun, promises to open the road for us. We've had to be very Mark Van Dorenish, if not Whittierish, in our comings and goings, carrying everything on our back or in bags.

The three boys are at home. I tutor the twins daily in English grammar, Margaret in French. Jonathan last night produced a book of short stories he had written, which showed some talent for writing I had not suspected in him.

I am revising and collecting my essays. In between, I am rereading the *Paradiso,* which I have not gone through entire for many years. My Muse is silent. But I am hoping that your poems will possibly start her going again.

About the letters. I think our correspondence might eventually find its way into the Princeton archives. But I don't like to give up my end as yet. There's nothing like old letters to recall the feel of times that are gone. I like from time to time to take yours out and peruse them, not only for the virtues they contain, but for the magic in them to give me myself again. I've felt in great danger lately of losing myself. The years seem to have stripped so much away. The wraith that's left seems thin and meagre.

I salute you in the name of Our Lord and the Virgin Mary and the cows and asses that looked on while the intruders in their stable prepared to receive their strange guest. John   AL

January 13, 1943

Dear John: I am painfully reconstructing a remote picture of my income which however remote is pressing me. Therefore I want to ask you whether I must pay an income tax on the fee for the anthology. It looks now as if the difference between a higher and a lower surtax bracket will be that $500.00. It is very discouraging.

I think my translation reads much better with the second comma in the refrain omitted—a slight change but one of considerable effect.

Edmund's new book (Colt Press) I find a little depressing except

for the Omlet and the Limperary Cripples.[1] His serious pieces strike
me as being too young for him. His meditation on Laurelwood is
moving but emotionally thin. Through it all runs a nostalgia for the
past glory of his family and class that ought to make us wicked
Southerners feel like amateurs in that field. Tereu.—Love to Margaret.   Aff. Allen   AL

1. *Notebooks of the Night* (1942).

January 17, 1943

Dear Allen: I am afraid there is no way you can escape paying an
income tax on money received from the government. Not even the
members of the Supreme Court, with all their knowledge of legal
exits and alleys, can do that. We are none of us going to have any
money ever again we can spend freely, taking our chances on our
own future. I saved what was for me a considerable sum from my
year with the CIAA—all has gone or will go March 15th next to the
Collector of Internal Revenue.

I feel like Poe's victim in *The Pit and the Pendulum.* I find myself
shrinking inwardly and outwardly and as through the action of time
my ability to enjoy life diminishes, the walls that enclose me narrow
and the very air I breathe is less than it was. What consolations I
might still find at my age are snatched from me. I am like Lorna
Lindsay's Cape Cod uncle who complained that age wouldn't even let
him enjoy sunsets as he once had. And sunsets are about the only
thing that aren't taxed as a pleasure.

I find my pleasure in your writing, however, withstands the time.
Your translation of the Vigil of Venus[1] is a remarkable contrast with
the translations—from the Spanish of Carrera Andrade—on which I
have been working. I have briefly compared it with the Latin original
and may presently have a few suggestions. But it has been impossible
for me to give myself to it, while working on this other job, which is
rather a futile one, since the book may never be published. However,
I am being paid for my time by the Coordinator and that gives me the
will to press on.

Carrera Andrade is really a charming poet, an Ecuadorian Francis
Jammes, without that complacency which made Jammes so tiresome
in his later years. He asked me to write an Introduction to a book of
his which Muna Lee has translated. The Coordinator agreed to pay
me for doing something I should have found hard to refuse doing. So
I am back at the old task of trying to make indifferent translations
sound like something. At that, Muna Lee was one of the best trans-

lators we discovered for the Fitts anthology. But none of our translators could tell when they had written an English sentence and when they had not. All were blinded by the Spanish.

I liked the *Notebooks of the Night* much better than I had liked the individual pieces when I first saw them. You are quite right about Bunny's nostalgia for his own past; that is really one of the reasons he likes us, who also have a past, however much he may attack the praisers of the past in public. I am now beginning to feel that no one has had a really good time since 1789; at least that seems to have been the latest date it was possible to enjoy a fifteen year old girl without private qualms or public fears.   Yours for Errol Flynn,[2] JPB   TLS

1. *The Vigil of Venus: Pervigilium Veneris,* trans. Allen Tate (Cummington, Mass.: Cummington Press, 1943).   2. Errol Flynn (1900–1959), the film actor, went on trial in Los Angeles on January 13, 1943, on charges of statutory rape involving two teen-aged girls. A jury of nine women and three men acquitted Flynn of all charges on February 6, 1943.

January 20, 1943

Dear John: There is still hope while the vigor of yours of the 17th belies its message. There is life in the old man yet. 1789 is as good a date as any. I feel a little humiliated that a movie actor should take on this vicarious suffering. We ought to be up to it ourselves. The trouble is that fornication (say since 1789) has been done mainly for therapeutic purposes, and has become for most men an obligation, which of course it is easy to avoid, like sulphur and molasses in the spring. No doubt the difference in our ages has let you in for this *ataxy* first. Never mind, I will catch you soon. My sense of the narrowing range of life is almost as acute as yours. We never had any reason to expect that we should be able, like the Duc d'Orleans (regent), to let the business of State languish while the whores filled the ante-chamber. Our State has never had any business, it has only made deals: a talent that you and I, as even private persons, have had no taste for.

Well, I think you must come down in the spring (say two months hence) and we shall see what we can make of it. I am still writing poetry: have just finished the first draft of a ballad (45 lines) which I will send you shortly.—There are no solutions, there is only writing to keep me out of the pattern of hereditary insanity which my ancestry considerately provided as an escape. I only wonder that so many of them took it in their time, while I have greater need of it than they. An excess of family pride.

I'd like to see some of your translations, though I should not be able to test them by the originals.   Aff. Allen   AL

January 26, 1943

Dear John: I am turning poems out so fast now that you will soon feel bombarded. Here are two more. The sonnets and the Ode were mere warming up, I believe. Jubilo I think, now at any rate, is my best since *The Mediterranean*.[1] But you tell me what I ought to think.

Edmund says my version of the *Pervigilium* is one of the best Latin translations he has ever seen; I am glad, and pleased too that he is going to try to sell it for me to the *Atlantic*. It is too good for that sheet, but I am not too good for the kind of money it can pay. Aff. Allen   AL

1. "Jubilo," *Kenyon Review* 5 (Spring, 1943), 184-86.

February 6, 1943

Dear Allen: I think you are quite right. These are the two finest poems you have done since *The Mediterranean*. *Jubilo* says completely what the address to the young proconsuls did not quite arrive at saying. And the *Dejected Lines* are not a whit inferior to it.[1] I think I prefer them, though that is perhaps because they so well express my own state at this time.

In Jubilo III 4, I don't like *machines*. Why not *roar* or some other trope signifying machines, but only one syllable? V 2, 4. I don't get the subject of 'incivility.' Are the poets the objects of incivility? Or both? In a way, it's the perfect word, and, as I take it, consciously ambiguous. VI 4. I don't think this line either properly completes the preceding one or prepares for the next stanza. VII 2, 5. What about exclamation points after both Jubilos?

In *Dejected Lines* I am worried by the pause indicated by the comma in II 7. I think it is really the verb 'like' followed by the weak 'it' that disturbs my ear. II 9. Is 'eats' right? The notion of eating is in 'food' in the following line. Shouldn't the verb in l. 9 be a preparation for eating? I think you should have some very violent verb here. IV 3. What about 'uncommonly' for 'exceedingly'? IV 7. I am not keen about 'sylvan,' or for that matter 'gentler.' That word, to my ear, should have a dominant 'd' sound in it to connect 'doom & door.' And just because 'In rational proration' is so abstract the door and the scene beyond should be concrete. V 3. Is 'wet' strong enough? V 5. 'With only fog' weak construction. Use a verb or participle. VI 7. I query 'last.'

But I am being absurdly captious. The poem is magnificent. I admire and envy you. Yours ever, John
I am trying to miscarry a cold. Hence the impersonal and perhaps impertinent character of this note.   AL

1. This poem appeared as "Winter Mask: To the Memory of W. B. Yeats," *Chimera* 1 (Spring, 1943), 2-3.

February 19, 1943

Dear John: Your commentary on the poems is very fine. I have adopted *uncommonly* for *exceedingly* in *Dejected Stanzas* (now entitled *Winter Mask*), and I only wish I could get a monosyllabic word for *machines* in *Jubilo*. You are absolutely right about it. I will keep plugging at it.

The *Dejected Stanzas* is a mere warming up for a poem of 240 lines 180 of which are written, in that same stanza, which I think of as a *little* canzone.[1] I rather like the rhyme scheme. It offers a chance for great variety of effect.

How are your translations coming?

If I can get a copy made of one of the sections of the long poem, I will send it. It is based on a recurrent dream.   Aff. Allen   AL

1. Tate is referring to "Seasons of the Soul," *Kenyon Review* 6 (Winter, 1944), 1–9. The stanzaic rhyme is A B A C B D E C D E.

February 25, 1943

Dear Allen: *Seasonal Confessions*[1] is superb—one of your best poems ever. I agree with you that the rhyme scheme is a good one for a long poem. It seems at the end of each stanza to stop only for another breath before going beautifully on.

I am going to make a few comments. I don't like the *brown* ceiling. You have kept the rest of the poem in tones of grey, with an occasional accent of blue. So the brown disturbs me simply as color and in any case doesn't seem to me to be the decisive epithet. III 3: Not inside. Say rather here was nor living nor dead. IV 4. I think a comma after *it*. IV 9. I would rather see aged instead of old, or aging, or some other dissyllable. VI 6. I wonder if day clothes would not convey the same literal meaning and have a more powerful implication.

I have had a difficult week. Having with some strain finished my introduction to Carrera Andrade's book of poems, a strain due to my fundamental ignorance of South America and its poetry, as well as to the fact that while I think him about the best down there, he is only a minor poet, no better (if as good) than his master Francis Jammes. I went off to Boston for a change of scene if not of air. I carried the mss with me, hoping to find a typist there who would save me the labor of making the four copies I needed. I didn't and brought it back. The first day home I went off to Town Meeting. The next day the mss had disappeared. It is something I have always dreaded—the losing of an only copy of something completed. The most extensive search failed to bring it to light. So I had, painfully, to reconstruct the whole thing from memory. I had worked hard to make the transitions smooth from biographical to critical material and they were the hardest to recover. Yesterday, it went off and I am feeling somewhat relieved, though not even yet serene.

I must now get to work on my income tax. O world, O life, O time!   Yours, John   TLS

1. Tate changed the title to "Seasons of the Soul" before the poem was published. It was dedicated to John Peale Bishop.

February 27, 1943

Dear John: Plans for my Eastern trip are made, and I hope you will be able to arrange to come back with me for a month or six weeks. I leave here on April 5th; will lecture at Princeton on the 8th; and on the 10th or 11th will go to New York for a few days. I plan at present to start back on the 14th or 15th. Why not meet me in New York for a mild binge, with headquarters as usual at the Little Hotel, and we can come down here together.

If we spend a night in Washington with friends of mine, we can save money* by taking from Washington a *de lux coach* train to Chattanooga. It is only fourteen hours.

Please think this over. I am counting on your coming.   Aff. Allen

*Round trip for this mode of travel, Washington-Chattanooga, is about $24.00—very cheap indeed.

                                                                    AL

March 1, 1943

Dear Allen: Nothing would give me more pleasure than to meet you in New York and to return with you South for a brief visit. I hope it can be arranged. Two things stand in the way. The first is money, of which, this being March and the first installment on the income taxes paid, I have something less than plenty. That end, I can probably take care of. The second is my garden, which this year I am taking very seriously, lest we fail to eat. There are as yet no signs of spring but lengthening days. But the time for first sowing in the hotbeds can't be far off. If I can have whatever is seasonable started in order I shall come with a clear conscience. Though I can't stay so long as you are kind enough to ask me.

Your return to Tennessee seems wonderfully to have invigorated you. I suppose one must go back from time to time and breathe the air that we first found life in. And wherever you are is, I have no doubt, as much the South as I shall ever find. Charles Town is for me as dead as Pompeii. As long as my sister continued to live there I could go back and still find a restoring air. But place is not everything. I lose communication with all my past. I am not at ease with these silent dead.

I learned lately that Ed Madden was dead—violently, that it was a shotgun, and probably by his own hand. He was my captain for a year in the last war and fascinated me as no other unreflective man has ever done. It was out of that fascination that I made the character of Charlie in Act of Darkness. And it seems odd now to recall that I at once seized that, endowed as he was for action, the determining impulse in his acts was a perverse will toward self-destruction. Imagination is always prophetic: if we see truly, we can always see what is about to happen.

I seemed to have a stir of poetic activity which was stopped by the damned necessity of working on the income tax. O Time! O fidgets! I shall keep your dates in mind and meet them if I can.

My compliments to Caroline.   Yours, John   AL

March 9, 1943

Dear John: At your leisure won't you look this over? This is the entire long poem I told you about.[1] You will see that I have benefitted by your criticism of II.

I am too close to it to judge it, but I suspect now it is the best poetry I have ever done.   Aff. Allen

I am hoping you will be able to join me in New York and come back with me.   AL

1. "Seasons of the Soul."

3/10/43

Dear John: I could easily become a nuisance! But I couldn't let you waste your time with the version of this poem which I sent you yesterday by mistake.   Yrs. A.T.   AL

March 12, 1943

Dear John: That's fine: get your hotbeds going (Caroline is preparing hers), forget the income tax, and meet me at the Little Hotel.

The time is getting short; so here is some information: From April 6th (Wednesday) to April 9th (Saturday) I will be at 58 Cleveland Lane, Princeton, in care of my host, Henry Church. From the 10th to the 13th, at the Little Hotel. I do hope you can make it.   Yrs. in haste, Allen   AL

March 17, 1943

Dear Allen: I think you are right in your estimate of *Seasonal Confessions*. It is a wonderfully sustained performance, on your highest and most serious level, and as a whole is impressive and moving.

The second section, curiously enough, brings out your descent from Poe. It is not written in his manner, thank God, but reveals the kinship.[1]

The matter in this section is obscure; the presentation clearer than in the other sections. Or is that an impression produced merely by the fact that I have now read it many times and am familiar with the empty hall. I continue to object to the adjective with ceiling in stanza 2. I don't think 'round' yet does the trick.

In the other sections there are lines which I do not feel are as clearly defined as they should be. In I, 1 why is the sky without head or tail? Is it the angel of the Lord? I prefer gloze to read for the sound's sake, but common clause is obscure in reference to Balaam. Are you, the poet, pronouncing a curse that is really a blessing?

I, 2: I question inching. The progress of that fire was rapid. I don't follow the metaphor implied by escheat. When a property is declared escheat, it is done by law, not illegally.

I, 3: The mind's tattering is better in the unrevised version. The line that follows troubles me in both versions. Hunting is better than sporting; it leads better to the lion.

I, 4: Why *stinking* ember? I like unrevised version better.

I, 5: Syntax not clear in opening lines. I offer this as a suggestion only:

When was it, then, that summer—
Daylong a liquid light—
And the child, a new-comer,
Bathed in the same green spray,
Could neither guess the night?
The summer had no reason,
Since, like the primal cause,

I, 6: Was Virgil 'saved'? I question 'humanly.' It's better than learnedly, but I would suggest a more emotional word. Shouldn't it be 'confounded . . . with'? 'Shadows curled' is not too good. Why not use an imperfect rhyme, there being so few true ones for world?

III, 1: Cold twilight is better than eddying. I like the repetition of 'cold.' Why not 'burned earth,' going back to I, 2. I question 'hangs.' A verb here is awkward. Use participle or adjective. 'Tin' is not clear except visually.

III, 2: The 'guerrila sharks' distub me. Why not

the hunting pair
That now displace your dover,
And haunt your company

III, 3: The relation of the line 'Cold soot upon the snow' is not clear. The word drop seems to apply better to soot than to wound.

IV, 1: I don't like refueling juice. It suggests gasoline.

IV, 2: All space, but no time. Why not all space, ignoring time.

IV, 4: Vertiginous chance fails to please my ear.

Please don't think me captious. We have been of some use to each other in the past in these matters. But they are better discussed face to face, above the poem, the pages spread between us. I have been working so long over translations that I question anything that happens not at once to be clear to me.

Anyhow, I here offer you a target to shoot your arrows into. I have done several poems recently, but this is the only good one.[2] It seems to me revealing about myself though the subject is remote.

Now about our seeing each other. I have noted your dates and will be in New York as certainly as one can promise anything in these uncertain and unpromising times. Could you possibly spare the time to come back here for as long as you care to stay? Spring is backward with us and I can offer you only an interior welcome. But I should like you to see where and how I live. And I should really like to see you and live with you a little while.   Yours ever, John   TLS

1. Bishop's remark here suggests the title of one of Tate's later essays, "Our Cousin, Mr. Poe," *Partisan Review* 16 (December, 1949), 1207–19.   2. "The Parallel" appeared with "The Spare Quilt" in *Poetry* 64 (April, 1944), 15–17.

March 22, 1943

Dear John: Your criticism of my Confessions is brilliant and what is even more interesting from my point of view, extremely helpful. I am adopting in toto your revision of I, stanza 5. Stanza 2 of I has nearly prostrated me: I've done ten versions of it and can't get it; it has gone dead on me, like the tenth fuck: the will is there but the potency is gone. I'll have to wait a while, and take vitamin D. (Is that the right one?)—You put your finger on all the weak spots, and had you done no more, that would have compelled me to face their weakness.

The Parallel just misses being one of your very best, and I can't quite make out what is missing. I believe something is wrong with the tone of the first two stanzas, or it may be that the symbolism of the sea and sand ought to be forced a little more; it comes out only after we've read the poem a second time, and know what follows. The last line is part of the trouble. (My offering is too much Tate, but I do think you've got to continue the sea in it.)

I wish you'd send me the others, or better still bring them to New York.—I suppose I have you to thank for the magazine containing your Phi Beta Kappa poem[1]—surely the best occasional poem of our time. I will go into it at length when we meet. Section two seems the best organized and most intense part of it. The whole thing hangs together by means of tone and the single image of the sea; but tone is the main thing.

I wish I could see my way to coming up to the Cape, but I know I can't; so I can only urge you anew to come to New York prepared to return here with me. My difficulty is that Nancy's school is eight miles away, and there is at least one day a week when the bus is late or doesn't run. It is impossible for the only chauffeur in our house to be away long.

I will be in New York three weeks from yesterday—April 11th.
Till then,   Aff. Allen   TLS

1. "A Subject of Sea Change," appeared in *American Scholar* 12 (April, 1943), 216–19.

April 28, 1943

Dear John: When I got back here with the malignant germs of the city I came down with the worst cold in five years; I am just now up and taking nourishment.—As I wired you I take most of the blame for our missing dates upon myself; but I think there is a slight responsibility that you ought to bear. My dates evidently misled you. I meant that I would arrive in N.Y. between the 10th and the 12th, and I gather that you thought I would get there before that, and would leave *by* the 12th. I am obviously to blame for this misunderstanding. But it never occurred to me that you were planning to spend just one evening in my society in the Great City: that would be the Saturday evening (the 10th) before you left. I assumed that you were coming prepared to stay several days, and I felt that there was no hurry about my getting there. My humiliation is all the greater because you took that long trip for just one evening; that is to say, the humiliation is in direct proportion to the compliment implied.

Well, you must forgive me, and hope with me for better luck in our next effort at a reunion.

I will be in the East, or at least Eastish, after August 1st. Archie has renewed his offer and this time he is making it good.[1] He knows how I feel about his recent politico-literary career, and he knows that he is not getting a yes-man; so I feel that my line is pretty plain, and not susceptible to any misinterpretation by anybody. The job is for one year, which pleases me; I don't want to be trapped in Washington, of all places.

I saw Dr. Wilson once in Princeton and twice in N.Y. He seemed to be in good shape, but hard up, as we all are; and I could not help seeing as ominous Mary's intention of staying on in N.Y. in some sort of job, while Edmund returns to the Cape. I hope I am wrong. When the child gets on its feet, then, Governor, the crisis appears.

I hope you will write me soon, and send more of your poems. I will do likewise.   Affectionately, Allen   TLS

1. Tate became consultant in poetry at the Library of Congress in September, 1943.

July 1, 1943

Dear John: You wanted prompt commentary on your new poem The Submarine Bed,[1] but I was simply not able to give it. I am up and doing at present but until a week ago I had been scarcely able to move for nearly two months. The story is sad and brief, even if the suffering is long: my guts refuse to function. Something has happened to my colon; it is inflamed and inert, as well as spastic. I have lost twelve pounds since the middle of May. I am putting up with the horse doctors hereabouts until I can get to Dr. Wolf early in September. I would go now but he must be leaving for his vacation.

We leave for Washington at the end of this month, and although we have a house—described to me as suburban Georgian—we are more and more depressed by the prospect.

I need not tell you that my burst of creative activity came to an end when my colitis began. I have done nothing since I returned from the East but take enemas.

Your poem is extremely good, and I have only a single suggestion. I believe you ought to make the tone of the next to last line more elevated, even rhetorical. The understatement seems to reduce the importance of the substance of the poem.—What about the other poems? Why not send them?

Ever since I agreed to go to Washington, butter has not succeeded in melting in Archie's mouth. But we shall see what we shall see. I surmise that he is going in for one of his non-political periods of penance for public excess. (I fall into his alliterative style even in discussing it.)

For heaven's sake write me and tell me your news and other news. I have had none for weeks. Love to Margaret.   Aff. Allen

P.S. A letter from Nannine informs me that Fischer has sold our anthology to Garden City. I wish I could find out how many copies

Fischer sold. Nannine has evaded three requests for this information.
Why don't you write her?   TLS

1. "The Submarine Bed" first appeared in *New Poems*, ed. Oscar Williams (1944).

| | The Library of Congress/Washington |
| August 5, 1943 | Reference Department |

Dear John: Here I am in the Seat of Poetry, Chaise de la Poesie, and
so far it isn't bad. The Librarian is all that you said he would be
personally, and Ada is nice too. We were taken practically from the
high road over to dinner *chez* MacLeish in Alexandria. I knew
Oronoco Street but I could not place the house that corresponded to
the number—607. As we drew up before it—horresco referens—my
hair stood up and a frisson passed down my spine. It is the boyhood
home of the old Confutterate ginral—R. E. Lee. When we exclaimed,
Archie looked restrained.

I am going to New London next Wednesday for a few days, and if
I can put off some jobs here I will stay a few days more, and that
might make a dashing trip up to you just possible. I will wire or
telephone you around next Friday, which God help us is the 13th.

Your new poem is excellent,[1] but I thought perhaps a stanza or so
too long for the dramatic effect. Love to Margaret.   Aff. Allen   TLS

1. Unidentified, but perhaps "The Spare Quilt."

Monday August 9, 1943

Dear John: I am afraid I can't take off any more time after next
Monday (16th); so I fear our meeting is out of the question now.—
Had I known you were going to the Entretiens de Pontigny, I should
have accepted their invitation.—There is just a chance that I could run
up to South Hadley on Friday or Saturday, but don't count on it. I'll
investigate trains and wire you.   Aff. Allen

P.S. I *might* take off more time if I received a sudden, last-minute
invitation to appear at one of the conferences. My address from Wednesday will c/o The Moorings, Groton, Conn.   AL

August 25, 1943

Dear John: I will get the biographical notes revised this week, and
send them to Loth. I had a letter from him, and talked [to] him on the
telephone this morning. Who in the hell is he?

I am a little confused about the point at which we were to receive royalties on American Harvest. Like you I remember acceding to the 8,000 figure, but I have no distinct recollection of 10,000. But maybe Nannine is right; maybe Nannine has sold us out. I have no confidence in literary agents. But I don't know what we can do unless we are willing to demand a showdown, and that might interfere with the payment of the money due from Garden City. I understand that we are to receive $750.00 apiece, less Nannine's 10 per cent. I am willing to settle for that figure, since I have felt from the beginning that Fischer would do us in if he could.

But if you want to demand an audit, I am perfectly willing. Think it over.

We are going to look for you in Washington in the fall. Our guest accommodations are primitive, consisting of a single bed in the game room; but it is warm and it has a private lavatory. The house is the size of a mousetrap, bourgeois Georgian in style, and the downstairs rooms were furnished in the best whorehouse manner. Caroline took it all up to the attic, and we feel better. The house is full of gadgets and thus easy to run. We brought a fine African "settled" woman with us, but she may get homesick and go back to Tennessee. Caroline spends her time creating a social life for her. Sunday she went to a nigger church with her, and yesterday she accompanied her to a colored beauty parlor, where she sat for four hours.

Yes, Nancy wants to get married in February, as soon as her young man gets his navy commission. I don't see how we can prevent it. She doesn't want to go to college, and she wants to get away from us. The boy is very handsome and of good enough family, and he dabbles in poetry, but that phase won't last. There is a good deal of insanity in his family, in spite of the fact that they are Mississippi extraverts, and when you add to that the insanity in mine, the prospect is not too good.[1] But again I don't know what we can do about it. I couldn't have foreseen all this eighteen years ago, the night we met at Marta's. I am already a great-uncle, my nephew having had a son last month—named for me, God help us all.

I think I wrote you that Archie is extremely pleasant. I am sure he is the best librarian in the world. Even the old professionals here are in awe of him.

And here at the end of this letter I recall something I meant to make a principal subject. Ernest and Archie and I—Ernest by air-mail from Cuba—are working on a plan to save Pound from being shot when our army occupies Italy. Archie says there is real danger that a provost marshal may get him and after a quick trial shoot him. I expect to see a transcript of his broadcasts today, and I have no doubt that he is technically guilty of treason. We feel that we ought to represent to the Attorney-General or to army headquarters that

Pound is really insane, and that he never to the slightest degree influenced anybody in America in favor of the Axis. We simply can't afford to have a poet martyr. What is your view? And will you join us in signing a petition? It will not be public: there is no public defense possible, since being a poet provides no immunity to the consequences of treason. We don't even want him pardoned. We feel that he should be allowed to fade out of the picture.

Love to Margaret. I feel very sad about missing a trip to the Cape, now for the third time, I believe. We may have more gasoline soon, and that will make it easier.   Aff. Allen

P.S. The State Department asked the Library to buy $200 worth of recent American poetry and criticism to send to Soviet Russia. I was detailed for the job. In my covering letter I pointed out that in including James T. Farrell's "A Note on Literary Criticism," a noted Marxian work, I felt that I was sending into the Soviet Union a piece of subversive literature. Do you think I will hold this job very long?   TLS

1. Nancy Tate became engaged and later married (on January 3, 1944) to Percy Wood, a young medical student who specialized in psychiatry.

August 31, 1943

Dear John: I don't know what will come of it but at any rate here's a possibility for you to think about.

Saturday I saw Huntington Cairns, who is on a Presidential Committee which has as its function the preservation of works of art and architecture throughout Europe from the American armies now about to invade the continent. Huntington has a special administrative job on the committee which will require assistance at the rate of about $6,500 a year. He asked me to recommend somebody. I mentioned you. He said he had already thought of you, and I believe you will hear from him shortly if he gets the money for the job—which he seemed confident of doing.

Washington isn't as bad as it has been painted, provided you don't get involved in a clique. By simply going home after my work in the Library I feel no more pressure here than anywhere else. Huntington would be a good man to be with. He has nothing of the bureaucrat about him. He is one of the pleasantest and most amiable men I know.

As I say, nothing may come of it, but it would not be a bad job; in fact, I think it would be one of the best here. I should have said that your office would probably be in the Mellon Gallery—sufficiently cut off from the Washington that runs people crazy.   Yrs. Allen

P.S. This should be kept confidential for a while.   TLS

September 6, 1943

Dear John: We are laboring on Labor Day, which as a matter of fact is what I have always done.

No, don't write anything publicly about Pound until we can see our way a little more clearly. Archie will be back here on Thursday or Friday, and I think he expects to have a private talk with the Attorney-General. Huntington Cairns, a very good lawyer who knows government procedures, advised me the other day to commit nothing whatever to writing for official use; and I think he's right, for the present. Huntington says that Archie will have to have a private understanding with the President, who can give orders to the army not to shoot Pound; but that we should not even suggest that the indictment be quashed. I am preparing a statement for Archie's use on Clement C. Wallandingham, the Ohio Copperhead, who was guilty of treason in precisely the way Pound is; but the Federal government merely sent him into the Confederate lines. (As you may recall, the Confederates didn't want him either, and expelled him, so that he had to go to Canada.) The best we can hope for is that he will never be prosecuted or that, if prosecuted, he will be given merely formal punishment, such as removal of citizenship, etc.

I agree with you that the later Cantos are pure [anti-]American doctrine, and that they are offensive to our "leaders" because he really believes it. But he was indicted strictly for his broadcasts. The treason is prima facie, since the fact of his broadcasting at all is a form of "giving aid and comfort to the enemy." He actually goes further than this: he mentions the "enemy," meaning us, and in some of the news broadcasts (as distinguished from his harangues) he describes Japanese victories just as a hired propagandist would describe them. So you see the case is serious. He is a man of intuitions and insights, but he has never had any intellectual power or even integrity. I have just reread his early books, The Spirit of Romance and Pavennes and Divisions—both intellectually shoddy, but in their time "useful" to people like us, younger by some ten to fifteen years. Vanity, as you say, is at the bottom of it. He got Confucius and Major Douglas scrambled together with J. Q. Adams and Jefferson, and when Mussolini flattered him (or responded to his flattery) he decided that Fascism was the realization of what we had betrayed in this country. The Corporate State has back of it a perfectly respectable political philosophy, which I don't find very sympathetic; but Pound, who has never had any critical reserve, had no trouble identifying practical Fascism with the theoretical model. It is a strange case, and in the long run I do not understand it. For example, I can imagine myself holding, as I have held and do hold, views of my country that go deeply against the current grain; but I cannot imagine myself, in time of war, emotionally identifying myself with my country's enemies, whatever the causes of the war may be. It is simply that the choice between one's own country and the opposed countries is unreal; for there is no choice. I base this feeling largely upon the belief that it can never be a good thing for a nation to lose a major war. We know all about that from our boyhood, which was under that peculiar cloud.

Wait, then, till the end of the week, and I will let you know what turn the discussion has taken here. Ernest's feeling is very much like yours. I have no direct, personal obligation to Pound; but I don't want him shot. I don't want a poet martyr.

I hope you will hear from Cairns this week.   Aff. Allen

P.S. I will see if I can get permission to send you the latest, unbound transcripts, April 24 to June 30. Have you heard the rumor that P. was confined as insane for a couple of months some time last winter? I am trying to have the rumor traced.   A. T.   TLS

October 11, 1943
Dear John: Archie called me this morning to say that you had accepted his offer, and I am simply delighted.[1] You may be mystified by the sudden nod from the Palace Guard, but it is really very simple. A couple of weeks ago Edmund wrote me you had been to see him and that you seemed depressed by the prospect of another cold winter on the Cape. I merely told Archie, and he set at once about the task of raising the money, which he did with remarkable speed. He tried to get more, but it was evidently impossible.

Your duties will be self-imposed, unless, as is likely, Archie finds for you a special project, such as mine, which is the editing of a quarterly journal of the acquisitions of the Library. I hope you will be given an office in our pavilion, which is remote from all the rest of the Library.

Do you want to get living quarters near the Library? They will be hard to find, but if you say the word I will start looking. Tell me what you want and I will see what you can get.

I wish we could bed you for the first few days, but now that Nancy is here, and the cook occupies the game room, we have only the living room sofa, which I do not recommend.

I am sending you a copy of my translation of the Pervigilium.[2] I like the printing.   Aff. Allen   AL

1. Archibald MacLeish had offered Bishop the newly-created post of Resident Fellow in Comparative Literature.   2. *The Vigil of Venus* (Cummington, Mass.: Cummington Press, 1943).

3418 Highwood Drive, S. E.
October 13, 1943   Washington 20, D.C.

Dear John: Archie has just telephoned me to say that you have asked him whether you could support your family on the $3,000 salary. I am afraid it would be impossible. My salary, after income tax deductions, comes to just about $5,000, and it will not be possible for us to live on it. We have a little additional money from the outside.

I suppose both Archie and I assumed that you would come down alone, and that Margaret would make you frequent visits, as she did winter before last in New York.

As an example of the high cost of living here, we have a house at $150.00 a month, furnished, which is considered a great bargain, but at the sacrifice of living off in a part of Washington that I never heard of, remote from friends and familiar haunts.

You could probably get a bedroom, a sitting-room, and small kitchen, furnished, for about $100.00, or perhaps slightly less near the Library.

I should say that it would cost you and Margaret six to eight thousand for twelve months, if you lived very economically. For this amount you could get a house, etc., pay for at least one servant provided you could get the servant. We brought one with us.

As you know, I am extremely anxious for you to come. I thought being here would do you a great deal of good, which would probably appear in new works after you left, as in my case after I left Princeton.   Aff. Allen   TLS

October 18, 1943

Dear John: Archie showed me his last letter to you, and I hope it will move you to come down at once. It seems to me that if Margaret is still much interested in her work she could find something very interesting to do here. I had got the impression from Edmund, who may have got it from Dos, that she would not want to leave the Cape on this account. As a matter of fact, if Margaret wanted to get a war job with a very good salary, it would be no trouble at all for a woman of her energy and very great ability. This is a new possibility that just occurred to me over the week end.

If you come down, I can drive you house hunting on some extra gasoline that a Navy captain gave me last night at a dinner party.

Archie is right—we will really be heartbroken if you don't come. We had set our hearts on it.

The other day I suggested you to Tom Matthews for the leading book reviewer of Time, but I hoped, if he offered you the job, you wouldn't take it, for the same reason that led me to decline it. We have a certain age, tempo, and distinction, and we want to live our lives in peace.   Aff. Allen   TLS

October 21, 1943

Dear John: I am relieved and delighted to know that you are coming.—I merely passed the word to Archie: he needed no argument.

I think your general plan is excellent, and I only wish a 3-bedroom house, furnished, that we heard of in Georgetown a week ago were still vacant. But there will be others, and we shall be looking out. Meanwhile, I am sure we can find you a boarding-house for the interim before Margaret's arrival. We might even get you a room with a German refugee across the street from us. You could have your meals with our family which is composed of the Tates and the Cheneys from Nashville.[1] I will know about this on Saturday. Archie's secretary is also looking for a boarding house for you.—I am sure you can get a house for $200.00. The Georgetown house was only $175.00.

We are very much pleased that you will both—or three of you—be here. We have been reluctant to meet new people in Washington, and an addition of old friends is what we need. I will inquire about schools for Robert.—I think I can get you an office in our pavilion which, although it does not imitate the Paris Opera, strongly resembles the lobby of a Southern chain hotel.   Aff. Allen
                                                                        AL

1. Frances and Brainard Cheney were working in Washington at this time.

October 22, 1943

Dear John: Your second letter (12th) clears everything up. I think on the whole you all had better try for a house in Alexandria, where there's a private day school whose rates are moderate, being run chiefly for army children. We will ask Ada to enquire there for a house, and we will do likewise. Even if you took a year's lease, you could not possibly get stuck with it beyond your stay. A line would form at the front door to take it off your hands.

If you say the word I will put an advertisement in one of the papers to the effect: house or apartment, furnished; 3 bedrooms, or 1 large and 1 small (this based on your letter of yesterday), preferably near Capitol but will consider elsewhere. This should be done as soon as possible.

I will not know till tomorrow whether you can get the temporary room across the street; but I think you can.   Yrs. Allen

P.S. Yes, I saw E. W. in N.Y., last week and urged him to take the *New Yorker* job.[1] The week before I was offered the corresponding post on *Time.* I promptly refused.   AL

1. Wilson succeeded Clifton Fadiman as the chief book reviewer for the *New Yorker,* beginning an association with the magazine that lasted for the rest of his life.

October 27, 1943

Dear John: Telegram and letter arrived together. The Neuberger room is reserved for you, but I don't know yet whether you can get breakfast there. But I take it there is no need for your knowing that till you get here.

We look for you Thursday. If you come in by 5:45 take a taxi to the Library and ride out with us; but later than that come direct to: 3418 Highwood Drive, S.E. Most taxi drivers don't know the street. Tell him to go out S.E. Penna. Ave. about 3 miles to Carpenter St., then turn left 2 short blocks to Highwood Dr.

It will be wonderful to have you here.—We go to N.Y. this week end. I wish you were going to be there.   In haste, Allen   AL

November 29, 1943

Dear John: It was a great relief to hear Margaret's voice a few minutes ago and to learn that you had stood the trip and felt better today.[1] Archie was much upset to know that you had for an instant felt you had "let us down" here; but I think he has wired you about that. I have just talked to Archie again, and we want to know whether there is anything we can do to make the time pass less heavily. At this distance we can only feel frustration in anything more substantial than that. If Margaret will send me a card when you are able to read, I will get you some books. At a somewhat further stage of convalescence I will suggest an exchange of limericks, such as we produced in 1932, that form of composition being best suited to the prone position and to the present state of the world.—Caroline joins me in best love, for a quick recovery.   Yrs. Allen   AL

1. After only two weeks in his Washington post, Bishop suffered a severe heart attack and had to return to his home in South Chatham, Massachusetts. He died on April 4, 1944.

December 14, 1943

Dear John: I was relieved to get your dictated letter; it was the first news I'd had for a week, when Archie passed on to me Margaret's letter to him. I am inclined very strongly to agree with you about your recuperative powers. Remember that the doctors have got to frighten you into discipline, and that is all to the good. Take their orders quite literally and I have no doubt that in six months you will be able to function again if you are careful.

Your *exemplum* so impressed me that I went to Dr. Dickens, the heart-specialist, this morning and had a thorough examination, including an electrocardiagram. Result: heart-action perfect but nervous; blood-pressure 125/70, which is perfect too for my age. I mentioned your case. Dr. Dickens asked whether you had high blood-pressure. I said yes. He remarked that my other symptoms—gas, spasticity, tension of solar plexus—could easily cause heart-trouble if my blood-pressure were high. So it's the low blood-pressure that is my present bulwark, as the high is your danger, I should surmise.— Stark [Young] (whom I wrote about your experiences with Wolf) says that Wolf likes new cases better than old, and has to be shaken to see anything new in an old patient. That plus your experience sent me to Dr. Dickens. I feel better already.

When you get the Pontigny ms. copied I will be glad to take it over if your strength has not sufficiently returned by that time.[1] Don't hesitate to let me do this.—Your trunk and suit-case went to South Chatham last week. Let me know if they haven't arrived.

I am going to New York this week end, where I expect to observe Dr. Wilson in his new luxury.   Aff. Allen   AL

1. "Entretiens de Pontigny: 1943," *Sewanee Review* 52 (Autumn, 1944), 493-98 [part I of a symposium].

December 23, 1943   3418 Highwood Drive, S.E./Washington

Dear John: Your letter brought good news indeed, and really shamed me into feeling better. Yesterday was my first day at the office since last Thursday when I went to N.Y., got into bed at the Hotel Gramercy Park with a sudden, jolting attack of flu, and then, on Saturday morning rose from the bed and took the train back; and upon arrival got directly into bed again. Nothing was accomplished in New York but some pleasant hours with Dr. and Mrs. Wilson, who nursed me with heart-warming zeal.—But at the office yesterday I had a "weak spell" and had to come home; so I'm resting one more day. Archie gave me his arm out to the car and made the predictable joke about the effect of the L. of C. on his past friends.

I hate to confess it but I grow more and more anxious about the results of Dr. Wolf's treatment in both our cases. It seems that in my case I was liberated from the migraine headaches only to fall victim to these attacks of tachycardia. My pulse yesterday reached about 120. It is strictly functional, if I may believe not only Wolf but other doctors including Dickens, the man here. The Gamma-Ray Machine haunts my fears. What *is* its effect? Does it upset the glands? Wolf says it "regularizes" the glands; but after we have lived for forty-odd years, to regularize the glands may be to disorganize other functions. We don't know enough to decide these questions, but I suspect that it is more than coincidence that both of us have developed acute ailments. So far I have been lucky in not having any organic trouble. I can't believe that your gardening and work about the house in the past year would cause heart disease; these light labors should normally have been good for you.—It all gives one to think but about what I do not know.

Wallace Stevens writes me that Henry Church mentioned to him the Sewanee Review for his Pontigny lecture. Stevens offered me the article, and I will be glad to copy your ms. if you will send it down. (And send you back an extra copy.)

Everybody here marvels at your quick comeback. I ponder your experience *in extremis:* I have never reached that nadir but I will sooner or later and when I do I shall not expect to "come back." That is our difference, and it provides you with your secret.

Christmas will be very quiet here. We have declined all invitations in the hope of a good rest, which Caroline especially needs, as she still has a remnant of flu, and has had for two weeks. Love to you both.   Aff. Allen   AL

                                    The Library of Congress/Washington
January 14, 1944   Reference Department

Dear John: I am glad you improve and glad you like the dedication which has its reason apart from sentiment: there's some of your work in the poem.[1]

I suspect that the announcement of Nancy's wedding which I sent the other day to South Chatham went astray. She was married on the 3rd, and I had to do it all, Caroline being away with her father in Florida. Mr. Gordon has since died, and Caroline took the body to Kentucky, where she now is and will remain till some time next week. A wedding and a death a week apart are more than our due. If Caroline had been able to fix a date for her return Nancy would have waited; but at the time it seemed that Mr. Gordon might linger for a month or more.

Nancy and Percy are now at Monteagle where Percy is studying for his examination; this passed, he will go to the Navy on March 1st. Now that it is done, I am both relieved and pleased. Percy is a fine boy.

I am sending back the Stevens ms because he had meanwhile sent me a carbon which will do nicely. I am sorry to have held you up. Today I wrote a letter to Nannine inquiring about our money. I need my part of it badly. There were only three days to prepare for the wedding, and it was very small; but I seem to have about $500.00 less than I had two weeks ago.

Take care of yourself. By the way, Archie, having created your position, wants to fill it again. Can you nominate a candidate?   Aff. Allen   AL

1. Tate had dedicated "Seasons of the Soul" to Bishop.

January 26, 1944

Dear John: Both Caroline and I cherish your fine letter about Nancy's marriage. Your compliment to us, particularly as it applies to me, is both a reproach and a reassurance. I have never made a conscious sacrifice for Nancy in terms of a design for my life; Caroline, of course, has. But I think we both felt from the beginning that all we should be able to do for Nancy would be to give her models of as little frustration in her parents as possible. Had we tried anything else, we should have failed; and there would have been nothing. There is no deeper satisfaction than the approbation of twenty years of one's life from an old and dear friend.

Katherine Anne is here to take your job, which I begin to think is Voodooed, because K. A. is in bed with a temperature of 102. It seems to be flu without complications, but we are anxious.

The box that you and Margaret sent Nancy was promptly forwarded. It will give her much pleasure.

Caroline's father died, or did I write you? She has been back just a week, but she has been in bed most of the time. She grows daily stronger and will doubtless be herself in a few days.

Your boredom is a good sign. But take it easy.   Aff. Allen   AL

March 1, 1944

Dear John: I am glad you are able to move. I saw you advertised on the Y.M.H.A. program for this Thursday, but I didn't believe it.

Nerves are certainly the trouble. Mine are better for the moment, but my fingers are crossed. I don't expect great improvement till I leave Washington. I am drinking too much and sleeping too little. And today I fear I am taking flu.

I wrote Nannine some time ago that I intended to sue Fischer if I didn't get the money soon. She replied with hurt feelings that Fischer would pay "after March 1st." How soon after? I have just written her again, and I will let you know what she replies.

I suppose you know that Katherine Anne came to fill your job. She nearly had pneumonia a week after she arrived, but is now up and about.

Let me know what the doctors tell you. And don't go too fast.   Yrs. Allen   AL

3/15/44

Dear John: Nannine says that Fischer will pay up on April 6. The delay has been due to delay at Doubleday Doran. I hope she is right. I was very hard-boiled about it, even threatening a lawsuit.—What did the doctor say about you? I've a very bad cold, but am pulling out of it. Everybody else well. Nancy is with us, Percy having gone to the Navy at San Diego.   Yrs. A. T.   AL

CHRONOLOGIES

JOHN PEALE BISHOP

1892	Born in Charles Town, Jefferson County, West Virginia, to Jonathan Peale and Margaret (Miller) Bishop.
1901	Father dies.
1906–1909	Attends high school in Hagerstown, Maryland.
1909–1910	Suffers temporary blindness lasting several months; develops strong liking for poetry.
1912	Publishes first poem, "To A Woodland Pool," in *Harper's Weekly*, September 28.
1913–1917	Briefly attends Mercersburg Academy in Pennsylvania; studies at Princeton, several years older than his classmates; publishes poetry in *Nassau Literary Magazine*; develops lifelong friendships with Edmund Wilson and F. Scott Fitzgerald; publishes his first book of verse, *Green Fruit* (1917).
1917–1919	After graduation from Princeton, accepts commission in the Army, serving in Europe during and after World War I.
1920–1922	Works for *Vanity Fair* in New York; becomes managing editor.
1922	With Edmund Wilson, publishes *The Undertaker's Garland*, a collection of verse and prose; marries Margaret Grosvenor Hutchins.
1922–1924	Travels in Europe; develops friendships with Archibald MacLeish, Ezra Pound, and E. E. Cummings.
1925–1926	Returns to New York, renewing association with *Vanity Fair*; meets Allen Tate September 23, 1925; writes a novel, *The Huntsmen Are Up In America*, which Scribner's encourages but later declines to publish.
1926	Returns to France for extended residence, purchasing the Chateau de Tressancourt outside Paris, where three sons are born over the next five years.

1928–1929   Beginnings of real friendship with Tate, who is in Paris on a Guggenheim fellowship. Spends an evening reading his poetry to Tate and Robert Penn Warren, who visits from Oxford.

1931   Publishes volume of short stories, *Many Thousands Gone;* wins 1930 *Scribner's Magazine* short fiction prize for the title story from the volume.

1932   Under Tate's prodding and criticism, begins to publish his poems in periodicals; friendship with Tate grows as Tate works in France for several months.

1933   Publishes *Now With His Love,* a collection of poetry; "The South and Tradition" appears; returns to the United States permanently, living for a time in Connecticut, later in New Orleans.

1935   Publishes *Act of Darkness,* a novel, and *Minute Particulars,* a collection of verse; publishes several poems in *Southern Review,* accompanied by Tate's essay, "A Note on Bishop's Poetry"; moves to South Harwich on Cape Cod.

1936   Publishes "Homage to Hemingway," and "The Golden Bough," both substantial critical essays.

1937   Supervises the building of a new home; publishes regular reviews in *Poetry* magazine.

1938   Moves into Sea Change, his new home in South Chatham, on Cape Cod; "The Discipline of Poetry" and "The Poetry and Prose of E. E. Cummings" appear.

1939   Attends Writers' Conference at Savannah, where he sees Tate, Warren, and others; publishes "The Sorrows of Thomas Wolfe" in the inaugural issue of *Kenyon Review.*

1940   Becomes chief poetry reviewer for *The Nation;* lectures at Yale and Princeton, where Tate is resident poet; with Tate's help, begins preparing a collection of his poetry; publishes "Finnegan's Wake."

1941   Publishes *Selected Poems;* appears on CBS radio program "Invitation to Learning."

1941–1942   Works in New York as director of publications for the Office of the Coordinator of Inter-American Affairs.

1942   Coedits and publishes, with Tate, *American Harvest,* an anthology of contemporary American poetry and prose.

1943   Accepts position as resident fellow in comparative literature at the Library of Congress, where Tate holds the poetry chair and MacLeish is the librarian; after two weeks' service, suffers severe heart attack and returns to Cape Cod.

1944   Dies on April 4, in Hyannis, Massachusetts, at the Cape Cod Hospital.

JOHN ORLEY ALLEN TATE (through 1944)

1899   Born in Winchester, Clark County, Kentucky, to John Orley and Eleanor Varnell Tate.

1906–1908   Lives in Nashville and attends the Tarbox School

1909   Attends Cross School, an academy emphasizing the classics, in Louisville, Kentucky.

1918   Admitted to Vanderbilt University, after having attended schools in Ashland, Kentucky, Evansville, Indiana, and the Georgetown Preparatory School. (He also took private lessons on the violin for a time.) At Vanderbilt, taught by W. C. Curry, John Crowe Ransom, Herbert Sanborn, and Herbert Cushing Tolman.

1919–1920   First published poems appear.

1921   Joins Fugitives.

1922   Forced to withdraw from school because of illness, works briefly for family coal business, and returns to Vanderbilt in February 1923; with Ridley Wills publishes *Golden Mean.*

1924   Teaches in Lumberport, West Virginia, before going to New York to undertake a career in literary journalism; meets Hart Crane, Gorham Munson, Slater Brown; spends summer in Guthrie, Kentucky, with Robert Penn Warren; meets Caroline Gordon, whom he marries in the fall; returns to New York and writes reviews and short literary features for the *Nation, New Republic,* the *Herald Tribune* and other publications.

1925   Employed as copy editor by Climax Publishing Company, publisher of *Rance Romances* and *Telling Tales.* Daughter Nancy Tate born September 23; on the same day, Tate meets John Peale Bishop in a New York speak-easy.

1926   Begins "Ode to the Confederate Dead."

1927   Publishes "Poetry and the Absolute," his first important critical essay.

1928   Publishes *Mr. Pope and Other Poems* and *Stonewall*

Jackson: The Good Soldier; receives Guggenheim fellowship; in Europe meets many of the important literary figures of England and France: T. S. Eliot, Herbert Read, L. A. G. Strong, Julian Green, Ernest Hemingway,F. Scott Fitzgerald, and Gertrude Stein; Robert Penn Warren visits him in Paris and they spend an evening with John Peale Bishop, which Bishop will later proclaim the most significant evening of his literary life. The three drink wine and Bishop reads his poems to Tate and Warren almost all night.

1929   Publishes *Jefferson Davis: His Rise and Fall;* writes "Message from Abroad"; begins regular correspondence with Bishop.

1930   On January 1, sails for New York; in April moves into "Benfolly," an antebellum farmhouse near Clarksville, Tennessee; contributes "Remarks on the Southern Religion" to *I'll Take My Stand.*

1931   "Sonnets of the Blood" appears; begins work on a biography of Robert E. Lee, which he never completes.

1932   Becomes Southern editor of *Hound and Horn* and edits Southern number of *Poetry;* returns to France in June and writes "Picnic at Cassis" (title later changed to "The Mediterranean") in the fall.

1933   Wins Midland Author's Prize from *Poetry* magazine; publishes the short story "The Immortal Woman."

1934   "Sonnets at Christmas" appear; becomes lecturer in English at Southwestern at Memphis, Tennessee.

1935   Makes first appearance at writers' conference (Olivet College, Michigan); publishes "The Profession of Letters in the South."

1936   With Herbert Agar edits *Who Owns America?* to which he contributes "Notes on Liberty and Property"; *The Mediterranean and Other Poems* published; resigns from Southwestern and returns to Benfolly; during summer lectures at Columbia University; "Narcissus as Narcissus" appears; with Anne Goodwin Winslow does dramatic version of "The Turn of the Screw" entitled "The Governess."

1937   Publishes *Selected Poems.*

1938   Accepts position at Woman's College of North Carolina at Greensboro; during summer completes *The Fathers,* which is published in the fall; "Tension in Poetry," one of his best known critical essays, is published; becomes advisory editor of *Kenyon Review.*

1939   Attends writers' conference at Savannah, Georgia; becomes resident poet in Creative Arts Program at Princeton; "The Trout Map" appears.

1940   Appears as panelist on CBS program "Invitation to Learning"; declines invitation to become consultant in poetry at Library of Congress; publishes "Understanding Modern Poetry."

1941   Publishes "Literature as Knowledge: Comment and Comparison," another of his most influential critical essays, and *Reason in Madness: Critical Essays.*

1942   With Bishop edits *American Harvest,* an anthology of recent American writing for South American readers, also a slightly modified version for readers of this country and England; publishes "*The Fugitive,* 1922–25, a Personal Recollection"; resigns at Princeton and returns to Monteagle, Tennessee, where he writes "More Sonnets at Christmas."

1943   Publishes "Jubilo" and "Winter Mask"; begins "Seasons of the Soul"; translates *Pervergilium Veneris* and publishes "More Sonnets at Christmas"; becomes consultant in poetry at Library of Congress; becomes involved in activities to save life of Ezra Pound.

1944   John Peale Bishop dies on April 4, after suffering heart attack in Washington several months before; Tate undertakes the editing of Bishop's *Collected Poems* (1948).

INDEX